BOWLING, BEATNIKS, AND BELL-BOTTOMS

Pop Culture of 20th- and 21st-Century America

BOWLING, BEATNIKS, AND BELL-BOTTOMS

Pop Culture of 20th- and 21st-Century America

VOLUME 1: 1900s–1910s

Cynthia Johnson, Editor
Lawrence W. Baker, Project Editor

U·X·L
A part of Gale, Cengage Learning

GALE
CENGAGE Learning·

Detroit • New York • San Francisco • New Haven, Conn • Waterville, Maine • London

JUL 0 3 2012

GALE
CENGAGE Learning·

Bowling, Beatniks, and Bell-
Bottoms: Pop Culture of 20th-
and 21st-Century America, 2nd ed.

Cynthia Johnson, Editor

Project Editor: Lawrence W.
Baker

Rights Acquisition and Management: Robyn Young

Composition: Evi Abou-El-Seoud

Manufacturing: Wendy Blurton

Imaging: John Watkins

Product Design: Kristine Julien

For product information and technology assistance, contact us at
Gale Customer Support, 1-800-877-4253.
For permission to use material from this text or product, submit all requests
online at www.cengage.com/permissions.
Further permissions questions can be emailed to
permissionrequest@cengage.com

Front cover photographs: (Left to right) The Game of Life, © CameraShots-
Concept/Alamy; Radio City Music Hall, © Sam Dao/Alamy; Slinky, © Garry Gay/
Workbook Stock/Getty Images; Hollywood sign, © Gavin Hellier/Alamy. Back
cover photographs: (Top to bottom) Nickelodeon, © Lewis Hine/Historical/Corbis;
Bobbysoxers, © Bettmann/Corbis; Man bowling, © H. Armstrong Roberts/
ClassicStock/Alamy.

While every effort has been made to ensure the reliability of the information presented in this publication, Gale, a part of Cengage Learning, does not
guarantee the accuracy of the data contained herein. Gale accepts no payment
for listing; and inclusion in the publication of any organization, agency, institution, publication, service, or individual does not imply endorsement of the editors or publisher. Errors brought to the attention of the publisher and verified to
the satisfaction of the publisher will be corrected in future editions.

LIBRARY OF CONGRESS CATALOGING-IN-PUBLICATION DATA

Bowling, beatniks, and bell-bottoms : pop culture of 20th- and
21st-century America / Cynthia Johnson, editor ; Lawrence W. Baker, project
editor. —2nd ed.
    v. cm. —
    Contents: v. 1. 1900s-1910s — v. 2. 1920s-1930s — v. 3. 1940s-1950s —
v. 4. 1960s-1970s — v. 5. 1980s-1990s — v. 6. 2000-2009.
    ISBN-13: 978-1-4144-1165-1 (set : alk. paper)
    ISBN-10: 1-4144-1165-0 (set : alk. paper)
    ISBN-13: 978-1-4144-1166-8 (v. 1 : alk. paper)
    ISBN-10: 1-4144-1166-9 (v. 1 : alk. paper)
    [etc.]
    1. United States—Civilization—20th century—Miscellanea—Juvenile
literature. 2. United States—Civilization—21st century—Miscellanea—
Juvenile literature. 3. Popular culture—United States—History—20th century—
Miscellanea—Juvenile literature. 4. Popular culture—United States—
History—21st century—Miscellanea—Juvenile literature. I. Johnson, Cynthia,
1969– II. Baker, Lawrence W.
    E169.1.B7825 2012
    306.097309′04—dc23   2012002579

Gale
27500 Drake Rd.
Farmington Hills, MI, 48331-3535

978-1-4144-1165-1 (set)   1-4144-1165-0 (set)
978-1-4144-1166-8 (vol. 1)   1-4144-1166-9 (vol. 1)
978-1-4144-1167-5 (vol. 2)   1-4144-1167-7 (vol. 2)
978-1-4144-1168-2 (vol. 3)   1-4144-1168-5 (vol. 3)
978-1-4144-1169-9 (vol. 4)   1-4144-1169-3 (vol. 4)
978-1-4144-1170-5 (vol. 5)   1-4144-1170-7 (vol. 5)
978-1-4144-1171-2 (vol. 6)   1-4144-1171-5 (vol. 6)

This title is also available as an e-book.
ISBN-13: 978-1-4144-1181-1   ISBN-10: 1-4144-1181-2
Contact your Gale, a part of Cengage Learning sales representative for ordering
information

Printed in China
1 2 3 4 5 6 7 16 15 14 13 12

Contents

Food and Drink

Music

Print Culture

Sports and Games

TV and Radio

The Way We Lived

The Way We Lived

The Way We Lived

VOLUME 6
2000s

Commerce

Fashion

Music

Print Culture

Sports and Games

Entries by Alphabetical Order

Entries by Topic Category

Food and Drink

Music

Sports and Games

TV and Radio

First-edition Contributors

Timothy Berg. Visiting assistant professor, Western Michigan University. Ph.D., History, Purdue University, 1999.

Charles Coletta, Ph.D. Instructor, Department of Popular Culture, Bowling Green State University. Contributing writer, *St. James Encyclopedia of Popular Culture* (2000).

Rob Edelman. Instructor, State University of New York at Albany. Author, *Baseball on the Web* (1997) and *The Great Baseball Films* (1994). Co-author, *Matthau: A Life* (2002); *Meet the Mertzes* (1999); and *Angela Lansbury: A Life on Stage and Screen* (1996). Contributing editor, *Leonard Maltin's Movie & Video Guide, Leonard Maltin's Movie Encyclopedia,* and *Leonard Maltin's Family Viewing Guide.* Contributing writer, *International Dictionary of Films and Filmmakers* (2000); *St. James Encyclopedia of Popular Culture* (2000); *Women Film-makers & Their Films* (1998); *The Political Companion to American Film* (1994); and *Total Baseball* (1989). Film commentator, WAMC (Northeast) Public Radio.

Tina Gianoulis. Freelance writer. Contributing writer, *World War I Reference Library* (2001–2); *Constitutional Amendments: From Freedom of Speech to Flag Burning* (2001); *International Dictionary of Films and Filmmakers* (2000); *St. James Encyclopedia of Popular Culture* (2000); and mystories.com, a daytime drama Web site (1997–98).

Sheldon Goldfarb. Archivist, Alma Mater Society of the University of British Columbia. Ph.D., English, University of British Columbia. Author, *William Makepeace Thackeray: An Annotated Bibliography, 1976–1987* (1989). Editor, *Catherine,* by William Makepeace Thackeray (1999).

Jill Gregg Clever, A.A., B.A., M.L.I.S. Graduate of Michigan State University, Thomas Edison State College, and Wayne State University. Business-technology specialist, Toledo–Lucas County Public Library.

Justin Gustainis. Professor of communication, State University of New York at Plattsburgh. Author, *American Rhetoric and the Vietnam War* (1993).

Audrey Kupferberg. Film consultant and archivist. Instructor, State University of New York at Albany. Co-author, *Matthau: A Life* (2002); *Meet the Mertzes* (1999); and *Angela Lansbury: A Life on Stage and Screen* (1996). Contributing editor, *Leonard Maltin's Family Viewing Guide.* Contributing writer, *St. James Encyclopedia of Popular Culture* (2000); *Women Filmmakers & Their Films* (1998); and *The American Film Institute Catalog of Feature Films.*

Edward Moran. Writer of American culture, music, and literature. Associate editor, *World Musicians* (1999); *World Authors* (1996); and *Random House Dictionary of the English Language* (1987; 1991). Contributing writer, *St. James Encyclopedia of Popular Culture* (2000). Editor, *Rhythm,* a magazine of world music and global culture (2001).

Sara Pendergast. President, Full Circle Editorial. Vice president, Group 3 Editorial. Co-editor, *St. James Encyclopedia of Popular Culture* (2000). Co-author, *World War I Reference Library* (2001), among other publications.

Tom Pendergast. Editorial director, Full Circle Editorial. Ph.D., American studies, Purdue University. Author, *Creating the Modern Man: American Magazines and Consumer Culture* (2000). Co-editor, *St. James Encyclopedia of Popular Culture* (2000).

Karl Rahder. M.A., University of Chicago Committee on International Relations. Author, several articles on international history and politics.

Chris Routledge. Freelance writer and editor. Ph.D., American literature, University of Newcastle upon Tyne (UK). Author, "The Chevalier and the Priest: Deductive Method in Poe, Chesterton, and Borges," in *Clues: A Journal of Detection* (2001). Editor, *Mystery in Children's Literature: From the Rational to the Supernatural* (2001).

Robert E. Schnakenberg. Senior writer, History Book Club. Author, *The Encyclopedia Shatnerica* (1998).

Steven Schneider. Ph.D. candidate, philosophy, Harvard University; Ph.D. candidate, cinema studies, New York University. Author, *An Auteur on Elm Street: The Cinema of Wes Craven* (forthcoming). Co-editor, *Horror International* (forthcoming) and *Dark Thoughts: Philosophic Reflections on Cinematic Horror* (forthcoming). Contributing writer, *British Horror Cinema* (2002); *Car Crash Culture* (2001); and numerous film journals.

Robert C. Sickels. Assistant professor of American film and popular culture, Whitman College. Ph.D., English, University of Nevada. Author, "A Politically Correct Ethan Edwards: Clint Eastwood's The Outlaw Josey Wales" in *Journal of Popular Film & Television* (forthcoming); "'70s Disco Daze: Paul Thomas Anderson's Boogie Nights and the Last Golden Age of Irresponsibility" in *Journal of Popular Culture* (forthcoming). Contributor, *St. James Encyclopedia of Popular Culture* (2000).

Reader's Guide

Popular culture—as we know it—was born in America, though historians disagree as to exactly when. Was it in 1893, when magazine publishers used new technologies to cut the costs of their magazines to a dime and sell hundreds of thousands of copies? Or was it in 1905, when the invention of the nickelodeon brought low-cost films to people all across the nation? Or was it back in 1886, when Richard Sears and Alvah Roebuck sent out their first catalog, which allowed people from all over to choose from among hundreds and then thousands of the same goods?

No matter the exact date, by the turn of the twentieth century, American magazine publishers, retailers, moviemakers, and other entertainers were bringing their goods before larger numbers of Americans than ever before. These magazines, movies, advertisements, shopping experiences, sports teams, and more were what we know as "popular culture," because they could be enjoyed firsthand by masses of Americans.

The story of America as revealed by its popular culture is complex and fascinating. Readers of *Bowling, Beatniks, and Bell-Bottoms: Pop Culture of 20th- and 21st-Century America* will discover, for example, that the comedic forms first developed by vaudeville comedians at the turn of the twentieth century lived on in film, radio, and finally television. They will learn that black musicians created the musical forms that are most distinctly American: blues and jazz. And they will realize that popular culture reacted to things like war and economic depressions in ways that were surprising and unexpected. The study of popular culture has a great deal to teach the student who is interested in how people use entertainment and consumption to make sense of their lives and shape their experience.

Bowling, Beatniks, and Bell-Bottoms gathers together essays that reflect the variety, diversity, and excitement of American popular culture of the twentieth and twenty-first centuries. This collection focuses more on events, fads, programs, performances, and products than on biographies of people, which are well documented in other sources. Even so, brief biographies of notables are sprinkled throughout. With approximately 850 essays on individual topics and dozens of overviews of pop culture trends, *Bowling, Beatniks, and Bell-Bottoms* covers a great deal of American popular culture, though not nearly enough. There are hundreds more people, bands, TV programs, films, and products that were worthy of mention but were left out due to space consideration. Our advisory board of media specialists, however, helped assure that the most prominent and studied subjects were included.

Have you ever wondered how the Slinky was invented, what Velveeta cheese is made of, or what people danced to before rock and roll? Those answers are in *Bowling, Beatniks, and Bell-Bottoms,* along with many others. It is our hope that this collection will bring both information and pleasure to all students of American culture.

Organization

Bowling, Beatniks, and Bell-Bottoms is arranged chronologically by decade over six volumes (two decades per volume for the twentieth century, and one volume covering the first decade of the twenty-first century). The approximately 850 entries are grouped into nine topic sections: Commerce, Fashion, Film and Theater, Food and Drink, Music, Print Culture, Sports and Games, TV and Radio, and The Way We Lived (though not all topics appear in every decade). Many subjects can easily appear in several different decades, so those essays are placed in either the decade in which the product was invented or the fad initiated, or in the decade in which the subject was most prominent or popular. In addition, several of the essays could have appeared under different topics (such as a book that was made into a movie), so those essays appear under the topic where it was best known. Users should make frequent use of the index or the two additional tables of contents (arranged alphabetically by entry name and by topic category) to locate an entry.

Essays range in length from 150 to 1000 words, with the majority averaging less than 500 words. Every essay aims to describe the topic and analyze the topic's contribution to popular culture. Each essay lists additional sources on the topic, including books, magazine or journal articles, and Web sites. Whenever possible, references to books are geared to younger readers. The editor and writers have personally visited every Web site mentioned and believe that these sites contain content that will assist the reader in understanding the subject. Due to the nature of the World Wide Web, it is possible that not all Web links will still function at the time of publication.

Bowling, Beatniks, and Bell-Bottoms also provides these features:

- A timeline that highlights key historic and pop culture events of the twentieth and twenty-first centuries
- A general overview of each decade
- A multipaged "At a Glance" box that breaks down "What We Said," "What We Read," "What We Watched," "What We Listened To," and "Who We Knew"
- An overview of each topic section in each decade
- Approximately 450 photos and illustrations
- Extensive use of cross references (pointing to decade, topic, and volume)

Acknowledgments

A thank-you encore goes to the advisors of this publication (their professional affiliation at the time of the publication of the first edition is noted): Catherine Bond, Department Chair, Library and Media Services, Conestoga High School, Berwyn, Pennsylvania; Cathy Chauvette, Assistant Regional Branch Manager, Fairfax County Public Library, Fairfax County, Virginia; Nancy Schlosser Garabed, Library Media Specialist, Council Rock High School, Newtown, Pennsylvania; Ann West LaPrise, Junior High/Elementary Media Specialist, Huron School District, New Boston, Michigan; and Nina Levine, Library Media Specialist, Blue Mountain Middle School, Cortlandt Manor, New York. Their input during the preparation of the first edition remains valuable.

The contributions of the writers from the first edition are noted on the contributors page (which reprints their background at the time of the first edition). For this second edition, much gratitude is given to writers David Larkins, Annette Petrusso, Maureen Reed, Patrick Walsh, and Greg Wilson.

Much appreciation goes to copyeditor Maxwell Valentine, proofreader Rebecca Valentine, indexer Theresa Murray, and typesetter

PreMediaGlobal. Additional thanks to Scott Rosen at the Bill Smith Group for permissions and imaging selection and Barry Puckett for image processing assistance.

Comments and Suggestions

We welcome your comments on *Bowling, Beatniks, and Bell-Bottoms.* Please send correspondence to: Editors, *Bowling, Beatniks, and Bell-Bottoms,* U•X•L, 27500 Drake Rd., Farmington Hills, MI 48331-3535; call toll-free: 800-877-4253; fax to 248-414-5043; or send e-mail via www.cengage.com.

Cynthia Johnson, Editor

Timeline

1900 On January 29, Ban Johnson forms the American League to compete against baseball's National League.

1900 In February, Eastman Kodak introduces the Brownie Camera.

1900 In March, the Good Roads Campaign tries to build support for better roads. At the time, there are only ten miles of paved roads in the nation.

1900 On March 31, the first ad for an automobile appears in the *Saturday Evening Post.*

1900 On April 23, Buffalo Bill Cody's *Wild West Show* opens at Madison Square Garden in New York City.

1900 On November 6, Republican William McKinley is reelected U.S. president, with New York governor Theodore Roosevelt as his vice president.

1900 On November 12, *Floradora,* one of the most popular theatrical musicals of the decade, premieres in New York. It runs for more than five hundred performances.

1901 On February 25, U.S. Steel is formed out of ten companies and becomes the world's largest industrial corporation.

1901 On March 13, steel tycoon Andrew Carnegie donates $2.2 million to fund a New York public library system.

1901 On September 6, President William McKinley is shot by an assassin in Buffalo, New York, and dies eight days later from complications from gangrene due to improperly dressed wounds. Theodore Roosevelt becomes president.

1901 On October 16, President Theodore Roosevelt starts a national controversy when he dines with black leader Booker T. Washington in the White House.

1902 The Teddy Bear is introduced, named after President Theodore Roosevelt.

1902 On January 1, in the first Rose Bowl football game, the University of Michigan defeats Stanford 49–0.

1902 On March 18, Italian opera singer Enrico Caruso produces his first phonographic recording.

1902 On April 16, Tally's Electric Theater, the first theater solely devoted to presenting motion pictures, opens in Los Angeles, California.

1902 On December 21, Guglielmo Marconi transmits the first wireless signals across the Atlantic Ocean.

1903 *Redbook* magazine is founded.

1903 The Portage Lakers of Houghton, Michigan—the first professional hockey team from the United States—win the International Hockey League championship.

1903 On January 22, the United States signs a 99-year lease on what will become the Panama Canal Zone, where it will build a canal that connects the Caribbean Sea to the Pacific Ocean.

1903 In February, the *Ladies' Home Journal* becomes the first American magazine to reach one million paid subscriptions.

1903 On May 23, two men make the first transcontinental automobile trip from San Francisco to New York in sixty-four days. Upon returning home, one driver is ticketed for exceeding the speed limit of six miles per hour.

1903 On August 14, Jim Jeffries defeats James J. "Gentleman Jim" Corbett to retain the world heavyweight boxing title.

1903 On September 12, Scott Joplin's ragtime opera *A Guest of Honor* begins a midwest tour.

1903 In October, the Boston Pilgrims defeat the Pittsburgh Pirates in the first World Series to pit an American League team against a National League team.

1903 On December 1, Edwin S. Porter's film *The Great Train Robbery* is considered the first Western and the first American film with a plot.

1903 On December 17, Wilbur and Orville Wright make the first sustained flight at Kitty Hawk, North Carolina.

1904 The Ford Motor Company sells fourteen hundred of its Model A cars.

1904 On April 20, the World's Fair opens in St. Louis, Missouri.

1904 On May 5, Cy Young pitches baseball's first perfect game.

1904 On November 8, Theodore Roosevelt is reelected president.

1905 The German navy launches the first submarine.

1905 African American leader W. E. B. Du Bois helps found the Niagara Movement, an organization to advance African American issues.

1905 On May 5, the *Chicago Defender,* the first major black newspaper, begins publication.

1905 In June, the era of the nickelodeon begins when Harry Davis's Pittsburgh, Pennsylvania, movie theater offers continuous movie showings. By the end of the decade, more than eight thousand nickel-admission movie theaters are in operation.

1905 On June 18, the Twentieth Century Limited begins train service between Chicago, Illinois, and New York City and boasts a travel time of only eighteen hours.

1906 Kellogg's Corn Flakes breakfast cereal is introduced.

1906 In February, Upton Sinclair publishes *The Jungle,* a novel depicting the horrible conditions in the meat-packing industry. The work prompts the passage of the Meat Inspection Act.

1906 On April 14, President Theodore Roosevelt coins the term "muckraking" when he criticizes journalists who expose abuses and corruption and miss the larger social picture.

1906 On April 18, a major earthquake and fire destroy much of San Francisco, California.

1906 On May 3, the First Annual Advertising Show in New York City heralds the beginning of an important American industry.

1906 On November 21, the first voice radio transmission travels eleven miles from Plymouth to Brant Rock, Massachusetts.

1907 Work begins on the Panama Canal.

1907 On January 23, in what newspapers call the "trial of the century," millionaire Harry K. Thaw is tried for the murder of world-famous architect Stanford White over the honor of Thaw's wife, showgirl Evelyn Nesbit.

1907 On June 10, French motion picture pioneers Auguste and Louis Lumière announce they have developed a method for producing color film.

1907 On July 8, Florenz Ziegfeld's musical revue, the *Ziegfeld Follies,* opens in New York.

1907 On December 3, actress Mary Pickford makes her stage debut in *The Warrens of Virginia.*

1908 The world's first skyscraper, the forty-seven-story Singer Building, is completed in New York City.

1908 The General Motors Corporation is formed and soon becomes the biggest competitor of the Ford Motor Company.

1908 In March, the Original Independent Show, organized in New York, includes works by American painters Edward Hopper, George Bellows, and Rockwell Kent.

1908 On September 6, Israel Zangwill's play *The Melting Pot* opens in New York City; the title becomes an internationally recognized description of the United States.

1908 On October 1, the Ford Motor Company unveils its Model T with a price tag of $825. It soon becomes the best-selling automobile of its time.

1908 On November 3, former U.S. secretary of war William Howard Taft is elected president.

1908 On December 26, Jack Johnson defeats Tommy Burns to become the first black world heavyweight boxing champion. His victory is considered an outrage by white racists.

1909 The fifty-story Metropolitan Life Insurance Tower in New York City becomes the world's tallest building.

1909 The Ford Motor Company manufactures nineteen thousand Model T cars.

1909 On March 16, the Federal Bureau of Investigation is created as a federal law enforcement agency.

1909 On March 23, former president Theodore Roosevelt leaves for a safari in Africa. He is paid $50,000 by *Scribner's Magazine* for his account of the trip.

1909 On April 6, U.S. Navy commander Robert Peary reaches the North Pole.

1909 On May 3, the first wireless press message is sent from New York City to Chicago, Illinois.

1909 On July 12, the U.S. Congress asks the states to authorize a national income tax.

1910 Western novelist Zane Grey's book *Heritage of the Desert* becomes a huge commercial success, starting his career of bringing the American West to the reading world.

1910 Levi Strauss and Company begins making casual play clothes for children.

1910 The Boy Scouts of America are founded in Chicago, Illinois.

1910 On February 28, Russian ballerina Anna Pavlova makes her American debut at the Metropolitan Opera House in New York City.

1910 On March 28, the first one-man show by artist Pablo Picasso opens at photographer and editor Alfred Stieglitz's 291 Gallery in New York City.

1910 In November, the National Association for the Advancement of Colored People (NAACP) publishes the first issue of the *Crisis* magazine, edited by W. E. B. Du Bois.

1910 On November 3, the Chicago Grand Opera opens with a production of *Aida,* by Giuseppe Verdi.

1911 Irving Berlin composes "Alexander's Ragtime Band," the song that popularized ragtime music.

1911 Air conditioning is invented.

1911 *Photoplay,* the first movie fan magazine, is published.

1911 On March 25, in New York City, 146 female workers are killed in the Triangle Shirtwaist Factory fire, alerting Americans to the dangers women face in industrial labor.

1911 On May 23, President William Howard Taft dedicates the New York Public Library.

1911 On May 30, the first Indianapolis 500 auto race is won by Ray Harroun with an average speed of 74.59 mph.

1911 On August 8, *Pathe's Weekly,* the first regular newsreel to be produced in the United States, is released to motion picture theaters.

1911 On December 19, the Association of American Painters and Sculptors is founded.

1912 New Mexico and Arizona become the forty-seventh and forty-eighth states.

1912 The Little Theater in Chicago, Illinois, and the Toy Theater in Boston, Massachusetts, the first influential little theaters in the United States, are founded.

1912 Dancers Irene and Vernon Castle start a craze for ballroom dancing.

1912 On April 15, the *Titanic* sinks on its maiden voyage from Ireland to the United States, killing 1,517.

1912 In August, photographer and editor Alfred Stieglitz devotes an entire issue of his periodical *Camera Work* to the modern art movement.

1912 On August 5, former president Theodore Roosevelt is nominated as the presidential candidate of the newly formed Progressive Party.

1912 On October 31, *The Musketeers of Pig Alley,* a film by D. W. Griffith that points out the social evils of poverty and crime on the streets of New York, is released.

1912 On November 5, New Jersey governor Woodrow Wilson is elected president.

1912 On December 10, the Famous Players Film Company registers for copyright of the five-reel feature film *The Count of Monte Cristo,* directed by Edwin S. Porter.

1913 The 792-foot-high Woolworth Building in New York City becomes the world's tallest building, a record it holds until 1930.

1913 The first crossword puzzle is published.

1913 The Jesse Lasky Feature Play Co., which later would become Paramount Pictures, is established in Hollywood, California.

1913 The Panama Canal is completed, and officially opens on August 15, 1914.

1913 On February 17, the International Exhibition of Modern Art, known as the Armory Show, opens in New York City. It is the first opportunity for many Americans to view modern art.

1913 On February 25, the Sixteenth Amendment to the Constitution is approved, authorizing a federal income tax.

1913 On March 24, the million dollar, eighteen-hundred-seat Palace Theatre opens in New York City.

1913 On May 31, the Seventeenth Amendment to the Constitution is approved, providing for the direct election of U.S. senators by citizens, rather than by state legislatures.

1914 On February 13, the American Society of Composers, Authors, and Publishers (ASCAP), an organization that seeks royalty payments for public performances of music, is founded in New York City.

1914 In March, comedian Charles Chaplin begins to evolve the legendary character of the Little Tramp in the film *Mabel's Strange Predicament.*

1914 On July 3, the first telephone line connects New York City and San Francisco, California.

1914 On August 3, World War I starts in Europe when Germany invades Belgium. Soon all of Europe is drawn into the conflict, though the United States remains neutral.

1914 On September 5, a German submarine scores its first kill, sinking the British cruiser *Pathfinder,* as World War I intensifies.

1914 In September, in the World War I Battle of the Marne, Germany's advance into France is halted.

1914 On November 3, the first American exhibition of African sculpture opens at the 291 Gallery in New York City.

1914 On December 3, the Isadorables, six European dancers trained by American dancer Isadora Duncan, perform at Carnegie Hall in New York City after escaping with Duncan from her war-torn Europe.

1915 The first taxicab appears on the streets of New York City.

1915 The first professional football league is formed in Ohio and is called simply the Ohio League.

1915 Modern dancers Ruth St. Denis and Ted Shawn found the Denishawn School of Dancing in Los Angeles, California.

1915 Five hundred U.S. correspondents cover World War I in Europe.

1915 On March 10, the Russian Symphony Orchestra plays the American debut performance of the symphony *Prometheus* by Aleksandr Scriabin at Carnegie Hall in New York City. Color images are projected onto a screen as part of the show.

1915 On December 10, the Ford Motor Company manufactures its one millionth Model T automobile.

1916 The Boeing Aircraft Company produces its first biplane.

1916 Newspaper publisher William Randolph Hearst inaugurates the *City Life* arts section as a supplement to his Sunday newspapers.

1916 In November, inventor and radio pioneer Lee De Forest begins to transmit daily music broadcasts from his home in New York City.

1916 On November 7, Woodrow Wilson is reelected president after campaigning on the pledge to keep the United States out of the war in Europe.

1917 The Russian Revolution brings communism to Russia, setting the stage for nearly a century of intermittent conflict with the United States.

1917 Showman George M. Cohan composes the song that was a musical call-to-arms during World War I: "Over There."

1917 Motion picture pioneer Cecil B. DeMille directs *The Little American,* a patriotic melodrama starring Mary Pickford.

1917 On April 6, the United States declares war on Germany after German submarines continue to attack U.S. merchant ships.

1917 On May 28, Benny Leonard wins the lightweight boxing championship, which he holds until his retirement in 1924 while building a record of 209–5; he makes a comeback in 1931.

1917 On August 19, the managers of the New York Giants and Cincinnati Reds are arrested for playing baseball on Sunday.

1917 On October 27, sixteen-year-old Russian-born violinist Jascha Heifetz makes his debut American performance at Carnegie Hall in New York City.

1918 The annual O. Henry Awards for short fiction are inaugurated in honor of short story writer O. Henry (a pseudonym for William Sydney Porter).

1918 On January 8, President Woodrow Wilson delivers his "Fourteen Points" address before Congress, outlining his plans for the shape of the postwar world.

1918 In March, *The Little Review* begins to serialize the novel *Ulysses,* by James Joyce, which features stream of consciousness techniques and a kind of private language.

1918 On November 11, Germany signs an armistice with the Allies, ending the fighting in World War I.

1918 In December, the Theatre Guild is founded in New York City.

1919 *Maid of Harlem,* an all-black-cast musical starring "Fats" Waller, Mamie Smith, Johnny Dunn, and Perry Bradford, draws enthusiastic crowds at the Lincoln Theatre in New York City.

1919 On January 29, Prohibition begins with the adoption of the Eighteenth Amendment to the Constitution, which bans the manufacture, sale, and transportation of intoxicating liquors.

1919 On February 5, United Artists, an independent film distribution company, is founded by Charles Chaplin, Douglas Fairbanks, D. W. Griffith, and Mary Pickford.

1919 On June 28, the Treaty of Versailles is signed by the Allied powers, officially ending World War I. Germany is forced to pay costly reparations for the damage it caused during the war.

1919 On July 4, Jack Dempsey defeats Jess Willard to win the world heavyweight boxing championship.

1919 On October 31, the Provincetown Players stage *The Dreamy Kid,* by Eugene O'Neill, with an all-black cast.

1919 On December 22, Attorney General A. Mitchell Palmer authorizes government raids on communists, anarchists, and other political radicals. These "Palmer raids" are part of a nationwide "red scare."

1920 Sinclair Lewis publishes the novel *Main Street.*

1920 Douglas Fairbanks stars in the film *The Mark of Zorro.*

1920 On January 5, the Radio Corporation of America (RCA) is founded and becomes a leading radio broadcaster.

1920 On February 12, the National Negro Baseball League is founded.

1920 On August 20, the first radio news bulletins are broadcast by station 8MK in Detroit, Michigan.

1920 On August 26, the Nineteenth Amendment to the Constitution gives women the right to vote.

1920 On September 28, eight Chicago White Sox players are charged with throwing the 1919 World Series in what becomes known as the "Black Sox Scandal." They are eventually banned from the game for life.

1920 On September 29, New York Yankee Babe Ruth breaks his own single-season home run record with 54 home runs.

1920 On November 1, Eugene O'Neill's play *The Emperor Jones* opens in New York City.

1920 On November 6, U.S. senator Warren G. Harding of Ohio is elected president.

1921 The Ford Motor Company announces a plan to produce one million automobiles a year.

1921 The Phillips Gallery in Washington, D.C., becomes the first American museum of modern art.

1921 In this year, 13 percent of Americans own telephones.

1921 On March 10, the first White Castle hamburger chain opens in Wichita, Kansas.

1921 On April 11, radio station KDKA in Pittsburgh, Pennsylvania, broadcasts the first sports event on radio, a boxing match between Johnny Ray and Johnny Dundee. Later that year, the World Series is broadcast.

1921 On May 23, *Shuffle Along* is the first black Broadway musical written and directed by African Americans.

1921 On July 29, Adolf Hitler is elected dictator of the Nazi Party in Munich, Germany.

1921 On September 8, the first Miss America pageant is held in Washington, D.C.

1921 On November 2, Margaret Sanger founds the American Birth Control League in New York City, raising the anger of many religious groups, especially Catholic groups.

1922 Robert Flaherty releases the documentary film *Nanook of the North.*

1922 Irish author James Joyce publishes *Ulysses,* which is banned in some countries for its alleged obscenity.

1922 F. Scott Fitzgerald publishes *Tales of the Jazz Age.*

1922 The American Professional Football Association changes its name to the National Football League (NFL).

1922 *Reader's Digest* magazine is founded.

1922 Al Jolson pens the popular song "Toot Toot Tootsie."

1922 On May 5, Coco Chanel introduces Chanel No. 5, which becomes the world's best-known perfume.

1922 On August 28, the first advertisement is aired on radio station WEAF in New York City.

1922 On December 30, the Union of Soviet Socialist Republics (USSR) is established with Russia at its head.

1923 Cecil B. DeMille directs the epic film *The Ten Commandments.*

1923 Charles Kettering develops a method for bringing colored paint to mass-produced cars.

1923 Bessie Smith's "Down Hearted Blues" is one of the first blues songs to be recorded.

1923 *Time* magazine begins publication.

1923 On April 6, trumpet player Louis Armstrong records his first solo on "Chimes Blues" with King Oliver's Creole Jazz Band.

1923 On August 3, President Warren G. Harding dies and Vice President Calvin Coolidge takes office.

1924 John Ford directs the Western film *The Iron Horse.*

1924 The Metro-Goldwyn-Mayer (MGM) film studio is formed in Hollywood, California.

1924 Evangelist Aimee Semple McPherson begins broadcasting from the first religious radio station, KFSG in Los Angeles, California.

1924 The stock market begins a boom that will last until 1929.

1924 On January 1, there are 2.5 million radios in American homes, up from 2,000 in 1920.

1924 On February 12, the tomb of King Tutankhamen, or King Tut, is opened in Egypt after having been sealed for four thousand years.

1924 On February 24, George Gershwin's *Rhapsody in Blue* is performed by an orchestra in New York City.

1924 On March 10, J. Edgar Hoover is appointed director of the Federal Bureau of Investigation.

1924 In June, the Chrysler Corporation is founded and competes with General Motors and Ford.

1924 On November 4, incumbent Calvin Coolidge is elected president.

1925 In one of the most famous years in American literature, F. Scott Fitzgerald publishes *The Great Gatsby,* Ernest Hemingway publishes *In Our Time,* and Theodore Dreiser publishes *An American Tragedy.*

1925 Lon Chaney stars in the film *The Phantom of the Opera.*

1925 The *WSM Barn Dance* radio program begins broadcasting from Nashville, Tennessee; the name is later changed to *Grand Ole Opry* and it becomes the leading country music program.

1925 The *New Yorker* magazine begins publication and features the prices paid for bootleg liquor.

1925 In February, the Boeing aircraft company builds a plane capable of flying over the Rocky Mountains with a full load of mail.

1925 On May 8, the Brotherhood of Sleeping Car Porters, founded by A. Philip Randolph, is one of the first black labor unions.

1925 In July, in the Scopes "Monkey" trial, a Tennessee teacher is tried and found guilty of teaching evolution in a trial that attracts national attention.

1925 On August 8, forty thousand Ku Klux Klan members march in Washington, D.C., to broaden support for their racist organization.

1926 Latin idol Rudolph Valentino stars in the film *The Son of the Sheik.*

1926 Ernest Hemingway publishes *The Sun Also Rises.*

1926 The Book-of-the-Month Club is launched to offer quality books to subscribers.

1926 On March 7, the first transatlantic radio-telephone conversation links New York City and London, England.

1926 On March 17, *The Girl Friend,* a musical with songs by Richard Rodgers and Lorenz Hart, opens on Broadway.

1926 On April 18, dancer Martha Graham makes her first professional appearance in New York City.

1927 Al Jolson stars in the film *The Jazz Singer,* the first film to have sound. Clara Bow—the "It" girl—stars in *It.*

1927 On January 1, the Rose Bowl football game is broadcast coast-to-coast on the radio.

1927 On April 7, television is first introduced in America, but investors are skeptical.

1927 On May 21, Charles Lindbergh completes his nonstop flight from New York City to Paris, France, and is given a hero's welcome.

1927 On May 25, the Ford Motor Company announces that production of the Model T will be stopped in favor of the modern Model A.

1927 On September 22, the heavyweight championship fight between Jack Dempsey and Gene Tunney becomes the first sports gate to top $2 million.

1927 On December 4, Duke Ellington's orchestra begins a long run at the Cotton Club nightclub in Harlem, New York.

1927 On December 27, the Jerome Kern and Oscar Hammerstein musical *Show Boat* opens on Broadway in New York City.

1928 On April 15, the New York Rangers become the first American team to win the National Hockey League Stanley Cup.

1928 On May 11, WGY in Schenectady, New York, offers the first scheduled television service, though the high price of televisions keeps most people from owning them.

1928 On July 30, the Eastman Kodak company introduces color motion pictures.

1928 On November 6, former U.S. secretary of commerce Herbert Hoover is elected president.

1928 On December 13, George Gershwin's *An American in Paris* opens at Carnegie Hall in New York City.

1928 On December 26, swimmer Johnny Weissmuller retires from competition after setting sixty-seven world records.

1929 Mickey Mouse makes his first appearance in *Steamboat Willie,* an animated film made by Walt Disney.

1929 Commercial airlines carry 180,000 passengers during the year.

1929 Ernest Hemingway publishes *A Farewell to Arms,* a novel set during World War I.

1929 Nick Lucas's "Tiptoe through the Tulips with Me" and Louis Armstrong's "Ain't Misbehavin'" are two of the year's most popular songs.

1929 On February 14, in the Saint Valentine's Day Massacre, gunmen working for Chicago, Illinois, mobster Al Capone gun down seven members of a rival gang.

1929 On October 29, the stock market collapses on a day known as "Black Tuesday," marking the start of what will become the Great Depression.

1930 Grant Wood paints *American Gothic.*

1930 The Continental Baking company introduces Wonder Bread to the nation, the first commercially produced sliced bread.

1930 Unemployment reaches four million as the economy worsens.

1930 On January 14, jazz greats Benny Goodman, Glenn Miller, Jimmy Dorsey, and Jack Teagarden play George and Ira Gershwin's songs, including "I've Got a Crush on You," in the musical *Strike Up the Band* at the Mansfield Theater in New York City.

1930 On March 6, General Foods introduces the nation's first frozen foods.

1930 On May 3, Ogden Nash, a poet who will become famous for his funny, light verse, publishes "Spring Comes to Murray Hill" in the *New Yorker* magazine and soon begins work at the magazine.

1930 On September 8, the comic strip *Blondie* begins.

1930 On October 14, *Girl Crazy,* starring Ethel Merman, opens at New York's Guild Theater. The musical features songs by George Gershwin, Walter Donaldson, and Ira Gershwin, including "I Got Rhythm" and "Embraceable You."

1931 The horror films *Dracula* and *Frankenstein* are both released.

1931 Nevada legalizes gambling in order to bring revenue to the state.

1931 On March 3, "The Star Spangled Banner" becomes the national anthem by congressional vote.

1931 On April 30, the Empire State Building, the tallest building in the world, opens in New York City.

1931 On June 3, brother-and-sister dancers Fred and Adele Astaire perform for the last time together on the first revolving stage.

1931 On July 27, *Earl Carroll's Vanities,* featuring naked chorus girls, opens at the three-thousand-seat Earl Carroll Theater in New York City.

1931 On October 12, the comic strip *Dick Tracy* begins.

1932 Edwin Herbert Land, a Harvard College dropout, invents Polaroid film.

1932 On May 2, *The Jack Benny Show* premieres as a variety show on radio and runs for twenty-three years and then another ten years on television.

1932 On July 30, the Summer Olympic Games open in Los Angeles, California, and feature record-breaking performances by Americans Babe Didrikson and Eddie Tolan.

1932 On July 31, in German parliamentary elections, the Nazi Party receives the most seats but is unable to form a government.

1932 On November 7, the radio adventure *Buck Rogers in the Twenty-Fifth Century* premieres on CBS and runs until 1947.

1932 On November 8, New York governor Franklin D. Roosevelt is elected president, promising to take steps to improve the economy. In his first one hundred days in office, Roosevelt introduces much legislation to use the government to aid those harmed by the Great Depression.

1932 On December 27, Radio City Music Hall opens at the Rockefeller Center in New York City.

1933 President Franklin D. Roosevelt presents the nation with his first radio address, known as a "fireside chat."

1933 Walt Disney releases the feature film *The Three Little Pigs.*

1933 On January 3, *The Lone Ranger* radio drama premieres on WXYZ radio in Detroit, Michigan.

1933 On January 30, Nazi leader Adolf Hitler becomes chancellor of Germany. Hitler soon seizes all power and sets out to attack his party's political enemies.

1933 On May 27, fan dancer Sally Rand attracts thousands with her performance at the Chicago World's Fair that celebrated the Century of Progress.

1933 On September 30, *Ah, Wilderness,* acclaimed American playwright Eugene O'Neill's only comedy, opens at the Guild Theater in New York City.

1933 On December 5, the Twenty-first Amendment to the Constitution puts an end to Prohibition.

1934 The first pipeless organ is patented by Laurens Hammond. The Hammond organ starts a trend toward more electrically amplified instruments.

1934 Dashiell Hammett publishes *The Thin Man,* one of the first hard-boiled detective novels.

1934 The Apollo Theater opens in Harlem, New York, as a showcase for black performers.

1934 German director Fritz Lang flees Nazi Germany to make movies in the United States.

1934 On May 5, bank robbers and murderers Bonnie Parker and Clyde Barrow are killed by lawmen in Louisiana.

1934 On July 1, the Motion Picture Producers and Distributors of America (MPPDA) association creates the Hay's Office to enforce codes that limit the amount and types of sexuality and other immoral behavior in films.

1934 On July 22, "Public Enemy No. 1" John Dillinger is shot and killed outside a Chicago, Illinois, theater by FBI agents and local police.

1934 On August 13, Al Capp's *Li'l Abner* comic strip debuts in eight newspapers.

1934 On August 19, Adolf Hitler is declared president of Germany, though he prefers the title Führer (leader).

1935 One out of four American households receives government relief as the Depression deepens.

1935 Twenty million Monopoly board games are sold in one week.

1935 The first Howard Johnson roadside restaurant opens in Boston, Massachusetts.

1935 The Works Progress Administration Federal Arts Projects, some of President Franklin D. Roosevelt's many New Deal programs, give work to artists painting post offices and other federal buildings.

1935 In April, *Your Hit Parade* is first heard on radio and offers a selection of hit songs.

1935 On April 16, the radio comedy-drama *Fibber McGee and Molly* debuts on NBC and runs until 1952.

1935 On May 24, the first nighttime major league baseball game is played in Cincinnati, Ohio.

1935 On October 10, *Porgy and Bess,* known as the "most American opera of the decade," opens in New York City at the Alvin Theater. The music George Gershwin wrote for the opera combined blues, jazz, and southern folk.

1936 American Airlines introduces transcontinental airline service.

1936 Ten African American athletes, including Jesse Owens, win gold medals in the Summer Olympics held in Berlin, Germany, embarrassing Nazi leader Adolf Hitler, who had declared the inferiority of black athletes.

1936 Dust storms in the Plains states force thousands to flee the region, many to California.

1936 Popular public-speaking teacher Dale Carnegie publishes his book *How to Win Friends and Influence People.*

1936 To increase feelings of nationalism, the Department of the Interior hires folksinger Woody Guthrie to travel throughout the U.S. Southwest performing his patriotic songs such as "Those Oklahoma Hills."

1936 In the Soviet Union, the Communist Party begins its Great Purge, executing anyone who resists the party's social and economic policies. By 1938, it is estimated that ten million people have been killed.

1936 Throughout Europe, countries scramble to form alliances with other countries for what seems to be a likely war. Germany and Italy join together to support the military government of Francisco Franco in Spain, while Great Britain and France sign nonaggression pacts with the Soviet Union.

1936 On July 18, the Spanish Civil War begins when Spanish military officers rise up against the Republican government of Spain.

1936 In October, the New York Yankees win the first of four World Series in a row.

1936 On November 3, Franklin D. Roosevelt is reelected as president of the United States.

1936 On November 23, the first issue of *Life* magazine is published.

1937 Dr. Seuss becomes a popular children's book author with the publication of *And to Think That I Saw It on Mulberry Street.*

1937 The Hormel company introduces Spam, a canned meat.

1937 A poll shows that the average American listens to the radio for 4.5 hours a day.

1937 *Porky's Hare Hunt,* a short animated cartoon by Warner Bros., introduces audiences to the Bugs Bunny character and the talents of Mel Blanc, the voice of both Bugs Bunny and Porky Pig.

1937 The first soap opera, *Guiding Light,* is broadcast. It continues as a radio program until 1956 and moves to television.

1937 British writer J. R. R. Tolkien publishes *The Hobbit.*

1937 On June 22, black boxer Joe Louis knocks out Jim Braddock to win the world heavyweight boxing championship.

1937 On December 21, *Snow White and the Seven Dwarfs,* the first feature-length animated film, is presented by Walt Disney.

1938 Glenn Miller forms his own big band and begins to tour extensively.

1938 On January 17, the first jazz performance at Carnegie Hall in New York City is performed by Benny Goodman and His Orchestra, with Duke Ellington, Count Basie, and others.

1938 In June, the character Superman is introduced in *Action Comics #1.* By 1939, he appears in his own comic book series.

1938 On August 17, Henry Armstrong becomes the first boxer to hold three boxing titles at one time when he defeats Lou Ambers at New York City's Madison Square Garden.

1938 On October 31, Orson Welles's radio broadcast of H. G. Wells's science fiction novel *The War of the Worlds* is believed by many listeners to be a serious announcement of a Martian invasion, resulting in panic spreading throughout the country.

1938 On November 11, singer Kate Smith's performance of "God Bless America" is broadcast over the radio on Armistice Day.

1939 Singer Frank Sinatra joins the Tommy Dorsey band, where he will soon find great success.

1939 Federal spending on the military begins to revive the economy.

1939 Pocket Books, the nation's first modern paperback book company, is founded.

1939 The National Collegiate Athletic Association (NCAA) holds it first Final Four championship basketball series, which is won by the University of Oregon.

1939 *Gone with the Wind,* David O. Selznick's epic film about the Civil War, stars Vivien Leigh and Clark Gable.

1939 *The Wizard of Oz* whisks movie audiences into a fantasyland of magic and wonder. The film stars Judy Garland and includes such popular songs as "Somewhere Over the Rainbow," "Follow the Yellow Brick Road," and "We're Off to See the Wizard."

1939 On May 2, baseball great Lou "The Iron Man" Gehrig ends his consecutive game streak at 2,130 when he removes himself from the lineup.

1939 On September 1, German troops invade Poland, causing Great Britain and France to declare war on Germany and starting World War II. Days later, the Soviet Union invades Poland as well, and soon Germany and the Soviet Union divide Poland.

1940 The radio program *Superman* debuts, introducing the phrases "Up, up, and away!" and "This looks like a job for Superman!"

1940 On February 22, German troops begin construction of a concentration camp in Auschwitz, Poland.

1940 The first issue of the comic book *Batman* is published.

1940 On May 10, German forces invade Belgium and Holland, and later march into France.

1940 On June 10, Italy declares war on Britain and France.

1940 On June 14, the German army enters Paris, France.

1940 On August 24, Germany begins bombing London, England.

1940 On November 5, President Franklin D. Roosevelt is reelected for his third term.

1940 On November 13, the Disney film *Fantasia* opens in New York City.

1941 "Rosie the Riveter" becomes the symbol for the many women who are employed in various defense industries.

1941 *Citizen Kane,* which many consider the greatest movie of all time, is released, directed by and starring Orson Welles.

1941 On January 15, A. Philip Randolph leads the March on Washington to call for an end to racial discrimination in defense-industry employment. President Franklin D. Roosevelt eventually signs an executive order barring such discrimination.

1941 On March 17, the National Gallery of Art opens in Washington, D.C.

1941 On July 1, CBS and NBC begin offering about fifteen hours of commercial television programming each week—but few consumers have enough money to purchase television sets.

1941 On October 19, German troops lay siege to the Russian city of Moscow.

1941 On December 7, Japanese planes launch a surprise attack on the U.S. naval and air bases in Pearl Harbor, Hawaii, and declare war against the United States.

1941 On December 11, the United States declares war on Germany and Italy in response to those countries' declarations of war.

1942 On January 1, the annual Rose Bowl football game is played in Durham, North Carolina, rather than the usual Pasadena, California, location, to avoid the chance of a Japanese bombing attack.

1942 Humphrey Bogart and Ingrid Bergman star in *Casablanca,* set in war-torn Europe.

1942 On February 19, President Franklin D. Roosevelt signs an executive order placing all Japanese Americans on the West Coast in internment camps for the rest of the war.

1942 On May 5, sugar rationing starts in the United States, followed by the rationing of other products.

1942 In June, American troops defeat the Japanese at the Battle of Midway.

1942 On December 25, the comedy team of Abbott and Costello is voted the leading box-office attraction of 1942.

1943 Gary Cooper and Ingrid Bergman star in *For Whom the Bell Tolls,* the film version of the novel by Ernest Hemingway.

1943 On January 25, the Pentagon, the world's largest office complex and the home to the U.S. military, is completed in Arlington, Virginia.

1943 On March 14, composer Aaron Copland's *Fanfare for the Common Man* premieres in Cincinnati, Ohio.

1943 On March 30, the musical *Oklahoma!* opens on Broadway in New York City.

1943 During the summer, race riots break out in Detroit, Michigan, and Harlem, New York.

1943 On September 8, Italy surrenders to the Allies.

1943 On November 9, artist Jackson Pollock has his first solo show in New York City.

1943 On December 30, *Esquire* magazine loses its second-class mailing privileges after it is charged with being "lewd" and "lascivious" by the U.S. Post Office.

1944 *Seventeen* magazine debuts.

1944 *Double Indemnity,* directed by Billy Wilder, becomes one of the first of a new genre of movies known as *film noir.*

1944 On March 4, American planes bomb Berlin, Germany.

1944 On June 6, on "D-Day," Allied forces land in Normandy, France, and begin the liberation of western Europe.

1944 On June 22, the Serviceman's Readjustment Act, signed by President Franklin D. Roosevelt, provides funding for a variety of programs for returning soldiers, including education programs under the G.I. Bill.

1944 On August 25, Allied troops liberate Paris, France.

1944 On November 7, Franklin D. Roosevelt is reelected for an unprecedented fourth term as president.

1945 Chicago publisher John H. Johnson launches *Ebony* magazine.

1945 The radio program *The Adventures of Ozzie and Harriet* debuts.

1945 On January 27, the Soviet Red Army liberates Auschwitz, Poland, revealing the seriousness of German efforts to exterminate Jews.

1945 On April 12, President Franklin D. Roosevelt dies of a cerebral hemorrhage and Vice President Harry S. Truman takes over as president.

1945 On April 21, Soviet troops reach the outskirts of Berlin, the capital of Germany.

1945 On April 30, German leader Adolf Hitler commits suicide in Berlin, Germany, as Allied troops approach the city.

1945 On May 5, American poet Ezra Pound is arrested in Italy on charges of treason.

1945 On May 8, Germany surrenders to the Allies, bringing an end to World War II in Europe.

1945 On August 6, the United States drops the first atomic bomb on the Japanese city of Hiroshima, killing more than fifty thousand people.

1945 On August 9, the United States drops a second atomic bomb on Nagasaki, Japan.

1945 On September 2, Japan offers its unconditional surrender onboard the U.S.S. *Missouri* in Tokyo Bay, bringing an end to World War II.

1946 The Baby Boom begins as the birthrate rises 20 percent over the previous year.

1946 *It's a Wonderful Life,* starring Jimmy Stewart and directed by Frank Capra, becomes one of the most popular Christmas movies of all time.

1946 On January 10, the first General Assembly of the United Nations meets in London, England.

1946 On June 19, Joe Louis retains his title by knocking out Billy Conn in the first heavyweight boxing match ever shown on television.

1946 On December 11, country singer Hank Williams cuts his first single, "Calling You."

1947 On January 29, Arthur Miller's play *All My Sons* opens in New York City.

1947 On March 12, President Harry S. Truman announces his "containment" policy aimed at stopping the spread of communism. It will later become known as the Truman Doctrine.

1947 On March 21, Congress approves the Twenty-second Amendment, which limits the president to two four-year terms in office. The amendment is ratified in 1951.

1947 On April 10, Jackie Robinson breaks the "color barrier" when he signs a contract to play for professional baseball's Brooklyn Dodgers. He is later named Rookie of the Year by the *Sporting News.*

1947 Beginning September 30, the World Series is televised for the first time as fans watch the New York Yankees defeat the Brooklyn Dodgers in seven games.

1947 On October 13, the Hollywood Ten, a group of film directors and writers, appears before the House Un-American Activities Committee (HUAC).

1947 On December 3, Tennessee Williams's *A Streetcar Named Desire* opens on Broadway in New York City.

1948 The Baskin-Robbins ice cream chain opens.

1948 On April 3, Congress approves $6 billion in Marshall Plan aid for rebuilding European countries.

1948 On May 14, the state of Israel is established.

1948 On May 29, the play *Oklahoma!* closes after a record 2,246 performances.

1948 On June 25, heavyweight boxing champion Joe Louis knocks out Joe Walcott for his twenty-fifth title defense; following the fight, he announces his retirement from boxing.

1948 On September 13, Margaret Chase Smith of Maine becomes the first woman elected to the U.S. Senate.

1948 On November 2, incumbent Harry S. Truman is elected president.

1949 Builder Abraham Levitt and his sons begin construction on a Long Island, New York, suburb called Levittown, which will become a symbol for the postwar housing boom.

1949 On February 10, Arthur Miller's *Death of a Salesman* opens on Broadway in New York City.

1949 On April 4, the North Atlantic Treaty Organization (NATO) is formed by the United States and twelve other mainly European countries to provide for mutual defense.

1949 On September 23, American, British, and Canadian officials reveal that the Soviet Union has successfully detonated an atomic bomb.

1949 On October 1, the Communist People's Republic of China is proclaimed.

1950 The first Xerox copy machine is produced.

1950 Miss Clairol hair coloring is introduced, making it easy for women to dye their hair at home.

1950 Desegregation continues when Charles Cooper becomes the first black player in the National Basketball Association and Althea Gibson becomes the first black woman to compete in a national tennis tournament.

1950 In March, the Boston Institute of Contemporary Art and New York's Metropolitan Museum and Whitney Museum release a joint statement on modern art opposing "any attempt to make art or opinion about art conform to a single point of view."

1950 On May 8, President Harry S. Truman sends the first U.S. military mission to Vietnam.

1950 On June 30, U.S. combat troops enter the Korean War.

1950 On October 2, *Peanuts,* the comic strip written and drawn by Charles Schulz, debuts in seven U.S. newspapers.

1951 *The Caine Mutiny,* a war novel by Herman Wouk, is published and soon becomes one of the longest lasting best-sellers of all time, holding its place on the *New York Times* list for forty-eight weeks.

1951 On April 5, Julius and Ethel Rosenberg receive death sentences for allegedly giving secret information to the Soviet Union.

1951 On June 25, CBS offers the first color television broadcast.

1951 On August 5, the soap operas *Search for Tomorrow* and *Love of Life* premiere on CBS.

1951 On October 15, the sitcom *I Love Lucy* premieres on CBS.

1951 On November 18, the news program *See It Now,* hosted by Edward R. Murrow, premieres on CBS.

1952 *Gunsmoke* debuts as a radio drama. In 1955, the Western drama moves to TV where it lasts until 1975. The show, which starred James Arness as Marshal Matt Dillon, becomes the longest running prime-time TV show with continuing characters.

1952 In January, *American Bandstand,* a popular teen-oriented music program, debuts as a local show in Philadelphia, Pennsylvania. Dick Clark, its most famous host, joins the show in 1956.

1952 On January 14, *The Today Show* debuts on NBC.

1952 In September, *The Old Man and the Sea,* a short novel by Ernest Hemingway, is printed in *Life* magazine and is the Book-of-the-Month Club's co-main selection.

1953 On October 5, the New York Yankees become the first team in history to win five consecutive World Series when they defeat the Brooklyn Dodgers.

1952 In November, *Bwana Devil,* the first 3-D movie, is released.

1952 On November 4, World War II general Dwight D. Eisenhower is elected president.

1953 *Playboy* becomes the first mass-market men's magazine and rockets to popularity when it publishes nude pictures of rising movie star Marilyn Monroe.

1953 IBM introduces its first computer, the 701.

1953 On January 1, Hank Williams, the father of contemporary country music, dies at age twenty-nine from a heart disease resulting from excessive drinking.

1953 On April 3, the first national edition of *TV Guide* is published.

1953 On July 27, the Korean War ends.

1953 On September 13, Nikita Khrushchev is named first secretary of the Soviet Union's Communist Party.

1953 In November, an eleven-day photoengravers strike leaves New York City without a daily newspaper for the first time since 1778.

1954 U.S. senator Joseph McCarthy of Wisconsin leads hearings into the presence of communists in the U.S. Army; his actions are later condemned by the Senate.

1954 *Sports Illustrated* becomes the first glossy weekly magazine about sports.

1954 Swanson Foods introduces the first TV dinners.

1954 On April 4, legendary conductor Arturo Toscanini makes his final appearance conducting the NBC Symphony Orchestra. The concert is broadcast on the radio live from New York City's Carnegie Hall.

1954 On April 4, Walt Disney signs a contract with ABC to produce twenty-six television films each year.

1954 On May 14, the Soviet Union joins with seven Eastern European countries to form the Warsaw Pact, a union of nations pledged to mutual defense.

1954 On May 17, with its *Brown v. Board of Education* decision, the U.S. Supreme Court ends segregation in public schools.

1954 In July, the Newport Jazz Festival debuts in Newport, Rhode Island.

1954 On July 19, "That's All Right, Mama" and "Blue Moon of Kentucky," the first professional records made by Elvis Presley, are released on Sun Records.

1954 On September 27, *The Tonight Show* debuts on NBC.

1954 In October and November, Hungary tries to leave the Warsaw Pact but is attacked and reclaimed by the Soviet Union.

1955 Velcro is invented.

1955 *The $64,000 Question* debuts and soon becomes the most popular game show of the 1950s.

1955 In January, Marian Anderson becomes the first black singer to appear at the Metropolitan Opera.

1955 On January 19, President Dwight D. Eisenhower holds the first televised presidential news conference.

1955 In March, *The Blackboard Jungle,* the first feature film to include a rock and roll song on its soundtrack—"Rock Around the Clock," by Bill Haley and The Comets—opens. The song becomes the country's number-one single in July.

1955 On April 12, large-scale vaccinations for polio are administered throughout the United States.

1955 On July 17, the Disneyland amusement park opens in Anaheim, California.

1955 On September 30, actor James Dean dies after his Porsche roadster slams into another car on a California highway.

1955 On October 13, poet Allen Ginsberg gives the first public reading of *Howl,* his controversial poem-in-progress.

1955 On December 5, Rosa Parks refuses to give up her seat to a white man on a bus in Montgomery, Alabama, sparking a bus boycott that will become a key moment in the Civil Rights Movement.

1956 On June 20, Loew's Inc. releases MGM's pre-1949 film library—excluding *Gone with the Wind* (1939)—for television broadcast.

1956 On November 6, President Dwight D. Eisenhower is reelected.

1956 On November 30, videotape is first used commercially on television, during the broadcast of CBS's *Douglas Edwards with the News.*

1957 On September 26, the landmark musical *West Side Story,* a modern-day adaptation of *Romeo and Juliet* by William Shakespeare, opens on Broadway at the Winter Garden Theatre in New York City.

1957 On October 5, the Soviet Union launches the satellite *Sputnik,* the first man-made satellite in space.

1958 On October 2, Leonard Bernstein begins his first season as director of the New York Philharmonic.

1958 On October 16, sponsors drop the NBC quiz show *Twenty-One* after a grand jury investigation determines that contestants were provided with pre-show answers.

1959 On January 2, revolutionary leader Fidel Castro assumes power in Cuba.

1959 On January 3, Alaska becomes the forty-ninth state.

1959 On February 3, rock and roll legends Buddy Holly, Ritchie Valens, and J. P. Richardson (known as "The Big Bopper") die in a plane crash outside Clear Lake, Iowa.

1959 On August 21, Hawaii becomes the fiftieth state.

1959 On October 21, the Solomon R. Guggenheim Museum, designed by architect Frank Lloyd Wright, opens in New York City.

1960 Designer Pierre Cardin introduces his first fashion designs for men.

1960 On January 3, the Moscow State Symphony begins a seven-week tour at New York City's Carnegie Hall, becoming the first Soviet orchestra to perform in the United States.

1960 On February 11, Jack Paar, host of *The Tonight Show,* walks off the show when an NBC censor deletes a joke from his performance without his knowledge.

1960 On February 20, black students in Greensboro, North Carolina, stage sit-ins at local lunch counters to protest discrimination.

1960 In April, the New York state legislature authorizes the City of New York to purchase Carnegie Hall, which was scheduled for demolition.

1960 On April 1, Lucille Ball and Desi Arnaz appear for the last time as Lucy and Ricky Ricardo on *The Lucy-Desi Comedy Hour.*

1960 On May 5, the Soviet Union announces the capture of American pilot Francis Gary Powers, whose U-2 spy plane was shot down over the Soviet Union.

1960 On September 26, U.S. senator John F. Kennedy of Massachusetts and Vice President Richard M. Nixon appear in the first televised presidential debate.

1960 On October 13, jazz trumpeter Louis Armstrong begins a goodwill tour of Africa, partially sponsored by the U.S. State Department.

1960 On November 8, U.S. senator John F. Kennedy of Massachusetts is elected president.

1961 On January 20, Robert Frost reads his poem "The Gift Outright" at the inauguration of President John F. Kennedy.

1961 On January 27, soprano Leontyne Price first performs at New York's Metropolitan Opera.

1961 In April, folk singer Bob Dylan makes his debut at Gerde's Folk City in New York City's Greenwich Village.

1961 On April 12, Soviet cosmonaut Yuri Gagarin becomes the first man to orbit the Earth.

1961 During the summer, Freedom Rides across the South are aimed at desegregating interstate bus travel.

1961 On August 15–17, East Germany constructs the Berlin Wall, separating communist East Berlin from democratic West Berlin.

1961 On October 1, Roger Maris sets a new single-season home run record with 61 homers.

1962 On February 10, Jim Beatty becomes the first person to run a mile in less than four minutes with a time of 3:58.9.

1962 On May 30, jazz clarinetist Benny Goodman begins a six-week, U.S. State Department–arranged tour of Russia.

1962 On July 10, the *Telstar* satellite is launched and soon brings live television pictures to American television viewers.

1962 On August 5, actress Marilyn Monroe dies from an overdose of barbiturates.

1962 On September 25, Philharmonic Hall, the first completed building of New York's Lincoln Center for the Performing Arts, is inaugurated by Leonard Bernstein and the New York Philharmonic.

1962 On September 29, *My Fair Lady* closes on Broadway after 2,717 performances, making it the longest-running show in history.

1962 In October, the United States and the Soviet Union clash over the presence of Soviet missiles in Cuba.

1962 On October 1, James Meredith becomes the first black person to enroll at the University of Mississippi as federal troops battle thousands of protesters.

1963 On January 8, *Mona Lisa,* by Leonardo da Vinci, is shown at Washington's National Gallery, the first time the painting ever has appeared outside the Louvre in Paris, France.

1963 On May 7, the Guthrie Theatre in Minneapolis, Minnesota, the first major regional theater in the Midwest, opens.

1963 On November 22, President John F. Kennedy is assassinated in Dallas, Texas, and Vice President Lyndon B. Johnson assumes the presidency.

1963 On November 24, the murder of alleged presidential assassin Lee Harvey Oswald is broadcast live on television.

1964 Ford introduces its Mustang, a smaller sporty car.

1964 On February 9, the Beatles make their first live appearance on American television, on *The Ed Sullivan Show.*

1964 On February 25, Cassius Clay (who later changes his name to Muhammad Ali) beats Sonny Liston to become the heavyweight boxing champion of the world.

1964 In May, the just-remodeled Museum of Modern Art in New York City reopens with a new gallery, the Steichen Photography Center, named for photographer Edward Steichen.

1964 On July 2, President Lyndon B. Johnson signs the Civil Rights Act of 1964, which bans racial discrimination in public places and in employment.

1964 On August 7, in the Gulf of Tonkin Resolution, Congress gives President Lyndon B. Johnson the power to use military force to protect U.S. interests in Vietnam.

1964 On November 3, incumbent Lyndon B. Johnson is elected president.

1965 In January, Bob Dylan plays an electric guitar on his new single, "Subterranean Homesick Blues."

1965 On February 21, black leader Malcolm X is murdered in Harlem, New York.

1965 On March 8, the first U.S. combat troops are sent to Vietnam.

1965 On April 26, *Symphony No. 4* by Charles Ives is performed in its entirety for the first time by the American Symphony Orchestra, conducted by Leopold Stokowski.

1965 On May 9, piano virtuoso Vladimir Horowitz returns to the Carnegie Hall stage after a twelve-year "retirement."

1965 On June 2, in a letter to President Lyndon B. Johnson, Pulitzer Prize–winning poet Robert Lowell declines an invitation to attend a White House arts festival, citing his "dismay and distrust" of American foreign policy.

1965 In July, Bob Dylan and his electric guitar are booed off the Newport Folk Festival stage.

1965 On September 29, President Lyndon B. Johnson signs into law the Federal Aid to the Arts Bill.

1965 On October 15, demonstrations against the Vietnam War occur in forty U.S. cities.

1965 On December 9, *A Charlie Brown Christmas* becomes the first *Peanuts* special to air on TV.

1966 The National Organization for Women (NOW) is established.

1966 On June 8, the National Football League and the American Football League merge.

1966 On July 12, rioting by blacks breaks out in twenty U.S. cities over racial discrimination.

1966 On August 29, the Beatles play their last live concert.

1966 On December 8, philanthropist, horse breeder, and art collector Paul Mellon donates his collection of British rare books, paintings, drawings, and prints, valued at over $35 million, to Yale University.

1967 On January 15, in the first Super Bowl, the Green Bay Packers defeat the Kansas City Chiefs, 35–10.

1967 On February 18, the National Gallery of Art arranges to purchase Leonardo da Vinci's *Ginevra dei Benci* for between $5 million and $6 million, the highest price paid to date for a single painting.

1967 In June, the Monterey International Pop Festival, an important early rock music event, is held in California.

1967 On June 20, Muhammad Ali is stripped of his boxing titles after being found guilty of tax evasion.

1967 On July 23, federal troops are called in to put a stop to rioting in Detroit, Michigan. Forty-three people are killed in the rioting, which lasts a week.

1967 On November 9, the first issue of *Rolling Stone* magazine is published. On the cover is a portrait of the Beatles' John Lennon.

1967 In December, Universal News, the last of the movie newsreel companies, closes because it is unable to compete with television news.

1968 On January 30, North Vietnam launches the Tet Offensive, escalating the war in Vietnam.

1968 On April 4, civil rights leader Martin Luther King Jr. is murdered in Memphis, Tennessee.

1968 On April 19, *Hair* opens on Broadway, at New York City's Biltmore Theatre.

1968 On June 5, presidential candidate and U.S. senator Robert F. Kennedy of New York is murdered in Los Angeles, California.

1968 On September 16, presidential candidate and former vice president Richard Nixon appears as a guest on TV's *Rowan and Martin's Laugh-In* and delivers one of the show's signature lines: "Sock it to me."

1968 On November 1, the Motion Picture Association of America inaugurates its film ratings system.

1968 On November 5, former vice president Richard Nixon is elected president.

1969 Hot pants make their first appearance.

1969 On July 20, U.S. astronaut Neil Armstrong becomes the first man to walk on the moon when the *Apollo 11* mission succeeds.

1969 On August 15–17, the Woodstock Music and Art Fair is held on a six-hundred-acre hog farm in upstate New York.

1969 On November 15, a quarter million Vietnam War protesters march in Washington, D.C.

1969 On December 6, a fan is murdered during the Altamont Rock Festival in California.

1970 Soviet cosmonauts spend seventeen days in space, setting a new record for space longevity.

1970 Across the nation, protests continue over the ongoing Vietnam War.

1970 Rock stars Jimi Hendrix and Janis Joplin die within three weeks of each other, both as a result of drug overdoses.

1970 In March, three women—Elizabeth Bishop, Lillian Hellman, and Joyce Carol Oates—win National Book Awards.

1970 On May 4, National Guard members shoot antiwar protesters at Kent State University in Ohio, killing four students.

1970 On April 10, the Beatles disband.

1970 On April 30, U.S. and South Vietnamese troops invade Cambodia, which has been sheltering North Vietnamese troops.

1970 On September 6, four airliners bound for New York are hijacked by Palestinian terrorists, but no passengers are harmed.

1970 On September 19, *The Mary Tyler Moore Show* debuts on CBS.

1970 On September 21, *Monday Night Football* debuts on ABC.

1970 On October 2, the Environmental Protection Agency (EPA) is created to regulate environmental issues.

1971 Disney World opens in Orlando, Florida.

1971 Hot pants become a fashion sensation.

1971 On January 2, cigarette advertising is banned from television and radio.

1971 On February 6, British troops are sent to patrol Northern Ireland.

1971 On February 9, the European Economic Community, a precursor to the European Union, is established.

1971 On March 8, Joe Frazier defeats Muhammad Ali to retain the world heavyweight boxing title.

1971 On April 20, the U.S. Supreme Court rules that students can be bused to end racial segregation in schools.

1971 In June, the Twenty-sixth Amendment to the Constitution lowers the legal voting age to eighteen.

1971 On June 13, the *New York Times* publishes the "Pentagon Papers," which reveal Defense Department plans for the Vietnam War.

1971 In September, a prison uprising in Attica, New York, ends with forty-three people killed, including ten hostages.

1971 On October 12, the rock musical *Jesus Christ Superstar* opens on Broadway in New York City.

1971 On October 13, the Pittsburgh Pirates and the Baltimore Orioles play in the first World Series night game.

1971 On December 25, "Christmas bombing" occurs in North Vietnam.

1972 In a sign of the cooling of Cold War tensions, East and West Germany and North and South Korea each enter into negotiations to normalize relations.

1972 *Ms.* magazine begins publication.

1972 *Pong*, the first video game available to play at home, becomes popular, as does the first video game machine, Odyssey, introduced by Magnavox.

1972 On February 14, the musical *Grease* opens on Broadway in New York City.

1972 On February 21, President Richard Nixon begins a seven-day visit to Communist China.

1972 On May 22, President Richard Nixon begins a nine-day visit to the Soviet Union.

1972 On June 17, the Watergate scandal begins with the arrest of five men caught trying to bug the Democratic National Committee headquarters at the Watergate building in Washington, D.C. The investigation soon reveals deep corruption in the Nixon administration.

1972 On July 24, the United Nations asks the United States to end its bombing of North Vietnam.

1972 On August 12, the last American combat troops leave Vietnam.

1972 On November 8, cable TV network HBO premieres in Pennsylvania with 365 subscribers.

1973 Three major American cities—Los Angeles, California; Atlanta, Georgia; and Detroit, Michigan—elect a black mayor for the first time.

1973 Investigations into the Watergate affair capture the public attention and shatter the Nixon administration.

1973 The Sears Tower (now known as the Willis Tower), at the time the world's tallest building, is completed in Chicago, Illinois.

1973 Ralph Lauren designs the costumes for the film *The Great Gatsby,* helping build his reputation.

1973 Fantasy-adventure game Dungeons and Dragons is created by Dave Arneson and Gary Gygax.

1973 The first Internet is set up by the U.S. Department of Defense as a way of connecting all the department's computers.

1973 On January 14, the Miami Dolphins win the Super Bowl and become the first professional football team to finish a season undefeated.

1973 On October 16, the Organization of Petroleum Exporting Countries (OPEC) declares an embargo (ban) on the export of oil to the United States and other Western countries.

1973 On October 23, the House of Representatives begins impeachment proceedings against President Richard Nixon.

1974 The Ramones launch the American punk movement with their performances at the New York City club CBGB.

1974 The streaking fad sweeps the country.

1974 President Richard Nixon tours the Middle East and the Soviet Union.

1974 On January 18, Israel and Egypt sign a peace accord that ends their long armed conflict.

1974 On April 8, Hank Aaron of the Atlanta Braves breaks Babe Ruth's lifetime home run record when he hits his 715th career homer.

1974 In May, screenwriter Dalton Trumbo, who had been blacklisted in the 1950s during the anticommunist crusades of U.S. senator Joseph McCarthy of Wisconsin, receives an Academy Award for the 1957 film *The Brave One.*

1974 On August 8, Richard Nixon announces that he would become the first U.S. president to resign from office, amid evidence of a cover-up of the Watergate affair.

1974 On August 9, Vice President Gerald Ford replaces Richard Nixon as president. Less than a month later, he officially pardons Nixon.

1974 On September 8, motorcycle stunt rider Evel Knievel tries to jump a rocket over the Snake River Canyon in Idaho but falls short.

1974 On October 3, Frank Robinson joins the Cleveland Indians as major league baseball's first black manager.

1974 On October 30, boxer Muhammnad Ali regains his world heavyweight boxing title by defeating George Foreman.

1974 In December, unemployment hits 6.5 percent amid a prolonged economic slump and rises to 8.9 percent by May 1975.

1975 The video cassette recorder (VCR) is invented by Sony Corporation in Japan.

1975 The first personal computer, the Altair 8800, is sold in a kit form.

1975 The cult film *The Rocky Horror Picture Show* is released.

1975 Skateboarding becomes popular, and mood rings and pet rocks are popular fads.

1975 Rock star Bruce Springsteen appears on the cover of both *Time* and *Newsweek* thanks to his popular album *Born to Run*.

1975 The Soviet Union and the United States cooperate in the manned *Apollo-Soyuz* space mission.

1975 On January 5, the all-black musical *The Wiz* opens on Broadway in New York City. It eventually tallies 1,672 performances.

1975 On April 30, Saigon, the capital of South Vietnam, is invaded by the communist North Vietnamese, ending the Vietnam War.

1975 On October 1, the Organization of Petroleum Exporting Countries (OPEC) raises crude oil prices by 10 percent.

1975 On October 11, *Saturday Night Live* debuts on NBC.

1976 The first personal computer, the Apple, is developed by Steve Jobs and Steve Wozniak. The Apple II, introduced a year later, offers color graphics.

1976 Model and actress Farrah Fawcett-Majors sets a trend with her feathered haircut and appears on millions of posters in her tiny red bathing suit.

1976 On July 4, the United States celebrates its bicentennial.

1976 On November 2, former Georgia governor Jimmy Carter is elected president.

1976 On November 6, *Gone with the Wind* is broadcast on TV for the first time.

1977 The film *Saturday Night Fever* helps make disco music popular.

1977 Studio 54 becomes New York City's hottest nightclub featuring disco music.

1977 Egyptian artifacts from the tomb of King Tutankhamen, or King Tut, draw huge audiences across the nation.

1977 Alex Haley's book *Roots* becomes a best-seller after the airing of the TV miniseries based on the book.

1977 On January 21, President Jimmy Carter signs an unconditional pardon for most Vietnam-era draft evaders.

1977 On February 8, *Hustler* magazine publisher Larry Flynt is convicted of obscenity.

1977 In April, the Christian Broadcasting Network (CBN) makes its debut.

1977 On August 16, Elvis Presley, the king of rock and roll, dies at Graceland, his Memphis, Tennessee, mansion.

1978 The Walkman personal cassette player is introduced by Sony.

1978 On July 25, the first human test-tube baby is born in England.

1978 On September 17, U.S. president Jimmy Carter hosts negotiations between Israeli prime minister Menachem Begin and Egyptian president Anwar Sadat at Camp David, Maryland.

1978 On October 13, punk rock musician Sid Vicious of the Sex Pistols is arrested for the stabbing death of his girlfriend.

1978 On November 18, Jim Jones and over nine hundred followers of his People's Temple cult are found dead after a mass suicide in Jonestown, Guyana.

1978 On December 5, the Soviet Union and Afghanistan sign a treaty of friendship, and within a year U.S. support for the Afghan government disappears.

1979 Eleven people are trampled to death at a Who concert in Cincinnati, Ohio.

1979 Jerry Falwell organizes the Moral Majority to lobby politicians regarding the concerns of Christian fundamentalists.

1979 On January 1, the United States and the People's Republic of China establish formal diplomatic relations.

1979 On March 28, a major accident in the nuclear reactor at the Three Mile Island power plant near Harrisburg, Pennsylvania, raises concerns about nuclear power.

1979 On November 4, Iranian militants seize the U.S. embassy in Tehran, Iran, and take fifty-two hostages, whom they will hold for over a year.

1979 On December 27, the Soviet Union invades Afghanistan, beginning more than two decades of war and disruption in that country.

1980 Post-it notes are created by 3M chemist Arthur Fry.

1980 On February 22, the U.S. Olympic ice hockey team wins the gold medal, sparking national celebration.

1980 On April 12, the United States votes to boycott the Summer Olympics in Moscow to protest the Soviet presence in Afghanistan.

1980 On April 21, the Mariel boatlift begins, bringing 125,000 refugees from Cuba to Florida before being halted in September.

1980 In June, the all-news CNN cable TV network debuts.

1980 On August 19, a report issued by the *Los Angeles Times* indicates that 40 to 75 percent of NBA players use cocaine.

1980 On November 4, former California governor Ronald Reagan is elected president.

1980 On November 21, the "Who Shot J.R.?" episode of *Dallas* draws the largest television audience of all time.

1980 On September 4, Iraq begins an eight-year war with Iran.

1980 On October 2, in his last fight, heavyweight boxer Muhammad Ali is defeated by World Boxing Council champion Larry Holmes.

1980 On December 8, former Beatles musician John Lennon is shot and killed in New York City.

1981 Nintendo's *Donkey Kong* is the most popular coin-operated video game.

1981 NASA launches and lands the first reusable spacecraft, the space shuttle.

1981 On January 13, the National Collegiate Athletic Association (NCAA) votes to sponsor women's championships in twelve sports after the 1981–82 season.

1981 On January 20, American hostages held at the U.S. embassy in Tehran, Iran, are released on the day of President Ronald Reagan's inauguration.

1981 On January 23, the United States withdraws support for the Marxist government of Nicaragua and begins to support antigovernment rebels known as Contras.

1981 On March 26, comedian Carol Burnett wins a $1.6 million libel lawsuit against the tabloid *National Enquirer.*

1981 On March 30, President Ronald Reagan and three others are wounded in an assassination attempt in Washington, D.C.

1981 On July 29, Great Britain's Prince Charles marries Lady Diana Spencer in an event televised around the world.

1981 On August 1, the Music Television Network (MTV) starts offering music videos that soon become as important as the actual music.

1981 On September 21, Sandra Day O'Connor is confirmed as the first woman to serve on the U.S. Supreme Court.

1982 The compact disc is introduced.

1982 The popular movie *E.T.: The Extra-Terrestrial* sets box office records.

1982 Michael Jackson's album *Thriller* is the year's most popular recording.

1982 Americans frustrate themselves trying to solve Rubik's Cube, a popular puzzle.

1982 On April 2, Argentina invades the Falkland Islands off its coast, sparking a short war with Great Britain, which claims the islands.

1982 On June 7, Graceland, the late Elvis Presley's Memphis, Tennessee, home, is opened as a tourist attraction.

1982 On July 27, acquired immune deficiency syndrome (AIDS) is officially named.

1982 On September 15, *USA Today* becomes the first national newspaper.

1982 On October 7, *Cats* opens on Broadway in New York City and will become the decade's most popular musical.

1983 First lady Nancy Reagan announces a "War on Drugs."

1983 Sally Ride becomes the first woman astronaut in space when she joins the crew of the space shuttle *Challenger.*

1983 Actor Paul Newman introduces his own line of spaghetti sauces to be sold in grocery stores; he uses the proceeds to benefit charities.

1983 On February 28, the farewell episode of the sitcom *M*A*S*H* is seen by 125 million viewers.

1983 On March 23, President Ronald Reagan proposes a space based antimissile defense system that is popularly known as "Star Wars."

1983 On April 18, terrorists bomb the U.S. embassy in Beirut, Lebanon, killing sixty-three.

1983 On September 1, the Soviet Union shoots down a Korean Air Lines flight that has strayed into its airspace, killing 269.

1983 On October 25, three thousand U.S. soldiers invade the Caribbean island nation of Grenada to crush a Marxist uprising.

1983 In November, Cabbage Patch Kids dolls, with their soft faces and adoption certificates, become the most popular new doll of the Christmas season.

1984 Trivial Pursuit becomes the nation's most popular board game.

1984 *The Cosby Show* debuts on NBC.

1984 Rap group Run-DMC is the first rap group to have a gold album.

1984 Apple introduces a new personal computer, the Macintosh, with a dramatic advertising campaign.

1984 On November 6, Ronald Reagan is reelected president.

1984 On December 3, a Union Carbide plant in Bhopal, India, leaks poison gas that kills two thousand and injures two hundred thousand.

1985 Nintendo Entertainment System, a home video game system that has brilliant colors, realistic sound effects, and quick action, is introduced to the United States.

1985 On March 16, U.S. journalist Terry Anderson is kidnapped in Lebanon; he will be held until December 4, 1991.

1985 In April, Coca-Cola changes the formula of its popular soft drink and the public reacts with anger and dismay, prompting the company to reissue the old formula as Classic Coke.

1985 On July 13, British rock star Bob Geldof organizes Live Aid, a charity concert and album to aid the victims of African famine.

1985 On October 2, the death of handsome movie star Rock Hudson from AIDS raises awareness about the disease.

1986 Country singer Dolly Parton opens a theme park in Tennessee called Dollywood.

1986 On January 28, the space shuttle *Challenger* explodes upon liftoff, killing the six astronauts and one teacher who were aboard.

1986 On February 26, Robert Penn Warren is named the first poet laureate of the United States.

1986 On April 26, a serious meltdown at the Chernobyl nuclear power plant near Kiev, Ukraine, releases a radioactive cloud into the atmosphere and is considered a major disaster.

1986 On May 1, in South Africa, 1.5 million blacks protest apartheid (the policy of racial segregation). Around the world, foreign governments place sanctions on South Africa.

1986 On June 10, Nancy Lieberman becomes the first woman to play in a men's professional basketball league when she joins the United States Basketball League.

1986 On July 15, the United States sends troops to Bolivia to fight against drug traffickers.

1986 On July 27, Greg LeMond becomes the first American to win France's prestigious Tour de France bicycle race.

1986 In October, it is discovered that members of the Reagan administration have been trading arms for hostages in Iran and illegally channeling funds to Contras in Nicaragua. This Iran-Contra scandal will eventually be investigated by Congress.

1986 On November 22, twenty-one-year-old Mike Tyson becomes the youngest heavyweight boxing champion when he defeats World Boxing Council champ Trevor Berbick.

1987 On March 19, televangelist Jim Bakker resigns after it is revealed that he has been having an adulterous affair with church secretary Jessica Hahn.

1987 On June 25, Soviet leader Mikhail Gorbachev announces *perestroika,* a program of sweeping economic reforms aimed at improving the Soviet economy.

1987 On October 3, Canada and the United States sign a free-trade agreement.

1987 On October 17, the stock market experiences its worst crash in history when it drops 508 points.

1987 On November 11, Vincent van Gogh's painting *Irises* is sold for $53.9 million.

1988 McDonald's opens twenty restaurants in Moscow, Russia.

1988 Singer Sonny Bono is elected mayor of Palm Springs, California.

1988 On February 5, former Panamanian dictator General Manuel Noriega is charged in a U.S. court with accepting bribes from drug traffickers.

1988 On February 14, Ayatollah Khomeini of Iran calls author Salman Rushdie's book *The Satanic Verses* offensive and issues a death sentence on him. The author goes into hiding.

1988 On April 14, Soviet forces withdraw from Afghanistan after ten years of fighting in that country.

1988 On July 3, believing it is under attack, a U.S. warship shoots down an Iran Air passenger liner, killing 290 passengers.

1988 On November 8, Vice President George Herbert Walker Bush is elected president.

1988 On December 21, Pan Am Flight 747 explodes over Lockerbie, Scotland, killing 259 on the flight and 11 on the ground. Middle Eastern terrorists are eventually charged with the crime.

1989 On March 24, the Exxon *Valdez* oil tanker runs aground in Alaska, spilling 240,000 barrels of oil and creating an environmental disaster.

1989 In May, more than one million Chinese demonstrate for democracy in Beijing.

1989 In June, Chinese troops crack down on demonstrators in Tiananmen Square, drawing attention to the repressive government.

1989 On August 9, Colin R. Powell becomes the United States' first black chairman of the Joint Chiefs of Staff.

1989 On August 23, the Soviet states of Lithuania, Latvia, and Estonia demand autonomy from the Soviet Union. Later, across the former Soviet-dominated region, Soviet republics and satellite countries throw off communist control and pursue independence.

1989 On August 24, former baseball star Pete Rose is banned from baseball for life because it is believed that he bet on games in which he was involved.

1989 On October 15, Wayne Gretzky of the Los Angeles Kings becomes the National Hockey League's all-time leading scorer with his 1,850th point.

1989 On October 17, a major earthquake hits the San Francisco, California, area.

1989 On December 16, American troops invade Panama and seize dictator General Manuel Noriega. Noriega will later be convicted in U.S. courts.

1989 On December 22, the Brandenburg Gate in Berlin is officially opened, allowing people from East and West Berlin to mix freely and signaling the end of the Cold War and the reunification of Germany.

1990 The animated sitcom *The Simpsons* debuts on the FOX network.

1990 Ken Burns's documentary *The Civil War* airs on PBS.

1990 British scientist Tim Berners-Lee invents the World Wide Web.

1990 On April 25, the Hubble Space Telescope is deployed in space from the space shuttle *Discovery.*

1990 On July 26, President George Herbert Walker Bush signs the Americans with Disabilities Act, which provides broad protections for those with disabilities.

1990 On August 2, Iraq invades Kuwait, prompting the United States to wage war on Iraq from bases in Saudi Arabia. Much of this conflict, called the Persian Gulf War, is aired live on television and makes CNN famous for its coverage.

1990 On October 3, East and West Germany are reunited.

1991 Mass murderer Jeffrey Dahmer is charged with killing fifteen young men and boys near Milwaukee, Wisconsin.

1991 On March 3, U.S. general Norman Schwarzkopf announces the end of the Persian Gulf War.

1991 In October, confirmation hearings for U.S. Supreme Court justice nominee Clarence Thomas are carried live on television and feature Anita Hill's dramatic accusations of sexual harassment. Despite the charges, Thomas is confirmed.

1991 On November 7, Los Angeles Lakers basketball star Earvin "Magic" Johnson announces that he has contracted the HIV virus.

1991 On December 8, leaders of Russia and several other former Soviet states announce the formation of the Commonwealth of Independent States.

1992 On April 29, riots erupt in Los Angeles, California, following the acquittal of four white police officers in the beating of black motorist Rodney King. The brutal beating had been filmed and shown widely on television.

1992 On May 21, Vice President Dan Quayle criticizes the CBS sitcom *Murphy Brown* for not promoting family values after the main character has a child out of wedlock.

1992 In August, the Mall of America, the nation's largest shopping mall, opens in Bloomington, Minnesota.

1992 On August 24, Hurricane Andrew hits Florida and the Gulf Coast, causing a total of over $15 billion in damage.

1992 On October 24, the Toronto Blue Jays become the first non-U.S. team to win baseball's World Series.

1992 On November 3, Arkansas governor Bill Clinton is elected president, defeating incumbent George Herbert Walker Bush and strong third party candidate H. Ross Perot.

1992 On December 17, the United States, Canada, and Mexico sign the North American Free Trade Agreement (NAFTA).

1993 Jack "Dr. Death" Kevorkian is arrested in Michigan for assisting in the suicide of a terminally ill patient, his nineteenth such action.

1993 On February 26, six people are killed when terrorists plant a bomb in New York City's World Trade Center.

1993 On April 19, more than eighty members of a religious cult called the Branch Davidians are killed in a mass suicide as leaders set fire to their compound in Waco, Texas, following a fifty-one-day siege by federal forces.

1993 In July and August, the Flood of the Century devastates the American Midwest, killing forty-eight.

1994 Tiger Woods becomes the youngest person and the first black to win the U.S. Amateur Golf Championship.

1994 Special prosecutor Ken Starr is appointed to investigate President Bill Clinton's involvement in a financial scandal known as Whitewater. The investigation will ultimately cover several scandals and lead to impeachment proceedings against the president.

1994 In January, ice skater Nancy Kerrigan is attacked by associates of her rival, Tonya Harding, at the U.S. Olympic Trials in Detroit, Michigan.

1994 On May 2, Nelson Mandela is elected president of South Africa. The black activist had been jailed for decades under the old apartheid regime and became the country's first black president.

1994 On August 11, major league baseball players go on strike, forcing the cancellation of the playoffs and World Series.

1994 On November 5, forty-five-year-old boxer George Foreman becomes the oldest heavyweight champion when he defeats Michael Moorer.

1995 On April 19, a car bomb explodes outside the Alfred P. Murrah Federal Office Building in Oklahoma City, Oklahoma, killing 168 people. Following a manhunt, antigovernment zealot Timothy McVeigh is captured, and later he is convicted and executed for the crime.

1995 On September 1, the Rock and Roll Hall of Fame opens in Cleveland, Ohio.

1995 On September 6, Cal Ripken Jr. of the Baltimore Orioles breaks the long-standing record for most consecutive baseball games played with 2,131. The total reaches 2,632 games before Ripken removes himself from the lineup in 1998.

1995 On October 3, former football star O. J. Simpson is found not guilty of the murder of his ex-wife and her friend in what many called the "trial of the century."

1996 Three years after the introduction of H. Ty Warners's Beanie Babies, the first eleven toy styles are retired and quickly become collector's items.

1996 On September 26, American astronaut Shannon Lucid returns to Earth after spending 188 days in space—a record for any astronaut.

1996 On November 5, Bill Clinton is reelected to the presidency.

1997 Researchers in Scotland successfully clone an adult sheep, named Dolly.

1997 The Hale-Bopp comet provides a nightly show as it passes by the Earth.

1997 Actress Ellen DeGeneres becomes the first openly gay lead character in her ABC sitcom *Ellen.*

1997 On January 23, Madeleine Albright becomes the first woman sworn in as U.S. secretary of state.

1997 On March 27, thirty-nine members of the Heavens Gate religious cult are found dead in their California compound.

1997 On April 13, Tiger Woods becomes the youngest person and the first black to win a major golf tournament when he wins the Masters with the lowest score ever.

1997 On June 19, the play *Cats* sets a record for the longest-running Broadway play with its 6,138th performance.

1997 On June 20, four major tobacco companies settle a lawsuit with states that will cost companies nearly $400 billion.

1997 On June 28, boxer Mike Tyson is disqualified when he bites the ear of opponent Evander Holyfield during a heavyweight title fight.

1997 On July 5, the *Pathfinder* spacecraft lands on Mars and sends back images and rock analyses.

1997 On August 31, Britain's Princess Diana is killed in an auto accident in Paris, France.

1998 Mark McGwire of the St. Louis Cardinals sets a single-season home run record with seventy home runs.

1998 The final episode of the popular sitcom *Seinfeld* is watched by an estimated audience of seventy-six million.

1998 On January 22, Unabomber Ted Kaczynski is convicted for a series of mail bombings and sentenced to life in prison.

1998 On March 24, the movie *Titanic* wins eleven Academy Awards, tying the record set by *Ben-Hur* in 1959.

1998 On April 10, a new drug for male impotence known as Viagra hits the market and is a popular sensation.

1998 On August 7, terrorists explode bombs outside the U.S. embassies in Nairobi, Kenya, and Dar es Salaam, Tanzania.

1998 In November, former professional wrestler Jesse "The Body" Ventura is elected governor of Minnesota.

1998 On December 19, the House of Representatives initiates impeachment proceedings against President Bill Clinton, but the U.S. Senate acquits Clinton on two charges in early 1999.

1999 The U.S. women's soccer team wins the World Cup by defeating China.

1999 On March 24, NATO launches a bombing campaign against Serbia to stop its actions in Kosovo.

1999 On March 29, the Dow Jones Industrial Average closes above 10,000 for the first time in history thanks to a booming stock market dominated by high-tech companies.

1999 On April 20, in Littleton, Colorado, two students go on a vicious shooting spree, killing themselves and twelve other students.

1999 On September 24, *IKONOS,* the world's first commercial, high-resolution imaging satellite, is launched into space; it can detect an object on Earth as small as a card table.

2000 The world wakes up on January 1 to find that the so-called "Y2K" computer bug had failed to materialize.

2000 In May, Eminem releases his *Marshall Mathers LP,* which sells 1.76 million copies in its first week, becoming the fastest-selling album by a solo artist of all time.

2000 The fourth Harry Potter book, *Harry Potter and the Goblet of Fire,* is released in July and sets new publishing sales records.

2000 Tiger Woods becomes the youngest golfer to win all four Grand Slam golf tournaments.

2000 The first inhabitants of the International Space Station take up residence in orbit over the Earth.

2000 In November, outgoing First Lady Hillary Rodham Clinton wins a seat in Congress as a senator representing New York state.

2000 On December 12, over a month after Election Day, Texas governor George W. Bush is declared the winner of the presidential race against Vice President Al Gore after contentious vote recounting in Florida is ordered stopped by the Supreme Court. Bush takes Florida by a margin of 527 votes and edges Gore in the Electoral College by only four votes.

2000 On December 28, squeezed by "big box" retailers like Wal-Mart, Montgomery Ward announces it will be closing its doors after 128 years in business.

2001 Wikipedia is launched.

2001 On April 1, a U.S. spy plane collides with a Chinese fighter jet and is forced to land on Chinese soil, causing an international incident.

2001 The first draft of the human genome, a complete sequence of human DNA, is published.

2001 The "dot com bubble" bursts, leading to widespread bankruptcies in the software and Internet industries.

2001 On September 11, nineteen terrorists hijack four planes, flying two into the twin towers of the World Trade Center in New York City and one into the Pentagon in Arlington, Virginia. The fourth plane goes down in a field in Pennsylvania during a fight over the controls and fails to reach its intended target, believed to be the White House.

2001 In October, Afghanistan, accused of harboring terrorist training camps and 9/11 mastermind Osama bin Laden, is invaded by the United States and its allies, initiating the so-called War on Terror.

2002 Europe introduces its first universal currency, the Euro, initially accepted in twelve countries.

2002 The U.S. State Department issues its report on state sponsors of terrorism, singling out seven countries: Cuba, Iran, Iraq, Libya, North Korea, Sudan, and Syria.

2002 The United States begins detaining suspected terrorists without trial at its military base in Guantanamo Bay, Cuba.

2002 Halle Berry wins the Academy Award for best actress, becoming the first African American to win the honor.

2002 Bulgaria, Estonia, Latvia, Lithuania, Romania, Slovakia, and Slovenia, all former Soviet bloc nations, are invited to join the North Atlantic Treaty Organization (NATO).

2003 On February 1, the space shuttle *Columbia* disintegrates during reentry, scattering the craft's debris across the United States and killing all seven astronauts aboard.

2003 SARS, a new respiratory disease, first appears in Hong Kong before spreading around the world.

2003 In the face of mass global protests, the United States invades Iraq on March 19 as part of its continuing war on terror. By April 9, the capital city of Baghdad is taken. The weapons of mass destruction that were reported to be harbored by Iraqi dictator Saddam Hussein and were the publicly stated reason behind the invasion are never found.

2003 On December 13, Saddam Hussein is found hiding in a bolt hole in an Iraqi village.

2004 Online social network Facebook is founded.

2004 On March 11, Madrid, Spain, is the target of the worst terrorist attacks since September 11, 2001; 191 people are killed and 2,050 wounded in a series of coordinated train bombings.

2004 George W. Bush is elected to a second term by a wider margin than in 2000.

2004 On December 26, a tsunami caused by an earthquake measuring 9.3 on the moment magnitude scale in the Indian Ocean kills over three hundred thousand people across eleven countries in Southeast Asia and Sri Lanka.

2005 The video-sharing Web site YouTube is launched.

2005 Prince Charles, the heir to the throne of Great Britain, marries his longtime love, Camilla Parker Bowles.

2005 In June, pop star Michael Jackson is acquitted of child molestation charges.

2005 On July 7, coordinated bombings on three trains and a bus kill fifty-six people in London, England.

2005 On July 26, American cyclist Lance Armstrong wins his record seventh-straight Tour de France.

2005 On August 29, Hurricane Katrina makes landfall on America's Gulf Coast. The resulting destruction, largely centered on New Orleans, Louisiana, after the city's levee system fails, leads to billions of dollars in damage and over eighteen hundred deaths. The federal government is widely criticized for its slow reaction to the disaster, with rapper Kanye West famously declaring on live television, "George Bush doesn't care about black people."

2005 In November, French surgeons perform the world's first face transplant.

2006 The issue of global warming becomes a mainstream subject of discussion with the release of former vice president Al Gore's film *An Inconvenient Truth* and the accompanying book of the same name.

2006 The *Oxford English Dictionary* adds the verb "google" to its pages.

2006 Online social network Twitter is launched.

2006 The United States reaches a population of three hundred million only thirty-two years after hitting the two hundred million mark.

2006 Pluto is downgraded from planetary status, reducing the number of planets in the solar system to eight.

2006 On February 22, the one billionth digital song is downloaded from Apple's iTunes store.

2006 Riding a backlash against the ongoing wars in Iraq and Afghanistan and dissatisfaction with the George W. Bush administration, the Democratic Party wins back majorities in both houses of Congress for the first time in twelve years.

2006 On December 30, Iraqis execute former president Saddam Hussein.

2007 President George W. Bush announces that 21,500 more troops will be sent to Iraq as part of a "surge" to stem the ongoing guerrilla attacks being carried out against U.S. troops and Iraqi civilians by Iraqi dissidents and Arab terrorists.

2007 On the night of February 17, pop star Britney Spears, increasingly under media scrutiny for her erratic behavior, shaves her head and lashes out against paparazzi and reporters who had been tailing her.

2007 Apple introduces the iPhone.

2007 In the wake of Barry Bonds setting a new home run record amongst whispers of his use of performance-enhancing drugs, the Mitchell Report is released, detailing a year-long investigation into the widespread abuse of steroids in major league baseball.

2008 The Iraq troop surge is judged largely a success by July, eighteen months after it was implemented.

2008 On August 17, swimmer Michael Phelps sets a new Olympic record when he wins his eighth gold medal.

2008 With the September 15 collapse of lending firm Lehman Brothers, a major panic sweeps the world financial markets. Along with the collapse of the housing bubble, these are the first clear signals of the onset of the Great Recession, the worst global economic crisis since the Great Depression.

2008 On November 4, U.S. senator Barack Obama of Illinois becomes the first African American elected president of the United States.

2009 Barack Obama's historic inauguration on January 20 draws over one million people to the National Mall in Washington, D.C.

2009 Upon assuming office, President Barack Obama orders the closing of the Guantanamo Bay detention center and passes a $75 billion economic stimulus package.

2009 On April 15 (tax day), protests break out across the country, marking the beginning of the loosely affiliated Tea Party movement. Although lacking a single guiding organization or national leader, the conservative, ostensibly grassroots, movement is united by its concern over certain types of government spending and increasing federal deficit levels.

2009 On June 25, pop star Michael Jackson is found dead of an apparent prescription drug overdose. His passing ignites worldwide mourning and an outpouring of grief from hundreds of millions of fans, despite the singer's legal and personal troubles through the 1990s and the first decade of the 2000s.

2009 On October 31, jobless claims break the 10 percent barrier for the first time since the Great Recession began.

2009 With the situation in Iraq less dire and attacks by the Afghan Taliban on the rise, President Barack Obama announces a surge of thirty thousand more troops in Afghanistan.

BOWLING, BEATNIKS, AND BELL-BOTTOMS

Pop Culture of 20th- and 21st-Century America

1900s

The Birth of the American Century

The United States entered the twentieth century during a period characterized by change and transformation in every sector of society. In fact, such broad reform was to become the norm in the first decade of what has since become known as the "American Century," during which the United States came to be the leading economic and military power in the world. American democracy became the model for political reform in countries around the world. American publishers, musicians, artists, film makers, and performers of all sorts participated in producing a tremendous collection of work that made American popular culture the popular culture of much of the Western world.

The social and economic changes occurring in the country were striking. Although it had once been a nation of small towns, rapid changes in living styles led to the concentration of more and more Americans into cities; by 1910, fully 54 percent of the nation's population lived in urban areas. The ethnic composition of America was changing dramatically as well, as some 8,795,386 immigrants arrived in the United States between 1901 and 1910. This surge in immigration accounted for a large portion of the 21 percent population growth that occurred in the decade, pushing the country's population from 75,994,575 to 91,972,266.

Many of these new immigrants lived in the major urban centers, such as New York City, where they worked in the giant factories that were beginning to characterize American industry. The United States

1900s At a Glance

WHAT WE SAID:
As Tom Dalzell, author of *Flappers 2 Rappers: American Youth Slang,* points out, slang did not become an important element of American speech until the 1920s. Slang, it should be remembered, is language that attains special meaning because of its use by a subgroup of the larger society. It was not until the rise of the youth, music, and racial subcultures in the 1920s that slang truly rose to its present importance as an element of popular culture. However, three of the more prevalent terms of the 1900s were:

"23 Skidoo!": The most popular expression of the decade, this phrase could be used to mean almost anything, though it was generally used to express approval.

Babe: A pretty girl.

"Good to the last drop" (1907): This enduring advertising slogan for Maxwell House Coffee was rumored to have been invented by President Theodore Roosevelt, who remarked that the cup of coffee he had just finished was "good to the last drop."

WHAT WE READ:
Sears, Roebuck catalog: Also known as the "Wish Book," this department store catalog was popular reading in many households. Started in 1891, it was so popular at the turn of the century that people often joked that the catalog and the Bible were the only two books rural people ever read.

Comic strips: The "funnies" became a daily part of many newspapers after the *New York Journal* published the first eight-page comics section on October 18, 1896.

Dime novels: These inexpensive, quickly produced stories were tremendously popular. Gilbert Patten wrote the adventures of Frank Merriwell for *Tip Top Weekly.* Starting in 1896, Patten's new stories reached about 125 million readers each week.

The Jungle (1906): Upton Sinclair wrote this damning account of the dangerous conditions in the meat packing industry. The nation responded to his discovery by pushing for new laws for food and drug handling. In the meantime, domestic meat sales dropped by half.

Ladies' Home Journal and Collier's Weekly: These two popular magazines were published to inform and entertain women. *Ladies' Home Journal* often included romantic stories.

WHAT WE WATCHED:
For the most part, people during this decade entertained themselves at public and private gathering places such as saloons, sporting clubs, private clubs, churches, and barbershops.

Traveling entertainment: Acts that visited towns throughout the country included vaudeville and

had once been dominated by small businesses, but a wave of mergers (the combining of companies) contributed to the growth of what was becoming known as "big business"—the reliance of the American economy on huge companies that had branches throughout the nation. The Ford Motor Company (cars), the Standard Oil Company (oil), the United States Steel Corporation (steel), the J. C. Penney Company

minstrel shows. During the decade, there were more than four hundred touring companies in the country. Almost every town had a vaudeville theater.

Circuses: Many circus companies toured the country, with the Ringling Bros. Circus and Barnum & Bailey Circus vying to become the "greatest." Some were supported by ninety railcars full of animals, entertainers, and props.

Sporting events: Crowds in cities across the country gathered to watch their favorite games. The first game of the first World Series was held on October 4, 1903, and drew a crowd of twenty-five thousand baseball fans in Boston. The American League's Boston Pilgrims beat the National League' Pittsburgh Pirates to win the series on October 14.

The Great Train Robbery (1903): Audiences loved the suspenseful drama provided by this flick. Five years after its release, there were ten thousand nickelodeons in towns across the nation, ready to offer moviegoers the latest entertainment.

World's Fair: The World's Fair of 1904 in St. Louis, Missouri, drew record crowds of over twenty million attendees.

Olympics: The third Olympics Games were held in 1904 to accompany the World's Fair.

Air meets: Once airplane pioneers Wilbur and Orville Wright proved in 1908 that humans could fly, some people tried to build their own flying machines in their backyards. Air meets, assemblies at which daredevils would gather to show off and demonstrate their latest inventions, were especially popular spectacles during the decade.

WHAT WE LISTENED TO:
"Meet Me in St. Louis" (1904): This hit song by Andrew Sterling and Kerry Mills was inspired by the World's Fair of 1904 that was held in St. Louis.

"In My Merry Oldsmobile" (1905): This song by Vincent Bryan and Gus Edwards demonstrated immense pride in the decade's new technology.

"You're a Grand Old Flag" (1906): This highly patriotic song by George M. Cohan became a permanent staple in marching band processions and political rallies.

WHO WE KNEW:
Henry Ford (1863–1947): Soon after the establishment of the Ford Motor Company in 1903, Henry Ford and his affordable cars became wildly popular with Americans. By the middle of the next decade, Ford would manufacture half of all the cars in the country.

Immigrants: In 1907 alone, 1.2 million immigrants landed at Ellis Island, near the island of Manhattan, New York. By 1910, one of every seven Americans included in the census was a first-generation immigrant.

(retail), and the Philip Morris Corporation (tobacco) were among the largest of such businesses.

Leading America during this time of change was its youngest president in history, Theodore "Teddy" Roosevelt (1858–1919). Speaking about America's role in the world, Roosevelt once told an older opponent: "You and your generation have had your chance…. Now let us of

1900s At a Glance (continued)

Jack Johnson (1878–1948): In 1908, Jack Johnson became the first black man to win the heavyweight boxing champion title.

Theodore Roosevelt (1858–1919): Upon the assassination of President William McKinley in 1901, Vice President Theodore Roosevelt assumed the presidency. His charismatic personality defined the age. He guided the country during the construction of the Panama Canal and was awarded the Nobel Peace Prize, among other noted accomplishments.

The Wright Brothers (Wilbur, 1867–1912; Orville, 1871–1948): Aviation pioneers, the Wright brothers are credited with the first motor-powered airplane flight, which took place at Kitty Hawk, North Carolina, on December 17, 1903.

this generation have ours!" When elected president William McKinley (1843–1901) was assassinated in 1901, Vice President Roosevelt assumed the presidency. He led the country though an era of political and economic reform known as the "Progressive Era." Progressive reformers tried to tame the growth of big business and sprawling cities by passing laws and creating government organizations to regulate various areas of American life; many of those laws and organizations remain intact today. In this decade, the United States also cultivated a more powerful military, which was immediately utilized as the country began to exert its power overseas, extending its influence in the Caribbean and Latin America and protecting its interests in China and the Far East.

In this era of political, economic, and population change, American popular culture was also going through a period of transformation. In the nineteenth century, limited transportation and communication networks kept forms of popular entertainment such as newspapers, magazines, and theater from being spread throughout the country. That began to change in the 1890s, however, when magazine publishers used new technologies to print and distribute hundreds of thousands—and then millions—of their publications to people across the country. These magazines, including the *Saturday Evening Post* and *Argosy,* contained a growing number of advertisements for products that were available nationwide, like Kellogg's cereals and the soft drink Coca-Cola. Syndication (the practice of placing of a single article or comic strip in many independent newspapers) brought comic strips such as *Mutt & Jeff* and *The Katzenjammer Kids* into homes across the country. Sears, Roebuck and Co. also took advantage of printing advances to send catalogs offering its goods to people all over the nation.

Older forms of entertainment still thrived in America. Buffalo Bill Cody (1846–1917) and his Wild West Show, a sensation in the nineteenth century, continued touring the country. Smaller circuses visited towns of all sizes. The popularity of such productions was threatened, however, as a new media began to take hold in the 1900s: film. The groundbreaking silent film *The Great Train Robbery* (1903) thrilled audiences with its realistic portrayal of a train robbery and helped drive the growth of nickelodeons, storefront theaters that showed the latest short silent films. For prices as low as a nickel, Americans could see the latest films from the nation's growing movie studios.

Advances in technology and innovation changed American popular culture, but widespread racism kept African Americans from joining in the growth of cultural activity. In fact, one popular form of entertainment—the minstrel show—was based on negative stereotypes of African Americans. The national forms of popular culture—magazines, advertising, films, sports, and book publishing—mostly excluded African Americans. There were some notable exceptions, however. Black boxer Jack Johnson (1878–1946) gained national fame when he beat a white boxer, James J. Jeffries (1875–1953), to gain the heavyweight championship; the ragtime tunes of African American composer Scott Joplin (1868–1917) were some of the most popular sheet music of the decade; and in towns across the South, Negro baseball leagues began to produce players every bit as talented as those in white baseball leagues, from which black players were excluded. It would be years, however, before African Americans were welcome participants in mainstream American popular culture.

The advances of the decade—and the century—allowed Americans to share a truly unified national popular culture in ways they never had before. They could read the same magazines and novels, go to the same movies, and buy the same brands of food, toys, and cars. In the 1900s, many Americans drank out of Dixie cups, drove Ford Model Ts, ate in local diners, read *National Geographic,* took pictures with their new Brownie cameras, and drank Coke. American kids ate Kellogg's cereals for breakfast, played baseball with Louisville Slugger bats, chewed gum and ate Cracker Jack popcorn, and went to bed at night with a companion named after their popular president, the teddy bear. This sharing of a common culture was just beginning. In the coming decades of the century, American culture would be further influenced by the movies, radio programs, TV shows, and other forms of entertainment that would provide enjoyment to people living in all regions of the country.

1900s

Commerce

In the last thirty years of the nineteenth century, the American economy had been wracked by a series of economic downturns. By the dawn of the twentieth century, business was booming. In most American industries, business owners were learning the lesson of the day: Bigger is better. When the United States Steel Corporation was incorporated at a value of $1 billion in 1901, it became the world's largest corporation. Other companies followed the lead of U.S. Steel in buying up or merging with competitors to give themselves the advantage of size. Many of the largest companies in existence at the beginning of the twenty-first century were founded in the 1900s, including the Firestone Tire and Rubber Company (1901), the Quaker Oats Company (1901), the J. C. Penney Company (1902), the Pepsi-Cola Company (1902), Texaco (1903), the Ford Motor Company (1903), the Harley-Davidson Motor Company (1907), the Hershey Chocolate Company (1908), and the General Motors Company (1908). These large companies employed a growing number of professional managers, a new occupation whose practitioners tried to bring logic and order to the huge operations they oversaw. New management techniques included building elaborate assembly lines, using machines to speed up production times, and encouraging worker efficiency.

Although the rise of big business increased economic activity in the nation, many worried that these large companies were becoming too powerful. Politicians used laws such as the Sherman Antitrust Act of 1890 to limit the power of large corporations to control the marketplace. In fact, President Theodore Roosevelt (1858–1919) gained a reputation as a "trustbuster" for his efforts to break the power of large trusts (a trust is a combination of companies that work together to reduce competition in an industry, often through price-fixing and collusion). Congress also passed laws to regulate business practices in the areas of transportation, consumer protection, and banking. Labor unions stepped up their efforts to protect the rights of workers, whom union leaders said were threatened by the growth of big companies. Unions staged many strikes against American businesses, including the famous Anthracite Coal Strike of 1902, which nearly crippled the entire American economy.

Though most Americans learned about the changing economic climate of the day through their newspapers, they also began to experience those changes directly as they purchased and used a variety of new products. The single most notable product to emerge from this decade was the Model T automobile, manufactured by the Ford Motor Company beginning in 1908. The self-propelled vehicle known as the car (short for "carriage," which was in turn a simplification of "motor carriage") was still in its infancy when Henry Ford (1863–1947) used his innovative assembly line process, (which involves individual, discrete tasks performed repeatedly) to make a car that was affordable to more Americans than ever before. The Harley-Davidson Motor Company began to manufacture its motorcycles in this decade as well, and both Ford and Harley-Davidson continued production into the twenty-first century. Though few consumers knew of it, two brothers named Wilbur (1867–1912) and Orville (1871–1948) Wright invented a product in 1903 that would revolutionize travel in the years to come: the airplane.

A range of other products that would have a lasting impact were also introduced in this decade. The Brownie camera, made by Kodak, allowed common citizens to create their own photographs rather than rely on a trained professional. The popular stereograph allowed them to view three-dimensional (3-D) images from around the globe. Both products changed the way people saw and interpreted the world.

The way that people bought things also changed. The dime store, especially retail giant Woolworth's, brought a version of the department store to lower-income Americans, providing a variety of low-cost goods. Sears, Roebuck and Co. used its famous catalog to offer Americans in even the most distant locations access to the growing array of consumer goods. By 1908, the company mailed out 3.6 million copies of a catalog offering ten thousand different items, from guns to pianos to—eventually—prefabricated houses assembled from a kit.

Aunt Jemima

Aunt Jemima is best known as a brand of pancake mixes and syrups sold by the Quaker Oats Company since 1889. The image of Aunt Jemima used for advertising campaigns and packaging has been controversial for over a hundred years. Based on the pre–Civil War (1861–65) stereotype of the fat, jolly, no-nonsense black "mammy," the character of Aunt Jemima was first introduced in **minstrel shows** (see entry under 1900s—Film and Theater in volume 1) in the late 1800s.

Quaker Oats is thought to have chosen the image of Aunt Jemima to promote the very first packaged pancake mix because the image of the kind and funny black mammy was comforting and safe to many white consumers. From the beginning, many African Americans found the image of the obese, smiling Aunt Jemima with a bandanna on her head to be an insulting glorification of slavery. Some fought to eliminate what they viewed as an offensive trademark. In response, Quaker Oats gave Aunt Jemima a make-over in the 1990s by removing the bandanna and making her fashionably thin. In 1994, the company hired African American singer Gladys Knight (1944–) as a spokesperson to advertise its products. Today, Aunt Jemima remains a controversial and recognizable brand of pancake mix and syrup.

Tina Gianoulis

The image of Aunt Jemima as a stereotypical black "mammy," viewed by many as offensive, was used to advertise pancake mixes and syrups for over one hundred years before being made-over in the 1990s.
© BETTMAN/CORBIS.

For More Information

Kern-Foxworth, Marilyn. *Aunt Jemima, Uncle Ben, & Rastus: Blacks in Advertising, Yesterday, & Tomorrow.* Westport, CT: Greenwood, 1994.

Manring, M. M. *Slave in a Box: The Strange Career of Aunt Jemima.* Charlottesville: University Press of Virginia, 1998.

Norris, Michele. *The Grace of Silence: A Memoir.* New York: Pantheon Books, 2010.

Patton, Phil. "Mammy: Her Life and Times." *American Heritage* (Vol. 44, no. 5, September 1993): pp. 78–86.

Quaker Oats Company. *Aunt Jemima.* http://www.auntjemima.com (accessed June 3, 2011).

Brownie Cameras

Easy to use and affordable, Kodak's Brownie camera made photography available to everyone. Here, a man holds the new box camera, circa 1910. © DAZO VINTAGE STOCK PHOTOS/IMAGES.COM/ALAMY.

In the 1800s, before the advent of the Brownie camera, photography was a difficult and often expensive process, which made it impractical for ordinary people to take pictures. When the Eastman Kodak Company introduced its new Brownie cameras in February of 1900, photography became instantly accessible to everyone, including children. In fact, the Brownie was designed and marketed especially for kids.

The Brownie camera was very easy to use. It was a simple box with an opening in the front for light to reach the film, a small viewing screen on top, and a switch to expose the film, which came on easy-to-load rolls. Kodak named the Brownie camera after popular characters created by Palmer Cox (1840–1924), a children's book author and illustrator, in the late 1800s. Using Cox's characters, Kodak marketed the camera in popular magazines where children would see them. Kodak encouraged kids to enter photography contests and to join Brownie clubs. Thanks to this aggressive and persuasive marketing campaign, along with the novelty and usefulness of the product, Brownie cameras were an instant success. They cost only one dollar, plus fifteen cents for each roll of film. Approximately 150,000 cameras shipped the first year, three times as many as had been shipped for Kodak's previous best-selling model. Kodak produced the Brownie for 70 years, eventually offering 125 different Brownie models. Brownies were usually brown or black, but some models were offered in bright colors. Some Brownies also had flash bulb attachments for taking pictures in dim light.

The Brownie cameras were such a success because they allowed everyone the option to take pictures. People could make photo albums of family pictures that captured parents, friends, relatives, and images of daily life. These photos helped preserve memories for generations of people. In a story told on the Kodak Web site, one man remembered, "During a recent family reunion, my aunt shared many of the pictures she had taken with that [Brownie] camera over the years. Those pictures brought back many cherished memories of all the good times that have passed. As she went through the pictures, my aunt told me a story about each one. I heard how my Uncle Tommy won a photo contest at the boys club back in the fifties using that camera." In bringing photography to everyone with its affordability and ease of use, the Brownie camera became a treasured part of American family life.

Timothy Berg

For More Information

Auer, Michel. *The Illustrated History of the Camera, from 1839 to the Present.* Boston: New York Graphic Society, 1975.

Collins, Douglas. *The Story of Kodak.* New York: Harry Abrams, 1990.

"Stories About the Brownie Camera: Mike Mannino." *Kodak.com.* http://www.kodak.com/US/en/corp/features/brownieCam/index.shtml (accessed June 9, 2011).

Dime Stores

The five- and ten-cent store, also called the five-and-dime, was one of the most popular institutions in the United States from the late 1880s to the middle of the twentieth century. The dime store was more than a place where shoppers met to find bargains and sip limeade at the lunch counter—it also sparked a revolutionary change in American shopping habits and was the direct ancestor of the modern discount store. Dime stores have figured in films, such as *Come Back to the Five and Dime, Jimmy Dean, Jimmy Dean* (1982), and in popular music, as in the 1920s song by Billy Rose (1899–1966) and Fred Fisher (1875–1942), "I Found a Million Dollar Baby (in a Five and Ten Cent Store)."

Woolworth's stores were a familiar sight in cities across the United States during most of the twentieth century. © AP IMAGES.

Although they have disappeared from American streets, the five-and-dime still has a firm place in American popular culture.

The father of the dime store was Frank Winfield Woolworth (1852–1919). As a youth, Woolworth did not enjoy working on his family's farm in upstate New York, so he eagerly accepted a job as a sales clerk at the local store, Moore and Smith. At that time, stores kept all their goods behind the counter with no prices marked. Customers had to ask a sales clerk for what they wanted and try to negotiate with the clerk if they were not satisfied with the stated price. Woolworth, who had heard of a new sales technique, placed a variety of items on a counter marked "Everything Five Cents." When that proved successful, he got the idea of opening an entire store selling items for five cents. His employers agreed that his idea was an interesting one and loaned him $315.41 to buy the inventory for his new store.

On February 22, 1879, F. W. Woolworth opened his first five-cent store in Utica, New York. On November 6, 1880, he raised the top price to a dime and opened the first five- and ten-cent store in Pennsylvania. The stores were popular among working people who needed to shop economically. By 1907, Woolworth had twenty-three stores nationwide, serving around a million customers a day. That year, the first Woolworth's lunch counter opened, serving inexpensive meals in an informal setting. By 1930, there were 2,247 Woolworth's around the world, along with many successful imitators, including Grant's, Kresge's, Murphy's, and McCrory's. In 1932, the ten-cent top price was dropped and dime stores became simply bargain stores.

Woolworth's gained an immortal place in the **civil rights movement** (see entry under 1960s—The Way We Lived in volume 4) in 1960 when four black college students sat down at a racially segregated Woolworth's lunch counter in Greensboro, North Carolina. Their action led to a statewide boycott of Woolworth's and eventually to civil rights reforms across the South. Part of the Greensboro lunch counter stands in the Smithsonian Institution's National Museum of American History in Washington, D.C.; the rest stands in its original location in the Greensboro Woolworth's building, which became the International Civil Rights Center and Museum in 2010.

By the 1980s, many dime stores had become shabby relics of the past. They were replaced on city streets by small "dollar stores" and in **malls** (see entry under 1950s—Commerce in volume 3) and suburban locations by huge modern discount stores like **Wal-Mart** (see entry under 1960s—Commerce in volume 4). In 1998, the last Woolworth's store closed its doors. Woolworth's eventually became Foot Locker, Inc., a corporation focused on chain shoe stores.

Tina Gianoulis

For More Information

Brough, James. *The Woolworths*. New York: McGraw-Hill, 1982.

Glassner, Lester, and Brownie Harris. *Dime-Store Days*. New York: Penguin Books, 1981.

Gustaitis, Joseph. "The Nickel and Dime Empire." *American History* (Vol. 33, no. 1, March 1998): pp. 40–48.

Hubbell, Sue. "You Can Still Get It at the 'Dime Store,' But Not for a Dime." *Smithsonian* (June 1994): pp. 104–12.

Pitrone, Jean Maddern. *F. W. Woolworth and the American Five and Dime: A Social History.* Jefferson, NC: McFarland, 2007.

Plunkett-Powell, Karen. *Remembering Woolworth's: A Nostalgic History of the World's Most Famous Five-and-Dime.* New York: St. Martin's Press, 1999.

Wolff, Miles. *Lunch at the 5 & 10.* Chicago: Ivan R. Dee, 1990.

Dixie Cups

The paper cup emerged in the early twentieth century as part of the battle to fight the spread of disease. Before the invention of the paper cup, individuals would often use a common drinking cup placed next to a sink in public places such as schools, courthouses, and trains. Legend has it that Kansas doctor Samuel Crumbine (1862–1954) saw a girl with tuberculosis (a contagious disease affecting the lungs) drinking from such a cup and called for the invention of disposable drinking cups. The first disposable cup was invented in 1904, and the device was perfected in 1908 by Lawrence Luellen, who marketed the "Luellen Cup & Water Vendor," which sold a cup of cold water for a penny.

Luellen's breakthrough invention fused two pieces of paper together with wax, which kept the water from ruining the paper. His water-vending units, soon sold in public places around the United States, were widely lauded for reducing or halting the spread of disease. Luellen's invention was marketed most famously by the Health Kup Company beginning in 1912, which changed its product name to the Dixie cup in 1919. Like Kleenex-brand facial tissue and the **Xerox copier** (see entry under 1960s—Commerce in volume 4), the Dixie brand name was so widely recognized that it soon came to be used interchangeably with the product itself. Dixie advertised and marketed its name widely. Although owned by different corporations through the twentieth century, Dixie was consistently the leading brand of paper cups, and today also lends its name to paper plates and napkins. Despite concerns about waste, single-use cups remain popular among American consumers even today.

Tom Pendergast

For More Information

King, Norman. "Dixie Cup." *The Almanac of Fascinating Beginnings.* New York: Citadel Press, 1994.

Freeman, Allyn, and Bob Golden. "Dixie Cup." *Why Didn't I Think of That? Bizarre Origins of Ingenious Inventions We Couldn't Live Without.* New York: John Wiley and Sons, 1997.

Lafayette College Libraries. "Dixie Cup Company History." *Hugh Moore Dixie Cup Company Collection, 1905–1986.* http://academicmuseum.lafayette.edu/special/dixie/company.html (accessed June 10, 2011).

Fuller Brush Company

Founded in 1906 by Alfred C. Fuller (1885–1973), the Fuller Brush Company has for many years been one of the world's most successful direct marketing companies, employing a large sales force that in the twentieth century sold brushes, brooms, and other household products door to door. Just as the "**Avon** Lady" (see entry under 1900s—The Way We Lived in volume 1) sold cosmetics by ringing doorbells, the "Fuller Brush Man" offered an array of more practical merchandise during an era when most women were at home during the day-time. Despite having doors slammed in his face by customers who resented being interrupted, the "Fuller Brush Man" gained a reputation for persistence and ingenuity in making his sales pitches. Comic strips and skits often satirized an aggressive Fuller Brush Man sticking his foot in a customer's door in a frantic attempt to make his plea. Comedian Red Skelton (1913–1997) starred in *The Fuller Brush Man,* a 1948 film about murder and mayhem in the world of door-to-door sales. A sequel, *The Fuller Brush Girl,* starring Lucille Ball (1911–1989), was released in 1950.

From its earliest days, the Fuller Brush Company adopted three basic principles to achieve its mission: "Make it work, make it last, and guarantee it no matter what." The company promotes the fact that its product line is made in the United States. In 2011, its five-hundred-thousand-square-foot plant near Great Bend, Kansas, was manufacturing more than two thousand items, including household cleaning aids, industrial cleaners, polishes and

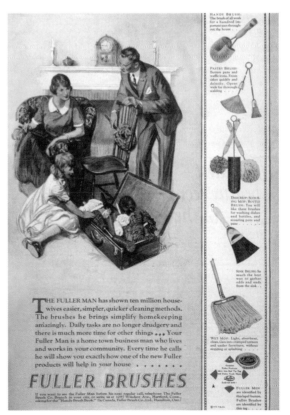

A typical Fuller Brush advertisement shows the ease of shopping at home, along with a line of products for sale. © MARY EVANS PICTURE LIBRARY/ALAMY.

wax products, mops, floor brushes, brooms, sponges, lotions and fragrances, hair-care aids, silk-screened graphics, aerosols, and chemicals. The company is now part of CPAC, Inc.

Sensitive to changing lifestyles that have all but eliminated the door-to-door salesman from American life, the Fuller Brush Company sells its products through factory outlets and mail order and has established an extensive online shopping catalog. Still, the company encourages one-on-one customer contact by offering distributorships to citizens or permanent residents who live in the continental United States. Historians credit Fuller Brush with developing strategies to increase consumer and employee loyalty that continue to see use in contemporary American business.

Edward Moran

For More Information

Friedman, Walter A. *Birth of a Salesman: The Transformation of Selling in America.* Cambridge, MA: Harvard University Press, 2004.

Fuller, Alfred Carl, as told to Hartzall Spence. *A Foot in the Door: The Life Appraisal of the Original Fuller Brush Man.* New York: McGraw-Hill, 1960.

Fuller Brush Company. http://www.fullerbrush.com (accessed June 14, 2011).

Fuller Brush Man (video). Burbank, CA: Columbia TriStar Home Video, 1991.

Harley-Davidson

In 1903, when William S. Harley (1880–1943) and Arthur Davidson (c. 1880–1950) produced their first motorcycle in their backyard in Milwaukee, Wisconsin, there were 15 motorcycle manufacturers in the United States. By 1911, there were 151 manufacturers. Today, Harley-Davidson is one of only a handful of American motorcycle makers remaining. Its bikes have become a major cultural icon around the world, representing not only efficient transportation but freedom, rebellion, and a romantic "outlaw" image. Harley-Davidson has successfully weathered the introduction of the cheap automobile in the mid-1920s and the emergence of the inexpensive, high-quality Japanese motorcycle in the mid-1970s to maintain its status as one of the most well-known American corporations in the world.

Harley and Davidson only produced one motorized bicycle during the first year they set up shop. The next year they made two; in 1905, eight. In 1910, thirty-two hundred motorcycles rolled away from

A Harley-Davidson motorcycle means the freedom of the open road to some riders, rebellion to others. © CAR CULTURE/CORBIS.

the Milwaukee factory. By 1920, Harley-Davidson was the largest motorcycle manufacturer in the world, producing twenty-eight thousand bikes. The military used twenty thousand "Harleys" during World War I (1914–18), and in World War II (1939–45), ninety thousand more joined the army. After the war ended, many returning soldiers bought Harleys for their personal use. Accustomed to bold wartime driving, these soldiers often drove their bikes recklessly and fast. When groups of them gathered to ride together, they formed the first motorcycle "gangs."

Motorcycle gangs have traditionally been associated with Harleys, perhaps because the loud rumbling of their engines and the high vibration of their ride appeals to bikers who wish to project a tough, wild image. Members of the Hell's Angels (founded in 1950), perhaps the most famous motorcycle gang, typically drive Harleys. However, in recent decades, Harley ownership has spread far beyond the outlaw bikers to those who wish to become "weekend outlaws." By 2010, according to company data, the average annual income of a Harley owner had exceeded $80,000. In recent years, Harley-Davidson has increased its marketing efforts to appeal to women, young adults, African Americans, and Hispanics. Many who don the customary leather jacket, helmet, and Harley T-shirt are now doctors, lawyers, and other professional people who call their bikes "hogs" and gather with other Harley riders at weekend rallies all around the country, two of the largest being in Daytona Beach, Florida, and Sturgis, South Dakota.

Tina Gianoulis

For More Information

Bolfert, Thomas C. *The Big Book of Harley-Davidson.* Milwaukee: Harley-Davidson, 1991.
Harley-Davidson Motorcycles. http://www.harley-davidson.com (accessed June 15, 2011).
Harley-Davidson Reader. Minneapolis: Motorbooks, 2010.
Henshaw, Peter, and Ian Kerr. *Encyclopedia of the Harley-Davidson.* London: Hermes House, 2010.
Scott, Missy. *Harley-Davidson Motor Company.* Westport, CT: Greenwood Press, 2008.

J. Walter Thompson Company

Headquartered in New York City, the J. Walter Thompson **advertising** (see entry under 1920s—Commerce in volume 2) agency is one of the world's largest, with more than 250 offices and affiliates in 88 countries. For half a century, from 1922 to 1972, it led the industry in billings (the amount of business done by an ad agency within a certain period of time). Founded in 1864 as Carlton & Smith, the agency was originally a broker of advertising space in religious periodicals. In 1877, William James Carlton (1838–1902), one of the original owners, sold the business to one of its employees, James Walter Thompson (1847–1928), for $500, plus $800 for the furniture. Over the next two decades, the J. Walter Thompson Company became the first full-service advertising agency. As a full-service agency, the company offered creative services like ad design and placement, package design, and logo design to its clients. One of its first logos, created in 1896, was the Rock of Gibraltar symbol for the Prudential Insurance Company, which is still in use.

During the first decades of the twentieth century, the company helped develop the catchy and concise advertising slogans that have since become a mainstay of consumer marketing. One of J. Walter Thompson's first successes was its 1912 campaign designed to convince women to use deodorant products, using the slogan "You can't vote. But you can smell nice." Under the direction of Stanley Resor (1879–1962), who purchased the agency in 1916, J. Walter Thompson commissioned market-research studies and was the first agency to open a research department. These moves helped define the way the advertising industry has functioned ever since. In 1920, the agency hired John B. Watson (1878–1958), a noted behavioral psychologist, to assist in the development of campaigns that would appeal to basic human wants and needs.

After World War I (1914–18), the J. Walter Thompson Company began representing some of America's most familiar brand-name products, such as Libby's, Kraft, **Aunt Jemima** (see entry under 1900s—Commerce in volume 1), and Fleischmann's. Its clients sponsored many popular **radio** (see entry under 1920s—TV and Radio in volume 2) shows during the 1930s, complete with clever jingles that described their products with a few memorable lines. In 1947, one client, Kraft Foods, sponsored the first network television program, "Kraft Television Theatre." Other major clients have been the Ford Motor Company, Pan American Airways, Nestlé, Eastman Kodak, Warner-Lambert, Rolex, Merrill Lynch, and Wendy's (for whom it coined the "Where's the Beef?" slogan). In 1988, the year after it was sold to the WPP Group, J. Walter Thompson did $665 million in new business, a one-year record for the agency. Today, the company, known as JWT, calls itself the "world's best-known marketing communications brand." Its increased reliance on online advertising reflects the larger digital media trends of recent years.

Edward Moran

For More Information

Fox, Stephen R. *The Mirror Makers: A History of American Advertising and Its Creators.* New York: Morrow, 1997.

J. Walter Thompson Corporation. http://www.jwt.com (accessed June 17, 2011).

Meyers, William. *The Image Makers: Power and Persuasion on Madison Avenue.* New York: Times Books, 1984.

Sivulka, Juliann. *Soap, Sex, and Cigarettes: A Cultural History of American Advertising.* 2nd ed. Boston: Wadsworth, 2011.

Strasser, Susan. *Satisfaction Guaranteed: The Making of the American Mass Market.* New York: Pantheon Books, 1989.

Kellogg's Cereals

With its headquarters in Battle Creek, Michigan, the Kellogg Company is the world's largest manufacturer of packaged, ready-to-eat breakfast cereals and related snack products. Many of the company's products, like Corn Flakes, Frosted Flakes, Froot Loops, and Rice Krispies, have become familiar breakfast foods around the globe. In 2010, the company reported more than $12 billion in sales worldwide.

Kellogg's evolved from the religion-based health industry of the late nineteenth and early twentieth centuries. The company traces its roots to the work of two brothers, John Harvey Kellogg (1852–1943) and Will Keith Kellogg (1860–1951). Both men were Seventh Day Adventists, although they were expelled from the church for worldliness and heresy in 1907. Seventh Day Adventists have traditionally adhered to high nutritional standards, and the Kellogg brothers were active in helping that denomination develop its early programs. John Harvey was medical

The Kellogg's Cereal City sign in Battle Creek, Michigan. © DENNIS COX/ALAMY.

superintendent of the Adventist Battle Creek Sanitarium, where he promoted a vegetarian diet, hydrotherapy (water therapy), and abstinence from alcohol, coffee, tea, and tobacco. He also served as editor of the church's monthly publication, *Good Health.*

In 1894, the Kellogg brothers invented flaked cereals, which they marketed as an easily digestible food product. In 1906, Will founded the Battle Creek Toasted Corn Flake Company to sell sweetened versions of these products as cereals, not just as health foods. By 1909, the brothers had become bitter rivals, and Will won the right to use the Kellogg's name as a trademark in 1920, after which he established the company as it is known today.

By the second half of the twentieth century, Kellogg's was arguably the nation's most recognizable cereal brand, with some thirty-five different products, ranging from All-Bran to Strawberry Mini-Wheats. It also manufactures Pop-Tarts and Nutri-Grain snack products. Many of the cartoon characters it developed to promote its various brands have become familiar icons, most notably Tony the Tiger (and his familiar slogan, "They're gr-r-reat!") from Frosted Flakes, and the "Snap!, Crackle!, and Pop!" gnomes from Rice Krispies. Kellogg's and other cereal manufacturers are often criticized by nutritionists and educators. Nutritionists disapprove of the high sugar content of their products, and educators protest how cereals are aggressively marketed to children, especially on **Saturday-morning television** (see entry under 1960s—TV and Radio in volume 4).

Edward Moran

For More Information

Hunnicutt, Benjamin Kline. *Kellogg's Six-Hour Day.* Philadelphia: Temple University Press, 1996.

Kellogg's Company. http://www.kelloggcompany.com (accessed June 18, 2011).

Lindsay, David. *House of Invention: The Secret Life of Everyday Products.* New York: Lyons Press, 2000.

Money, John. *The Destroying Angel: Sex, Fitness & Food in the Legacy of Degeneracy Theory, Graham Crackers, Kellogg's Corn Flakes & American Health History.* Buffalo: Prometheus Books, 1985.

Louisville Slugger

Baseball (see entry under 1900s—Sports and Games in volume 1) is called America's National Pastime, and Louisville Slugger is the name of the most famous and popular wooden bat employed by professional

The Louisville Slugger Factory and Museum in Louisville, Kentucky. The company has been supplying bats to professional baseball players for over a century. © WALTER BIBIKOW/ JON ARNOLD IMAGES LTD./ ALAMY.

ballplayers to smash singles, bash doubles, belt triples, and pound home runs at the ballpark.

The roots of the Louisville Slugger date to 1884 and involve John A. "Bud" Hillerich (1866–1946). Hillerich's father operated a woodworking shop that produced bedposts, bowling pins, handrails, and ornaments. At the time, most ballplayers whittled their own bats and often owned only one. The story goes that Hall-of-Famer-to-be Pete Browning (1861–1905), playing for the Louisville Eclipse of the American Association (predecessor to the National League), broke his bat during a game. Additionally, he was in the middle of a batting slump. Young Hillerich, who was just eighteen at the time, happened to be at the game and offered to produce a bat for Browning. The ballplayer agreed, and Hillerich spun one out of white ash, made to Browning's specifications. The following day Browning busted out of his slump, getting three hits in three at-bats, and requested that Hillerich produce additional bats. Soon other ballplayers began ordering Hillerich's product. At first, they were known as Fall City Sluggers, but in 1894 Hillerich copyrighted the name Louisville Slugger, which was imprinted in an oval on every bat. Each ballplayer's signature was also burned into each bat, allowing him to keep track of his lumber.

In 1905, another future Cooperstown inductee, Pittsburgh Pirate shortstop Honus Wagner (1874–1955), became the first professional athlete to earn endorsement money for allowing his name to be linked to a product when he signed a contract with Hillerich that resulted in bats with his name burned into them to be sold in stores. Ten years later, the Hillerich factory was destroyed in a fire. During the rebuilding process, Frank W. Bradsby (1878–1937), a former purveyor of athletic equipment, was hired to market the bats. In 1916, the company name became Hillerich & Bradsby (H&B).

To this day, H&B still produces bats for major leaguers, designed to the specifications of each ballplayer. The history of the company—and the history of its baseball bats—is chronicled in the Louisville Slugger

Museum. Located in downtown Louisville, Kentucky, visitors to the museum can observe actual bat production. Despite the present-day use of aluminum bats by school teams and Little Leagues, H&B produces 1.8 million wooden bats per year. Major leaguers who choose Louisville Sluggers use an average of seventy-two bats per season.

Rob Edelman

For More Information

Arnow, Jan. *Louisville Slugger: The Making of a Baseball Bat.* New York: Pantheon Books, 1984.

Louisville Slugger. http://www.slugger.com (accessed June 18, 2011).

Magee, David, and Philip Shirley. *Sweet Spot: 125 Years of Baseball and the Louisville Slugger.* Chicago: Triumph Books, 2009.

Model T

The Ford Motor Company's mass-produced and affordable Model T made the car an essential part of American life. Before the Model T, cars were luxury items that could be purchased only by the richest portion of American society. With the Model T, Henry Ford (1863–1947), who founded the Ford Motor Company in 1903, figured out how to make the car a necessary component of everyday life for regular working people.

To construct the Model T, Henry Ford devised labor-saving techniques that would increase production and reduce costs. Unlike his competitors, Ford Motor Company offered only one type of car. The parts for the Model T were interchangeable, and Ford said that people could buy the Model T "in any color they want, so long as it's black." As the popularity of the car grew, Ford continued to fine-tune his production line, implementing a system of management that would become known as "Fordism." Fordism was based on the assembly line and increased wages for his workers. Ford's assembly line divided labor into small tasks that required less skill and craftsmanship from each individual employee. Insightfully, Ford reasoned that workers would only accept the more mundane positions if they were paid well. The Ford Motor Company paid more than double the average daily wage of other industries. When Ford introduced the eight-hour, five-dollar day in 1914, job seekers flocked to the company. Henry Ford's genius revolutionized the automobile industry and helped increase sales.

A Sunday drive in the family Model T, around 1915. © HULTON ARCHIVE/ARCHIVE PHOTOS/GETTY IMAGES.

Although people had been fascinated with motorized vehicles since they were first produced, cars had only been affordable for the very wealthy. The Model T was introduced for $850, a price far lower than other cars and within the reach of many people. For the first time, working men and women could afford a motorized vehicle and Ford aggressively marketed the Model T to them. Ford publicized the Model T by winning a transcontinental race with it. Even though the Model T's victory was later disqualified (the drivers had changed the engine mid-race), the public had already fallen in love with it. It was fast, it was cheap, and it was truly American.

Produced from 1908 to 1927, the Model T changed the way people thought about traveling, distances, and time. The Model T became the best-selling car in history (at the time). By 1915, Ford Motor Company had produced one million Model Ts. By the mid–1920s, the Model T had made the car an essential component of American life. The car promoted the development of the **suburbs** (see entry under 1950s—The Way We Lived in volume 3) during the 1920s. Americans began to demand the paving of million of miles of roads. By the time of the stock market crash in 1929 that initiated the **Great Depression** (1929–41; see entry under 1930s—The Way We Lived in volume 2), the Model T had become so much a part of American life that as people began losing their jobs and savings, they held on to their cars, sometimes pulling them with horses when they could not afford gas. The Model T had made America a nation of drivers.

Sara Pendergast

For More Information

Brooke, A. Lindsay. *Ford Model T: The Car That Put the World on Wheels.* St. Paul, MN: Motorbooks, 2008.

Casey, Robert H. *The Model T: A Centennial History.* Baltimore, MD: Johns Hopkins University Press, 2008.

Collins, Tom. *The Legendary Model T Ford.* Iola, WI: Krause, 2007.

Gourley, Catherine. *Wheels of Time: A Biography of Henry Ford.* Brookfield, CT: Millbrook Press, 1997.

McCalley, Bruce W. *The Model T Ford: The Car That Changed the World.* Iola, WI: Krause, 1994.

Plastic

Plastic is a synthetic material made out of petroleum products that can be shaped and molded into an infinite variety of shapes without breaking. Few other products have influenced American culture as much as plastic. In the early twentieth century, plastic proved that it could be used as a substitute for all kinds of natural materials. It soon began to appear in all kinds of products that Americans used. Americans' use of plastic as a cheap imitation of natural substances led some to call American culture a "plastic" or artificial culture, focused on cheap imitations rather than on items of genuine quality. Whether or not that was true, plastics became a part of most Americans' daily lives.

Plastic was the result of the search for a man-made alternative to natural materials such as marble, ivory, and bone. Those items were used in all kinds of consumer goods in the 1800s and earlier, but they could be somewhat rare and expensive. The first plastic-like substance was celluloid, invented in 1869 by John Wesley Hyatt (1837–1912) as a substitute for ivory. That discovery led to later innovations, including the development of chemically synthetic plastics in the early twentieth century. The invention of other plastic forms such as **nylon** (see entry under 1930s—Fashion in volume 2), rayon, polyvinyl chloride, vinyl, lucite, plexiglas, and teflon followed.

The development of plastic as a part of history is important, but, like many scientific inventions, its use by ordinary people is what made plastic such an important part of everyday American life. As the twentieth century progressed, plastics crept into American life in increasingly unique ways. For instance, celluloid, the first plastic substance, revolutionized photography, enabling film to be used easily in portable cameras by all kinds of people. No longer did one need to be a professional photographer to take pictures. Celluloid was also crucial to the development of motion pictures. All of the classic images Americans enjoyed on the screens of their local movie theaters were due to plastic celluloid. Cellophane, a close relative of celluloid, was used as a plastic wrap to help keep food fresh and in such products as adhesive tape. Plastics found their way into clothing in the form of **nylon stockings** (see entry under 1930s—Fashion in volume 2), or nylons, for women's legs; in rayon dresses that simulated natural (and therefore more expensive) silk; and in **polyester** (see entry under 1970s—Fashion in volume 4) suits for men.

Plastics also entered the home with increasing regularity. People spoke into new, one-piece plastic telephone receivers and sat on Naugahyde (artificial leather) recliners. Plastics were especially popular in the kitchen. Vinyl flooring stood up to lots of rough treatment and spills wiped up easily from its surface. Plastic **Tupperware** (see entry under 1940s—Commerce in volume 3), kitchen bowls made out of plastic, proved very popular in the 1940s and after. Plastic could form all kinds of convenient shapes for bowls, glasses, and containers. Plastic kitchenware could be dropped without breaking, and it was inexpensive to buy. Teflon proved it could be used as a nonstick cooking surface. As a result of these innovations, homeowners loved plastic. Plastic was also found elsewhere in the home—in children's toys, such as **LEGO** blocks (see entry under 1950s—Sports and Games in volume 3) and **Fisher-Price toys** (see entry under 1930s—Commerce in volume 2); in teenagers' bedrooms, with vinyl rock-and-roll records; in plastic swimming pools in the backyard; and in plastic doormats that resembled green grass.

By the 1960s, plastics were an inescapable part of American life. The substance was even immortalized in the 1967 film *The Graduate* (see entry under 1960s—Film and Theater in volume 4), starring Dustin Hoffman, when an older neighbor tells Hoffman's character that he could describe a bright future for him in one word: "plastics." By that time, however, although millions of people were using plastic in their everyday lives, some people became disturbed by the American tendency to replace natural things with synthetic plastics. As early as the 1920s, plastic was used as a negative word for artificial. Living in a "plastic society" meant living in an artificial world cut off from nature. Indeed, plastics had been phenomenally successful in replicating natural materials. But by the 1970s, the true costs of this material were slowly becoming known. Plastics, it turned out, caused cancer in many workers who inhaled fumes while manufacturing them. They also proved to be a big environmental problem. Plastic enabled Americans to adopt a "throwaway" lifestyle that centered around convenience. Many items, like Styrofoam cups, were used once and then thrown away, piling up along roadsides as litter and taking up precious space in landfills. Plastics also do not degrade into their base materials as natural substances do, so the plastic cup disposed of in a landfill in 1955 still exists today. More recently, government agencies have become increasingly concerned about the health effects of plastics used in food packaging and baby bottles. These problems even led some local and state governments to ban Styrofoam, plastic shopping bags, and other plastic products and to urge people to reconsider their use of plastic.

By the beginning of the twenty-first century, plastics were an integral aspect of American life. Plastics helped make life easier in a multitude of ways but also proved that few, if any, innovations come without some cost to society.

Timothy Berg

For More Information

Fenichell, Stephen. *Plastic: The Making of a Synthetic Century*. New York: HarperBusiness, 1996.

Katz, Sylvia. *Plastics: Common Objects, Classic Designs*. New York: Harry N. Abrams, 1984.

Meikle, Jeffrey L. *American Plastic: A Cultural History*. New Brunswick, NJ: Rutgers University Press, 1995.

Sparke, Penny. *The Plastics Age: From Bakelite to Beanbags and Beyond*. Woodstock, NY: Overlook Press, 1993.

Underwood, Anne. "The Chemicals Within." *Newsweek* (February 4, 2008): p. 50.

Sears, Roebuck Catalog

From the time of its origin in 1888, the Sears, Roebuck catalog was more than just a listing of store merchandise. Called the "Big Book" or the "Wish Book" by the millions of people who eagerly awaited its arrival each year, the catalog brought the wider world into the isolated homes of rural America. From it, working-class Americans who lived far from

The Sears, Roebuck catalog helped connect Americans by bringing the latest fashions, appliances, and more to everyone's doorstep. © BETTMANN/ CORBIS.

cities or even stores, could order anything from shoes, clothes, furniture, and appliances to wagons and machinery. More than this, they could keep up to date on advances in equipment, technology, and fashion. Through its mail-order shopping business, Sears, Roebuck and Co. was able to reach out to the seventy percent of Americans who lived in the rural United States at the end of the nineteenth century. Many of these Americans joked that the Bible and the Sears, Roebuck catalog were the only books that they read.

Richard W. Sears (1863–1914) was working as a station agent for a railroad, passing the time by reading the various catalogs that came through on mail trains, when he began to think that he could develop his own successful mail-order business. He and his partner Alvah C. Roebuck (1864–1948) issued their first catalog in 1888, selling jewelry and watches. Each year the two expanded their catalog and their inventory, offering free trials and money-back guarantees to boost sales. Cleverly, they designed their catalog a little smaller than that of their biggest competitor, Montgomery Ward. That way, the company reasoned, its catalog would be placed on top when the catalogs were stacked. By 1895, the company had incorporated, and the catalog had grown to over 500 pages with the addition of items such as clothes, guns, farm equipment, and furniture. In 1908, Sears, Roebuck began to sell mail-order houses, with a selection of 450 models. Houses were shipped in thousands of parts, with detailed instructions for assembly. By the early 1900s, Sears, Roebuck and Co. was earning $10 million in sales.

The Sears, Roebuck catalog continued to represent a successful mail-order business for over a century. In 1993, finally overwhelmed by competition and changing shopping habits, the catalog portion of Sears, Roebuck and Co. closed. Although specialty catalogs, for markets including weddings and tools, can still be ordered from the company, the Sears Web site has now assumed the traditional duties of the famous mail-order catalog.

Tina Gianoulis

For More Information
Emmett, Boris, and John E. Jeuck. *Catalogues and Counters: A History of Sears, Roebuck and Company.* Chicago: University of Chicago Press, 1950.
Gustaitis, Joseph. "Closing the Book." *American History Illustrated* (Vol. 28, no. 3): pp. 36-42.

Hicks, L. Wayne. "The House Is in the Mail." *American History* (Vol. 35, April 2000): pp. 38–43.

Katz, Donald R. *The Big Store: Inside the Crisis and Revolution at Sears, Roebuck.* New York: Viking, 1987.

Liggett, Lori. "The Founders of Sears, Roebuck and Company." *Bowling Green State University American Culture Studies Program.* http://www.bgsu.edu/departments/acs/1890s/sears/sears.html (accessed June 18, 2011).

McGinty, Brian. "Mr. Sears and Mr. Roebuck." *American History Illustrated* (Vol. 21, no. 2, June 1986): pp. 34–8.

Sears. http://www.sears.com (accessed June 18, 2011).

Worthy, James C. *Shaping an American Institution.* Champaign: University of Illinois Press, 1984.

Stereoscopes

Stereoscopes were the first mass-produced viewing devices for three-dimensional (3-D) photography. Stereoscopes allowed people to view two photographs of a single scene taken from slightly different perspectives (called stereographs) as one 3-D image. The 3-D images brought a realism and a depth to photography that had never been seen before.

Stereoscopy, popular from 1850 to 1920, was a forerunner of cinema and **television** (see entry under 1940s—TV and Radio in volume 3). From the comfort of their own homes, people could use the stereoscope to see images of important people, places, and historic events. The device also enabled them to entertain themselves with erotica (pictures

meant to arouse sexual interest), images of tourist destinations, and fine works of art. Invented by British physicist Charles Wheatstone (1802–1875) in 1832, the stereoscope truly became popular when it was introduced to America. Between 1860 and 1890, more than four hundred million stereographs were produced in assembly-line fashion in large factories in America. Stereographs were the main source of visual information about the American West, the Civil War (1861–65), the Spanish-American War (1898), and the world in general. With the rise in popularity of cinema in the 1920s, however, stereoscopes soon lost their adult audience. Stereoscopic images were relegated to children's toys like the View-Master, which was introduced in 1939.

The stereoscope was the first device that allowed people to view 3-D images. © BRAND X PICTURES/GETTY IMAGES.

Stereoscopic imagery has never ceased to fascinate viewers. It enjoyed a brief revival in the 1950s with **3-D movies** (see entry under 1950s—Film and Theater in volume 3 and entry under 2000s—Film and Theater in volume 6) and **comic books** (see entry under 1930s—Print Culture in volume 2). In the 1990s, computer-generated Magic Eye stereograms, which allowed viewers to see stereoscopic images without a viewer, became tremendously popular, selling more than twenty-five million books of images by 1995. Computerized holographic and virtual-reality technologies have broadened the usefulness and appeal of stereoscopic imagery to interactive games and even to military training programs for surveillance, weapons targeting, and flight schools.

Sara Pendergast

For More Information

Earle, W. E., ed. *Points of View: The Stereograph in America—A History.* Rochester, NY: Visual Studies Workshop, 1979.

Jones, John. *Wonders of the Stereoscope.* New York: Knopf, 1976.

Magic Eye. http://www.magiceye.com (accessed June 20, 2011).

Wing, Paul. *Stereoscopes: The First One Hundred Years.* Nashua, NH: Transition, 1996.

Teddy Bears

Most Americans carry fond memories of a childhood teddy bear. Although contemporary stuffed animals are manufactured in the form of every creature from aardvarks to zebras, the bear remains the most popular and iconic option available.

The teddy bear has its origins both in the United States and in Europe. When U.S. president Theodore Roosevelt (1858–1919) took a hunting trip to Mississippi in 1902, one of his companions captured a black bear cub and brought it to Roosevelt to shoot. The president saw no sport in such an act and refused to shoot it. A *Washington Post* reporter traveling with the hunting party wrote a story about the incident, which was printed with an illustration showing Roosevelt declining to shoot the helpless cub. A Brooklyn variety store owner, Morris Michtom, saw the cartoon and got an idea about how to sell some stuffed bears that his wife had made. He placed them in his shop window with a sign reading "Teddy's Bears." Demand for the bears was so great that

Teddy bears, often a child's first toy, trace their origins to President Theodore "Teddy" Roosevelt, an avid hunter, who chose not to shoot a bear cub.
© IAN SHAW/ALAMY.

Michtom founded the Ideal Novelty and Toy Corporation and immediately began mass-producing them.

The same year, German Richard Steiff saw trained bears performing at a circus and thought a toy based on the creatures might sell. He took his idea and some drawings to his aunt, Margarete Steiff (1847–1909), who was a well-known toy and doll maker. She designed and made a few sample bears, which she took to the 1903 Leipzig Toy Fair. European dealers were uninterested, but an American distributor ordered several thousand bears for export to the United States.

Today, teddy bears are big business, with millions of collectors in the United States alone. The industry distinguishes between two kinds of bears: toys (which have huggable, soft stuffing) and collectibles (with firm interiors and jointed limbs). Gund, Inc., is the premier maker of cuddly toy bears, whereas Germany's Steiff company remains the leader in collectibles. Some of Steiff's classic bears have fetched as much as $10,000 at auction.

Justin Gustainis

For More Information

Brown, Michele. *The Little History of the Teddy Bear.* Stroud, UK: Tempus, 2006.

Bull, Peter. *The Teddy Bear Book.* New York: Random House, 1970.

Pfeiffer, Günther. *The Story of the Steiff Teddy Bear: An Illustrated History from 1902.* Philadelphia: Courage Books, 1995.

Mullins, Linda. *The Teddy Bear Men: Theodore Roosevelt and Clifford Berryman.* 2nd ed. Cumberland, MD: Hobby House Press, 2002.

Severin, Gustav. *Teddy Bear: A Loving History of the Classic Childhood Companion.* Philadelphia: Courage Books, 1995.

1900s

Film and Theater

The first decade of the twentieth century was one of the last decades in which entertainment was still largely local and noncommercial, owing to several factors. Movies were still in their infancy. Broadway had not yet gained a reputation as the center of serious and popular theater. Most Americans sought their entertainment in small local theaters, at vaudeville shows, and, in a growing number of cities, at storefront nickelodeons. Although wealthier Americans in large cities could attend serious professional performances of opera and of classic plays, such as the works of Shakespeare, most Americans enjoyed rougher, less refined fare. In the 1900s, twenty-first-century-style film and theater—polished productions that can be enjoyed by the masses in a variety of locations—simply did not exist.

The most popular form of entertainment in the decade was vaudeville. The core of a vaudeville show was variety: Each show contained nine to twelve acts, with comedy, stunts, dramatic skits, and singing. Vaudeville acts toured from city to city, and performers from the best and most famous troupes garnered considerable public stature. The impact of vaudeville on later forms of popular culture was enormous, as many vaudeville performers went on to become the first stars of radio and TV. Another popular form of live entertainment was the minstrel show, a form of variety show in which the performers often presented stereotypical and racist impersonations of African Americans. Many white actors performed "blackface" minstrelsy (MIN-strul-see), which meant that they applied makeup to look black, but minstrel shows also offered a rare opportunity for African Americans to appear on stage, albeit often in a degrading context. Buffalo Bill Cody (1846–1917) and his Wild West Show provided another form of entertainment, a variety show meant to dramatize the mythical American West.

Film was in its infancy at the beginning of the decade, but it soon made great strides. Technological constraints only allowed films to be about thirty seconds long, limiting the ability of film to tell a story, and they contained no sound. Early films were thus novelties, and they were often shown along with live entertainment, as in a vaudeville show. The creation of the silent film *The Great Train Robbery* in 1903 revolutionized the industry, however. At about twelve minutes long, the film told a dramatic story about a train robbery and was received enthusiastically by audiences across the country. Throughout the decade more and more Americans began to see short films in nickelodeons, which were essentially storefront theaters that charged a small admission fee. By 1908, it was estimated that eighty million nickelodeon tickets were sold every week. By the 1910s, the rise of more skilled directors and famous "movie stars" would make film one of the most popular forms of entertainment.

Broadway

Even though the roadway named "Broadway" extends the length of the New York City borough of Manhattan, the name has come to indicate the area, in midtown Manhattan, in which a majority of the city's primary theaters are located. The word "Broadway" has come to represent bright, flashing lights and oversized billboards towering over playgoers as they crowd around theater entrances most every evening just before 8 PM (and on Wednesday and Saturday for matinees, or afternoon performances). For those who choose to devote their life to the stage, appearing on Broadway is a significant accomplishment and starring on the Broadway stage is a dream come true.

New York City's status as the hub of American theater dates to 1826, when the three-thousand-seat Bowery Theatre opened; it was the first

The Great White Way—Broadway—in midtown Manhattan, New York City. © DAVID R. FRAZIER PHOTOLIBRARY, INC./ALAMY.

playhouse to feature glass-shaded gas-jet lighting. By the 1880s, "Broadway" had become the general term for American theater, and the New York theater district was nearby, only farther downtown, at East 14th Street and Union Square. As the city expanded, clusters of playhouses opened further uptown, in what today is midtown Manhattan. Eventually, most were constructed in the crosstown streets of the West Forties, by and directly above Times Square. The first major playhouse in the area arrived in 1893, when the American Theatre opened on West 42nd Street.

In the early twentieth century, revues featuring music, dance, and comedy were especially popular on Broadway. As the American musical theater evolved, scores of significant composers and performers earned fame writing music for and appearing in Broadway hits. Before **radio** (see entry under 1920s—TV and Radio in volume 2) and **television** (see entry under 1940s—TV and Radio in volume 3), countless popular songs originated on Broadway. For example, during World War

I (1914–18), "Over There," a patriotic national rallying cry composed by George M. Cohan (1878–1942), was introduced at the New Amsterdam Theatre before becoming a hit record. Musical theater flourished on Broadway during a good portion of the twentieth century, but serious dramas and nonmusical comedies were increasingly staged as well. One notable Broadway dramatist, who gained infamy for his emphasis on realism in his writing, was Eugene O'Neill (1883–1953), who during the 1920s authored *The Emperor Jones, Anna Christie,* and *Strange Interlude.*

Many film actors started out on Broadway. Marlon Brando (1924–), for one, became a theater legend in 1947 with his riveting performance as Stanley Kowalski in *A Streetcar Named Desire.* Brando made his screen debut in 1950, replayed Kowalski in the film version of *Streetcar* the following year, and never came back to Broadway. Meanwhile, other actors preferred stage over screen, even though successful movie actors enjoyed far more international fame than their stage-exclusive counterparts. Broadway legends such as Laurette Taylor (1884–1946), Eva Le Gallienne (1899–1991), Katherine Cornell (1893–1974), Alfred Drake (1914–1992), and the husband-and-wife team of Alfred Lunt (1892–1977) and Lynn Fontanne (1887–1983) became major stage personalities, while barely, if ever, appearing on screen.

Broadway—also known as the Great White Way—remains one of New York's top tourist attractions and still symbolizes American theater. In recent years, many smash hits and long-running favorites have continued to thrill audiences, including *Chicago, The Phantom of the Opera,* and *The Producers.*

Rob Edelman

For More Information

Atkinson, Brooks. *Broadway.* Rev. ed. New York: Limelight Editions, 1985.

Bloom, Ken. *Broadway: Its History, People, and Places.* New York: Routledge, 2004.

Brown, Gene. *Show Time: A Chronology of Broadway and the Theatre from Its Beginnings to the Present.* New York: Macmillan, 1997.

Dunlap, David W. *On Broadway: A Journey Uptown over Time.* New York: Rizzoli, 1990.

Frommer, Myrna Katz, and Harvey Frommer. *It Happened on Broadway: An Oral History of the Great White Way.* New York: Harcourt, 1998.

The Internet Broadway Database. *The Internet Broadway Database.* http://www.ibdb.com (accessed June 20, 2011).

Buffalo Bill's Wild West Show

The mythology of the Old West is an essential part of American folklore. While much of this vision is derived from countless dime novels (inexpensive, melodramatic books that originally cost ten cents) and Hollywood movies that depict the settling of the American West, the origin of this mythology may be traced to one man: William F. Cody (1846–1917), more commonly known as Buffalo Bill. Cody was a U.S. cavalry scout, buffalo hunter, Indian fighter, Pony Express rider, gold miner, ox team driver—and entertainer. He created Buffalo Bill's Wild West Show, a traveling extravaganza that celebrated and glorified the settling of the American West.

Legend has it that Cody was dubbed "Buffalo Bill" after being hired to help supply buffalo meat to workers building the cross-country railroad; he claimed to have personally killed 4,280 buffalo. His fame was spread by Ned Buntline (1823–1886), a dime novelist who made him the hero of a series of stories published in *The New York Weekly.* Buntline was not a chronicler of Cody's real-life deeds; he fictionalized and exaggerated them, thus creating the mythology surrounding his subject.

In 1872, Buntline persuaded Cody to act in his play, *The Scouts of the Plains,* which was Buffalo Bill's debut in show business. Supposedly, upon observing a Nebraska Independence Day celebration in 1883, Cody concocted the idea of Buffalo Bill's Wild West Show, which recreated a Pony Express ride, a stagecoach attack, and various rodeo events. The finale included a spectacle involving cowboys, Indians, and stampeding animals. Wherever possible, Cody hired real-life Western notables to appear in his show.

For an 1884 appearance at the Cotton Exposition in New Orleans, Louisiana, Cody acquired the services of famed sharpshooter Annie Oakley (1860–1926). The following year, he hired Sitting Bull (1831–1890), fabled chief of the Teton Sioux Indians, who had led the final major Indian resistance against western settlement. In retrospect, Cody's employment of Indians is controversial; his depiction of them attacking stagecoaches and settlers perpetuated the image of the Indians as dangerous savages.

Cody's extravaganza reached its height in popularity in 1887, when he took it to London, England, to celebrate the fiftieth anniversary of the reign of Queen Victoria (1819–1901). Two years later, Cody toured

Late-nineteenth-century program cover from Buffalo Bill's Wild West and Congress of Rough Riders of the World show. William F. "Buffalo Bill" Cody's show toured around the world, thrilling audiences. © SMITHSONIAN INSTITUTION/CORBIS.

throughout Europe, beginning with a performance in Paris. After returning to the United States in 1893 and savoring one last successful season, Cody's show began to decline, its luster fading because of competition from similar traveling extravaganzas and internal upheaval. However, Cody did manage to keep the show afloat until his death in 1917.

Rob Edelman

For More Information

Buffalo Bill and the Indians, Or Sitting Bull's History Lesson (film). United Artists, 1976.

The Buffalo Bill Historical Center. http://www.bbhc.org/home (accessed June 20, 2011).

Cody, William F. *An Autobiography of Buffalo Bill (Colonel W. F. Cody).* New York: Cosmopolitan Book Corp., 1923.

Cody, William F. *The Business of Being Buffalo Bill: Selected Letters of William F. Cody, 1879–1917.* New York: Praeger, 1988.

Kasson, Joy S. *Buffalo Bill's Wild West: Celebrity, Memory, and Popular History.* New York: Hill and Wang, 2000.

Warren, Louis S. *Buffalo Bill's America: William Cody and the Wild West Show.* New York: Alfred A. Knopf, 2005.

The Great Train Robbery

The Great Train Robbery (1903) is one of the most popular and important early silent films. It was directed by Edwin S. Porter (1869–1941) for the Edison Company and enjoyed by audiences for several years after its initial release. What makes this film outstanding is its ambitious length and style of storytelling. Most films of the period lasted only two or three minutes and contained less than a handful of different shots. *The Great Train Robbery* told its story in about twelve minutes, linking fourteen individual shots together to complete a cohesive plot-line. It is also often called the first recognizably modern **Western** film (see entry under 1930s—Film and Theater in volume 2).

The original publicity for this audience-pleaser stated that it was meant to present "a faithful duplication of the genuine 'Hold Ups' made famous by various outlaw bands in the far West." The plot is action packed. Bandits enter a telegraph office and tie up the telegraph operator. Then they stop a train and rob the express car and its passengers before escaping on horseback. Next, the telegraph operator's daughter finds her father and unties him. He alerts the people of the town, and they form a

The Great Train Robbery, *shot in 1903, was one of the most popular silent films of all time.* © HULTON-DEUTSCH COLLECTION/CORBIS.

posse (PAH-see; a group of people who search for someone) to capture the bandits. The posse chases the bandits and succeeds in exacting justice.

The film made use of interesting special effects to highlight parts of the story. Two new techniques were especially thrilling to the audience. First, Porter created a sense of realism by stopping the action to insert a dummy for a real-life actor and restarting the camera as the dummy was tossed from a moving train. To tell the story, Porter filmed all the action from a distance, in a series of long shots. Then, after the completion of the story, he zoomed in for a close-up. In a close-up, the camera is placed so close to the subject that the viewer sees him or her only from the chest up; in the movie theater, Porter's closeup shot showed a bandit firing a gun at the camera—and simultaneously at the audience! Early movie audiences had not experienced seeing close-ups and were quite entertained by this powerful final shot.

Compared to today's films, *The Great Train Robbery* might not appear to be an example of clever editing or technological innovation, but it is an illustration of a highly entertaining, longer narrative film that offered early cinema audiences a more detailed story-telling format.

Audrey Kupferberg

For More Information

Durks, Tim. *The Great Train Robbery.* http://www.filmsite.org/grea.html (accessed June 20, 2011).

Fenin, George N., and William K. Everson. *The Western: From Silents to the Seventies.* Rev. ed. New York: Grossman, 1977.

Musser, Charles. *The Emergence of Cinema: The American Screen to 1907.* Berkeley: University of California Press, 1990.

Harry Houdini (1874–1926)

During the early twentieth century, Harry Houdini was the world's most celebrated illusionist and escape artist. He earned world renown performing death-defying stunts that captured media attention and the imaginations of his audiences.

Houdini was born in Budapest, Hungary, in 1874; his birth name was Erich (or Ehrich) Weiss. His family came to America in 1878. He first became intrigued by trickery and illusion while a teenager and renamed himself after famed French magician Jean Eugene Robert-Houdin (1805–1871). Determined to forge a career as a magician, he labored for several years in obscurity before winning national acclaim in **vaudeville** (see entry under 1900s—Film and Theater in volume 1) and, then, international acclaim upon performing in England.

Houdini started out his career executing simple magic tricks but eventually developed and perfected the escape acts that won him notoriety. In these acts, he would free himself from straitjackets, prison cells, packing crates, coffins, mail pouches, milk cans, giant paper bags, and so-called "Chinese Water Torture" chambers (large glass boxes filled with water). Often, he would be tied with rope, handcuffed, or manacled. As his fame grew, Houdini also became known for exposing fake spiritualists.

In 1918, Houdini began acting in movies. In 1925, he opened on Broadway in *Magic,* a two-and-a-half-hour extravaganza. He died the following year. Legend has it that his death was the direct result of his being punched in the stomach by an overenthusiastic college student

Harry Houdini prepares to perform another death-defying trick, probably the "overboard box escape." © ARCHIVE PICS/ALAMY.

who wished to test the strength of Houdini's abdominal muscles. In the Hollywood biography *Houdini* (1953), his demise comes as he fails to complete an underwater escape trick. In fact, Houdini died of peritonitis, caused by a ruptured appendix—which may or may not have been connected to the stomach punch.

Rob Edelman

For More Information

Cobb, Vicki. *Harry Houdini.* New York: DK, 2005.

Fleischman, Sid. *Escape! The Story of the Great Houdini.* New York: Greenwillow, 2006.

Hass, E. A. *Houdini's Last Trick: The Amazing True Story of the World's Greatest Magician.* New York: Random House, 1995.

*Houdini Tribute.*http://www.houdinitribute.com (accessed June 20, 2011).

Kalush, William. *The Secret Life of Houdini: The Making of America's First Superhero.* New York: Atria, 2006.

Library of Congress. "Variety Stage: Harry Houdini." *American Memory Project.* http://lcweb2.loc.gov/ammem/vshtml/vshdini.html (accessed July 8, 2011).

Silverman, Kenneth. *Houdini!!! The Career of Erich Weiss.* New York: HarperCollins, 1996.

Minstrel Shows

Minstrel shows were an extremely popular form of entertainment in which white performers wearing blackface makeup impersonated African Americans. The shows originated in the nineteenth century as professional stage productions. In the first half of the twentieth century professional productions disappeared, but putting on a minstrel show became a popular activity for amateur groups.

Impersonations of African Americans became popular in the northern United States around 1830. Thomas D. Rice (c. 1808–1860) performed songs and dances as the plantation slave Jim Crow. George Washington Dixon (c. 1801–1861) gained fame by pretending to be a northern black man named Zip Coon. Out of these individual acts developed the full-fledged minstrel show, with the first one generally said to be the performance by Dan Emmett (1815–1904) and his Virginia Minstrels on February 6, 1843, in New York City (Emmett gained greater fame years later, when he wrote the popular Southern anthem "Dixie.").

The Virginia Minstrels were a great success. Soon there were dozens of minstrel troupes, including the Christy Minstrels, led by E. P. Christy (1815–1862). The Christy Minstrels established the standard pattern for the minstrel show: four or more performers in a semi-circle on stage, with a banjo player and a fiddler in the middle and two "endmen," one playing the tambourine and one the bone castanets. The endmen, called Mr. Tambo and Mr. Bones, wore outlandish clothes and makeup and made jokes at the expense of themselves and the somewhat pompous master of ceremonies, or Interlocutor, seated in the middle.

In the mid-nineteenth century, the minstrel show was the most popular form of entertainment in America. After 1900, the professional version of it disappeared, losing out in competition with **vaudeville** (see entry under 1900s—Film and Theater in volume 1), **radio** (see entry under 1920s—TV and Radio in volume 2), and the movies. But blackface performers continued to appear in vaudeville shows, in movies like

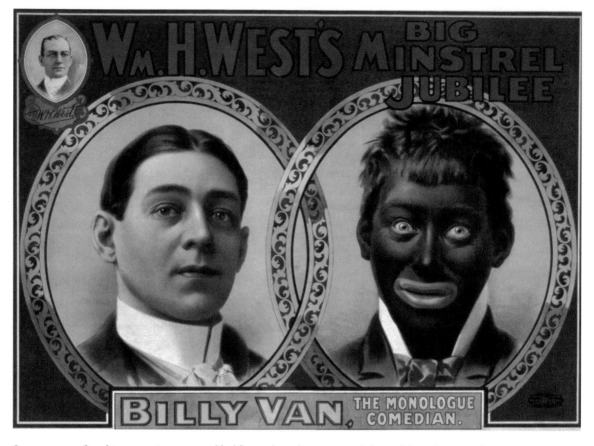

It was common for white entertainers to wear blackface makeup during minstrel shows of the early twentieth century. Here, comedian Billy Van is shown before and after makeup. © EVERETT COLLECTION/ALAMY.

The Jazz Singer (1927; see entry under 1920s—Film and Theater in volume 2), and in the popular radio show *Amos 'n' Andy* (1928–55; see entry under 1930s—TV and Radio in volume 2). There continued to be a craze for amateur minstrel shows until, after the **civil rights movement** (see entry under 1960s—The Way We Lived in volume 4) of the 1960s, they came to be regarded as racist.

Some commentators have defended the minstrel shows, saying that they expressed not just racist derision but also admiration and sympathy for African Americans. Some say the performances were less about race than about the liberating effect of putting on a mask. The general view by the end of the twentieth century, however, was that the minstrel shows were a shameful but important part of American history.

Sheldon Goldfarb

For More Information

Comer, Jim. *Every Time I Turn Around: Rite, Reversal, and the End of Blackface Minstrelsy.* http://www.angelfire.com/oh/hydriotaphia/crow.html (accessed June 20, 2011).

Huggins, Nathan Irvin. "Personae: White/Black Faces—Black Masks." In *Harlem Renaissance.* New York: Oxford University Press, 1971, pp. 244–301.

Lhamon, W. T., Jr. *Raising Cain: Blackface Performance from Jim Crow to Hip-Hop.* Cambridge, MA: Harvard University Press, 2000.

"Minstrel Shows: 'That Shuff-a-lin' Throng.'" *Musicals101.com.* http://www.musicals101.com/minstrel.htm (accessed June 20, 2011).

Toll, Robert C. *Blacking Up: The Minstrel Show in Nineteenth-Century America.* New York: Oxford University Press, 1974.

Nickelodeons

During the first decade and a half of the twentieth century, movies were fast becoming a diversion for the masses. However, the popular venues for watching movies, from the thousand-seat **movie palaces** (see entry under 1910s—Film and Theater in volume 1) built during the 1910s and 1920s to the present-day multiplex theaters, had not yet come into being. So motion pictures were projected in nickelodeons—small storefronts that were converted into makeshift theaters. The term "nickelodeon" derived from two words: "nickel," their usual admission price; and "odeon," the Greek word for theater.

Nickelodeons played a key role in the popularization of film not only because they served to exhibit early motion pictures but also because they were one of the first forms of affordable entertainment available to the general public. Legend has it that the first nickelodeon surfaced in Pittsburgh, Pennsylvania, in 1904, when a local businessman converted his store into a theater. As motion pictures then were **silent** (see entry on silent movies under 1900s—Film and Theater in volume 1), the businessman installed a piano to be used for musical accompaniment. Before the year was out, over one hundred similar establishments had opened across the city. By

Before the development of large movie houses, motion pictures were shown in small storefronts converted into makeshift theaters known as nickelodeons. © CORBIS.

1908, between eight thousand and ten thousand nickelodeons were in use nationwide. Many were located in immigrant and working-class communities, allowing those with modest incomes to indulge in the pleasures of moviegoing. Nickelodeons thus acted to spread the development of motion pictures as a form of mass entertainment.

As befitting their status as amusement halls, nickelodeon exteriors were usually brightly painted and lit. They were decorated with posters advertising current and future programs. Live barkers (people who advertise at a show entrance) shouted the latest attractions to passersby. Inside, paying customers sat on wooden benches or folding chairs and watched the movies' images flicker on a canvas screen. The projection booth, located in the rear, was a small box, six feet square, with sufficient room for the projector and projectionist who cranked the film by hand. A nickelodeon's seating capacity ranged from fifty to six hundred seats.

The average nickelodeon program lasted about thirty minutes, consisting of three separate films, each one reel (approximately ten minutes) long. Programs often changed daily, to encourage a steady flow of return customers. The content of these one-reelers included adaptations of Shakespeare and the Bible, dramatizations of current events as well as famous novels and plays, depictions of the realities of everyday working-class life, and scenes from exotic locations.

Several of Hollywood's business pioneers started out as nickelodeon operators. Among them were Marcus Loew (1870–1927), Adolph Zukor (1873–1976), and William Fox (1879–1952) as well as the Warner brothers Harry (1881–1958), Albert (1884–1967), Sam (1888–1927), and Jack (1892–1978). Eventually, nickelodeons gave way to more spacious and comfortable movie houses. During the short time of their existence, however, they played an essential role in offering the working and immigrant classes their first exposure to mass entertainment and American popular culture.

Rob Edelman

For More Information

Bowers, Q. David. *Nickelodeon Theatres and Their Music.* Vestal, NY: Vestal Press, 1986.

Nasaw, David. *Going Out: The Rise and Fall of Public Amusements.* New York: BasicBooks, 1993.

Wagenknecht, Edward. *The Movies in the Age of Innocence.* Norman: University of Oklahoma Press, 1962.

Silent Movies

In the early twenty-first century, the age of digital recording and surround-sound, it is difficult to imagine a time when movie actors did not speak on screen. Yet during the first twenty-five years of the twentieth century, it was difficult to imagine them ever doing so. Silent movies were watched in silence or accompanied by live musicians in the theater. Speech was displayed in print (known as intertitles) on the screen between the action sequences.

Thomas Edison (1847–1931) and his assistant William Dickson (1860–1935) were the first to make moving pictures possible with their Kinematograph in 1891. Dickson later designed the Kinetoscope, a box-like apparatus that allowed a single viewer to watch moving pictures. Early silent films, known as "actualities," lasted only a few seconds and recorded events as they happened using a fixed camera. In the late 1990s and into the twenty-first century, **reality TV** (see entry under 1990s—TV and Radio in volume 5) shows used similar filming techniques. For around twenty-five cents—the hourly wage for a skilled worker in 1894—spectators could view a short film on one of the Kinetoscopes set up in "parlors" around the country.

Before long, small movie theaters charging a nickel a time were set up in storefronts. By 1910, there were over ten thousand of these **nickelodeons** (see entry under 1900s—Film and Theater in volume 1) in America. Future movie businessmen such as the Warner brothers (Harry, 1881–1958; Albert, 1884–1967; Sam, 1888–1927; and Jack, 1892–1978) and William Fox (1879–1952) began as nickelodeon owners. However, some people thought movies were immoral. Edison's film *The Kiss,* which simply shows a couple kissing, caused a scandal in 1908. A small number of films did contain nudity, but as titles such as *The Chinese Laundry* and *Dancing Bears* suggest, most early silent films were tame by the standards of twenty-first-century cinema.

Storytelling in American movies began around 1902 with the short *The Life of an American Fireman* by Edwin S. Porter (1869–1941). In 1905, his fifteen-minute adaptation of the abolitionist tale *Uncle Tom's Cabin* was one of the longest and most expensive movies yet made. America's racist past is evidenced by many early silent movies such as *The Cheat* (1915) by Cecil B. DeMille (1881–1959) and the *Sambo* series of comedies. Even in 1915, many people found the classic **The Birth of a Nation** (see entry

Actor Harold Lloyd hangs from a clock in a scene from the 1923 silent movie Safety Last. © KOBAL COLLECTION.

under 1910s—Film and Theater in volume 1), directed by D. W. Griffith, (1875–1948) shockingly racist. It was banned in several states.

Film shorts used a single reel of film and lasted a maximum of around fifteen minutes. By 1914, "features" used up to twelve reels and lasted over two hours. Classic novels and plays began to be adapted for film on a large scale. Techniques of editing and camera movement improved quickly. By the 1920s, studios had adopted the practice of making movies using tested formulas. The formula **Western** (see entry under 1930s—Film and Theater in volume 2) and "swashbuckling" adventure movies such as *The Three Musketeers* and the *Zorro* (see entry under 1910s—Print Culture in volume 1) series emerged in the 1920s. **Rudolph Valentino** (1895–1926; see entry under 1920s—Film and

Theater in volume 2), Douglas Fairbanks (1883–1939), and young Greta Garbo (1905–1999) were the movie stars of the time. Scandals in Hollywood related to immoral behavior eventually led to heavy-handed censorship, but in Europe directors continued to experiment. From 1918 onwards, German filmmakers like Carl Meyer (1894–1944) and Fritz Lang (1890–1976) and Russian Sergei Eisenstein (1898–1948) treated film as more than just entertainment. Eisenstein is widely described as the most important filmmaker of the silent era. His *Battleship Potemkin* (1925) is one of the most influential films of all time.

Slapstick comedy and mime are silent film's lasting legacy. Early professional actors such as Buster Keaton (1895–1966) and Harold Lloyd (1893–1971) enjoyed huge silent success. **Charlie Chaplin** (1889–1977; see entry under 1910s Film and Theater in volume 1) crafted brilliant and profitable comedies; *The Immigrant* (1917) and *The Kid* (1921) remain classics.

The first "talkie" film, ***The Jazz Singer*** (see entry under 1920s—Film and Theater in volume 2), marked the end of an era in movie history when it was released in 1927. In it, Al Jolson (1886–1950) heralded the coming of the "talkie" with the famous spoken line: "Wait a minute. Wait a minute. You ain't heard nothing yet!" Although "talkies" quickly made films more popular than ever, some people clung to the silent film format. Many stars of the silent era had terrible speaking voices and the arrival of sound ended their careers. *Sunset Boulevard* (1950) tells the dark story of Norma Desmond, an ex–silent screen star washed up in the era of sound. When told she used to be a big star, Desmond declares: "I *am* big. It's the pictures that got small." Famously, Chaplin resisted the arrival of sound. His almost-silent film *Modern Times* (1936) is partly an attack on the sound film.

Despite the efforts of the studios to turn out silent films in a production-line process, talkies soon became the twentieth century's greatest form of entertainment. Sound simply made movies more powerful. Yet during the transition to sound, many argued that silent movies were the purer form of filmmaking. Some of the most highly praised movies of all time come from the silent era.

Chris Routledge

For More Information

Acker, Ally. *Reel Women: Pioneers of the Cinema 1896 to Present.* New York: Continuum, 1991.

Cook, David A. *A History of Narrative Film.* 4th ed. New York: W. W. Norton, 2004.

Everson, William K. *American Silent Film.* New York: Da Capo, 1978.

Karney, Robyn, ed. *Chronicle of the Cinema: 100 Years of the Movies.* Rev. ed. London: Dorling Kindersley, 1997.

Kobel, Peter, and the Library of Congress. *Silent Movies: The Birth of Film and the Triumph of Movie Culture.* New York: Little, Brown, 2007.

"Welcome to Silent-Movies.com." *Silentmovies.com.* http://www.silentmovies. com (accessed June 20, 2011).

Silvester, Christopher. *The Penguin Book of Hollywood.* New York: Viking, 1998.

Vaudeville

For the transitionary decades during the late nineteenth and early twentieth centuries, vaudeville was a primary means of spreading mainstream entertainment in the United States. Vaudeville came before the establishment of the popular dramatic theater movement on **Broadway** (see entry under 1900s—Film and Theater in volume 1), and before movies, **radio** (see entry under 1920s—TV and Radio in volume 2), and television gained footholds in American popular culture. Vaudeville programs consisted of diverse groups of performers—including singers, dancers, actors, comedians, jugglers, acrobats, animal acts, and magicians—who were hired by talent bookers to tour through regions of the country, performing live on the vaudeville circuit.

The term vaudeville was derived from one of two sources. The first source was the French *Val de Vire* (or *Vau de Vire*), the valley of the Vire River in Normandy. The valley was famed for the comic songs and ballads originating in the region back in the fifteenth century. The second possible source is the *voix de ville* ("voice of the city"), the French term for urban folk songs. Vaudeville came to the forefront during the 1880s, when forward-thinking entrepreneurs (perhaps the best known was Benjamin Franklin Keith [1846–1914]) began to market entertainment for the masses. These entrepreneurs remodeled their theaters, sometimes to lavish specifications, and booked better-quality performers. Some vaudeville theaters were "small time." These theaters were the less ornate venues (sites of events), many located in smaller towns, where lesser-known performers worked longer hours and earned more modest paychecks. Meanwhile, others were "big time." These theaters, located in the major cities, were large, extravagantly designed entertainment palaces. The most popular, highest-salaried performers worked the major theaters, where schedules were less grueling and working conditions were far superior. Part of a vaudevillian's professional status depended upon whether he or she worked a three-a-day or five-a-day schedule, referring to the number of performances put on per day.

A typical vaudeville bill consisted of between nine and twelve individual acts. Shows were generally fast paced. As the decades passed, styles and standards were altered to fit the changing American scene. Into the early 1900s, even with an emphasis on bringing in family audiences, sensationalism was a great attraction in vaudeville. Customers were treated to such scandalous theatrics as wiggling exotic dancers removing layers of clothing while performing the "dance of the seven veils." Customers attended the theater for glimpses of such notorious beauties as Evelyn Nesbit (1884–1967), who had been the "other woman" in a celebrated murder case, and swimming champion Annette Kellerman (1887–1975), who had been arrested in Boston for wearing a one-piece bathing suit that had been deemed indecent.

In addition, the humor occasionally was off-color. Vaudeville programs featured songs and jokes that involved ethnic slurs against Irish, German, Italian, and Jewish immigrants. These insults provided laughs for both deeply rooted Americans and recent European immigrants. Nor were African Americans spared from being stereotyped; however, many songs spotlighting black behavior actually were sentimental, particularly those that waxed nostalgic for a peaceful life down South. These numbers were performed mainly by white performers who "corked up" (used the black ash from burned corks as makeup) and appeared in blackface, which then was an acceptable practice.

Among the many great stars of early vaudeville were singing comediennes Nora Bayes (1880–1928), Elsie Janis (1889–1956), and Eva Tanguay (1878–1947); juggler-comedian W. C. Fields (1879–1946); Julian Eltinge (1883–1941), a female impersonator; the comedy teams of Joe Weber (1867–1942) and Lew Fields (1867–1941) and Joe Smith (1884–1981) and Charlie Dale (1881–1971), specialists in ethnic humor; and Bert Williams (1874–1922), a renowned African American comedian. Around the turn of the twentieth century, motion picture shorts were added to many vaudeville bills. These were considered novelties, and few vaudevillians realized that the growth of the motion picture industry would eventually result in the death of vaudeville. While many vaudevillians made appearances in early motion pictures, W. C. Fields and other stars became movie headliners. Joining Fields were singer-comedian Eddie Cantor (1892–1964); and the comedy teams of Bert Wheeler

(1895–1968) and Robert Woolsey (1889–1938), the husband-and-wife duo of George Burns (1896–1996) and Gracie Allen (1902–1964), and the **Marx Brothers** (see entry under 1930s—Film and Theater in volume 2). The Marx Brothers consisted of Harpo (1888–1964), Groucho (1890–1977), Chico (1886–1961), and Zeppo (1901–1979).

Vaudeville began its decline in the late 1920s, with the expanding mass popularity of motion pictures. Back then, a typical screen program included two feature films and, perhaps, a newsreel or travelogue, a comedy short, and a cartoon. When compared with the easy profits that could be made showing films to the public, the coordination and presentation of live vaudeville shows became financially prohibitive. Thus, "canned entertainment" won the day.

Audrey Kupferberg

For More Information

Cullen, Frank, Florence Hackman, and Donald McNeilly. *Vaudeville, Old & New: An Encyclopedia of Variety Performers in America.* New York: Routledge, 2007.

Gilbert, Douglas. *American Vaudeville: Its Life and Times.* New York: Dover, 1940, 1968.

Green, Abel, and Joe Laurie Jr. *Show Biz: From Vaude to Video.* New York: Henry Holt, 1951.

Laurie, Joe, Jr. *Vaudeville: From the Honky Tonks to the Palace.* New York: Henry Holt, 1953.

Slide, Anthony. *The Encyclopedia of Vaudeville.* Westport, CT: Greenwood Press, 1994.

Snyder, Robert. *The Voice of the City: Vaudeville and Popular Culture in New York.* New York: Oxford University Press, 1989.

Staples, Shirley. *Male/Female Comedy Teams in American Vaudeville, 1865–1932.* Ann Arbor, MI: UMI Research Press, 1984.

Vaudeville! http://xroads.virginia.edu/~ma02/easton/vaudeville/vaudevillemain.html (accessed June 20, 2011).

Ziegfeld Follies

Between 1907 and the early 1930s, the *Ziegfeld Follies* was the most spectacular and famous American revue (a theatrical production consisting of songs, skits, and dance numbers). The *Follies* was conceived by theatrical impresario (the promoter and manager of a theater company) Florenz Ziegfeld (1869–1932) and his first wife, European performer Anna Held (1873–1918). The revues featured singers introducing the

New York City's Winter Garden Theatre hosts the Ziegfeld Follies *in 1936.* © HULTON ARCHIVE/ARCHIVE PHOTOS/GETTY IMAGES.

day's top musical numbers, dancers performing elaborately choreo-graphed routines, comedians tickling funny bones, and actors perform-ing one-act plays. Most of all, however, the *Ziegfeld Follies* was fabled for featuring scores of young, beautiful, elaborately costumed showgirls, who often would do little more than parade about or pose prettily, amid settings that formed a living picture, or tableau.

The *Follies* began as an American version of sophisticated yet ris-qué (bordering on indecent) French revues such as the *Folies Bergère.* The American *Follies* quickly created a formula all its own: the produc-tion of romantic musical performances as well as the inclusion of more low-brow fare. The romantic musical performances featured ornate art-nouveau settings designed by artist Joseph Urban (1972–1933) (The term *art nouveau* refers to a movement in art, lasting from the 1890s to about 1914, that evolved into a decorative style.). The more unrefined low-brow fare highlighted the pretty showgirls, whose costumes included elaborate accessories such as headdresses but were quite revealing of the wearer's body. Other revues might spotlight a couple dozen showgirls, but a typical *Ziegfeld Follies* would feature more than 120 attractive women. During the course of a show, there might be five or six costume changes. All the clothes, and the materials from which they were made, were handpicked by Ziegfeld. These showgirls came to be known as the Ziegfeld Girls.

However, the Ziegfeld Girls' performances were far from the entire show. Dozens of legendary singers, dancers, and comics appeared in the *Follies,* among them Bob Hope (1903–2003), **Will Rogers** (1879–1935; see entry under 1910s—Film and Theater in volume 1), Bert Lahr (1895–1967), Eddie Cantor (1892–1964), Fanny Brice (1891–1951), Marilyn Miller (1898–1936), Bert Williams (1874–1922), and Leon Errol (1881–1951). Famed song-writers Irving Berlin (1888–1989), Oscar Hammerstein (1895–1960), and Jerome Kern (1885–1945) composed musical numbers for Ziegfeld. Many of the songs that debuted in the *Follies* went on to become standards of popular American music.

The initial revue was called *The Follies of 1907.* Ziegfeld kept the *Follies* going for the next twenty-three years, until the beginning of the **Great Depression** (1929–41; see entry under 1930s—The Way We Lived in volume 2). The Depression made the expensive productions impractical for both Ziegfeld to fund and potential ticket buyers to afford. His life and his Follies were captured on screen in several films: *The Great Ziegfeld* (1936), a biography featuring William Powell (1892–1984) in the title role, which became a Best Picture Academy Award winner; *Ziegfeld Girl* (1941), a tale of three *Follies* showgirls; and *Ziegfeld Follies* (1946), which featured skits, dances, and songs, all introduced by a fantasized Ziegfeld (played again by Powell) who now resided in heaven.

Audrey Kupferberg

For More Information

Cantor, Eddie. *The Great Glorifier.* New York: A. H. King, 1934.

Carter, Randolph. *Ziegfeld: The Time of His Life.* Rev. ed. London: Bernard Press, 1988.

Farnsworth, Marjorie. *The Ziegfeld Follies.* New York: Bonanza Books, 1956.

The Great Ziegfeld (film). Metro-Goldwyn-Mayer, 1936.

Higham, Charles. *Ziegfeld.* Chicago: Regnery, 1972.

Mordden, Ethan. *Ziegfeld: The Man Who Invented Show Business.* New York: St. Martin's Press, 2008.

Ziegfeld Follies (film). Metro-Goldwyn-Mayer, 1946.

Ziegfeld Girl (film). Metro-Goldwyn-Mayer, 1941.

1900s

Food and Drink

Like much else in America during the first decade of the twentieth century, the ways Americans prepared and ate their meals were also changing. At the heart of these changes was the movement from preparation of food in the home from scratch, using primitive appliances, to the preparation of prepackaged foods using modern, electric appliances. Although these changes occurred over the first thirty years of the century, they trace their beginnings to the 1900s.

Here is a look at this transition from the vantage point of a typical middle-class kitchen. In 1901, Mrs. Jones, a middle-class housewife (a woman who did not work outside the home), spent the majority of her day cooking and cleaning. She tended a small garden that produced food for the family. In the fall, she canned fruit and vegetables to last through the winter. Mrs. Jones kept a fire burning in the wood-or coal-burning stove on which she cooked the meals, although getting the heat level right was never easy. She fetched water in a bucket from the well out behind the house. She bought unbranded foods in bulk from the local grocer.

By 1910, keeping house was beginning to get easier. The Jones family moved to the city, and their new apartment had running water, indoor toilets, and a gas stove (Electric stoves were available, but usually too expensive for the average family). Now Mrs. Jones did not have to spend most of her day tending a fire or fetching water—she simply turned on the flame or the faucet. Though she no longer had a garden, Mrs. Jones was lucky that a new A&P grocery store had opened just down the block. The A&P carried all types of dry food, fruits and vegetables (both fresh and canned), and refrigerated goods. Now that canned goods were readily available, Mrs. Jones no longer canned food of her own. She did not have to worry about the quality of the canned foods, because Congress had passed the Pure Food and Drug Act in 1906 to ensure the safety of mass-produced food. Among the Jones family's favorite branded foods were products that were introduced in this decade: Coca-Cola, Cracker Jack popcorn, and Jell-O gelatin. When the Joneses wanted a change of pace, they could walk three blocks to the local diner, a low-cost restaurant that served good family food, or head out to the amusement park, where they could buy a hot dog and an ice-cream cone—new, popular fast foods.

The A&P Grocery Company pioneered the concept of the grocery chain, but it soon faced competition from regional and, later, national grocery chains. In diners and at hot dog stands, Americans got their first taste of fast food. The growth of mass-produced, branded food products began to make life easier in this decade, and the food industry would expand dramatically through the century.

Chewing Gum/Bubble Gum

The practice of chewing gum dates back thousands of years, but only in the last two centuries has it become a widespread phenomenon, enjoyed by children and adults alike. With the mass marketing of chewing gum, and later bubble gum, those in need of fresh breath, sweet taste, and what the commercials called "pure chewing satisfaction" have many options from which to choose.

The Ancient Greeks were probably the first gum chewers. They chewed a resin from the lentisk, or mastic tree. During the same period, the Mayans of Central America chewed chicle (pronounced CHI-kull), the milky sap of the sapodilla tree. More than twenty centuries later, some companies still used chicle as one of the primary ingredients of modern chewing gum (though many now use a synthetic rubber). Other chewers of olden times include the native North Americans, who chewed the sap from red spruce trees. European colonists later picked up the habit and began trading the resin.

The birth of modern chewing gum can be traced back to the mid-nineteenth century, when chicle, imported to the United States, was combined with waxes and various additives to enhance its chewability. In 1848, John B. Curtis (1827–1897) made and sold the first commercial chewing gum, called the State of Maine Pure Spruce Gum. Shortly thereafter, chewing gum began being produced in a variety of flavors. U.S. troops serving in Europe in World War I (1914–18) introduced chewing gum to the local population. It proved an immediate hit, and a multimillion dollar industry was born. Popular brands of chewing gum have included Chiclets, Wrigley's Spearmint, Doublemint, and Big Red. There are a wide variety of sweet, sugarless, and breath-freshening varieties.

Gum technology took a major step forward when bubble gum was invented in 1928. Walter Diemer (c. 1904–1998), an accountant for the Fleer Chewing Gum Company in Philadelphia, Pennsylvania, was experimenting with new gum recipes when he hit upon the bubble gum formula by accident. "I was doing something else," Diemer later explained, "and ended up with something with bubbles." He colored his concoction pink because that was the only color he had on hand. The result, dubbed Dubble Bubble, became a hit with consumers and remains on the market in the twenty-first century.

Throughout the twentieth century and into the twenty-first, bubble gum has been marketed in a variety of novel and interesting ways. It has been included in packets of baseball cards, nested inside lollipops, and packaged with a humorous comic strip chronicling the adventures of the fictional character "Bazooka Joe." However it is made or sold, it continues to win the hearts and exercise the jaws of children of all ages.

Robert E. Schnakenberg

For More Information

Landau, Elaine. *Chewing Gum: A Sticky Treat.* Vero Beach, FL: Rourke Press, 2001.

Mathews, Jennifer P. *Chicle: The Chewing Gum of the Americas, from the Ancient Maya to William Wrigley.* Tucson: University of Arizona Press, 2009.

Wardlaw, Lee. *Bubblemania: A Chewy History of Bubble Gum.* New York: Aladdin, 1997.

Young, Robert. *The Chewing Gum Book.* Minneapolis: Dillon Press, 1989.

Coca-Cola

In 1886, an Atlanta, Georgia, pharmacist named John "Doc" Pemberton (1831–1888) concocted a thick, sweet brown syrup that he claimed would cure headaches and upset stomachs. Mixed with carbonated water and served for a nickel a glass at the counter of his pharmacy, Doc Pemberton's drink grew in popularity and soon he was selling up to nine glasses a day. He named his creation Coca-Cola, after its most powerful ingredients, cocaine from the coca plant of South America and caffeine from the kola nut of Africa.

From such humble beginnings, Coca-Cola has grown to become one of the most powerful corporations on earth. Sold in 195 countries, Coca-Cola is the largest selling soft drink, and the Coca-Cola bottling system is the most widespread production and distribution network in the world. More than that, "Coke" has come to represent American culture and lifestyle in both positive and negative ways at home and abroad.

Pemberton may have been a creative inventor, but he was not an aggressive businessman. Soon after he introduced Coke in Atlanta, ownership of the product passed to Asa Candler (1851–1929), who was a sharp businessman and increased sales dramatically. He improved the original recipe, removing the cocaine, which was beginning to be recognized as a dangerous drug. By 1895, Candler was distributing Coca-Cola in every state and territory in the United States. In 1919, Candler sold the business for $25 million to a group of investors headed by Ernest Woodruff. It was Woodruff's son, Robert (1889–1985), who would make Coke an international household word.

When he assumed the presidency of the company in 1923, Robert Woodruff concentrated on creating the Coca-Cola image. His first step was the mystification of the "secret formula" for the drink. Mostly as an advertising trick, he made a very public show of hiding the handwritten copy of Pemberton's original formula in a

Coca-Cola has grown over the years to be the most successful soft drink and a symbol of the American way of life. This Coca-Cola poster by N. C. Wyeth is from 1937. © K. J. HISTORICAL/CORBIS.

bank vault. Only two or three Coke executives would have access to the formula, he said, and their identities would be secret. Supposedly, these executives would not be allowed to travel together, so that in case of a car, train, or airplane crash, the formula would not be lost. The American public responded well to Woodruff's little drama. He followed up by producing hundreds of products with the Coca-Cola logo. Trays, glasses, napkins, and calendars bearing the red-and-white script logo appeared in thousands of homes across the United States. However, it was the role of Coke in World War II (1939–45) that established the soft drink globally.

When the United States joined World War II in 1941, Woodruff continued his campaign to identify the soft drink with basic American values. One of his smartest marketing moves was to supply Cokes to American servicemen at the U.S. price of five cents a bottle, no matter how far away they were stationed. Though this policy cost the company money, it was money well spent. Coca-Cola became a patriotic symbol of home to homesick soldiers, and the journalists who wrote about the war gave the drink priceless advertising in their stories. In 1943, General Dwight D. Eisenhower (1890–1969) set up ten Coca-Cola bottling plants in Northern Africa to supply American troops there. Although other soft drink companies, most notably Pepsi-Cola, tried to compete, none achieved the popularity of Coke. By the time the war ended, the Coca-Cola company had sixty-three bottling plants set up in Europe, Africa, and Asia, ready to begin peacetime soft drink sales.

Woodruff's aggressiveness in advertising lived on at the company after his death, and the company's advertising slogans have become almost as much a part of American culture as the soda itself. Coke has been called "the real thing," "the pause that refreshes," and "it." A 1971 ad campaign identified Coke with world peace by gathering dozens of singers on an Italian hillside to sing "I'd like to teach the world to sing in perfect harmony. I'd like to buy the world a Coke and keep it company." More than a soda with dubious health benefits and some peculiar uses— bottles of Coca-Cola syrup are still offered by some pharmacies as a remedy for indigestion, and many household-hints books recommend its acid for cleaning automobile battery terminals—Coca-Cola has become a symbol of the American way of life. As such, many people outside the United States view the soft drink as a symbol of an American invasion of their country, both culturally and economically.

Coca-Cola is now a gigantic corporation that also produces Sprite and Minute Maid products, along with sport drinks, bottled water, and coffee drinks. However, that fizzy brown soda pop that some southerners call "Georgia champagne" continues to convince generations of Americans that, as the old ad said, "things go better with Coke."

Tina Gianoulis

For More Information

Allen, Frederick. *Secret Formula: How Brilliant Marketing and Relentless Salesmanship Made Coca-Cola the Best-Known Product in the World.* New York: HarperBusiness, 1994.

Brands, H. W. "Coca Cola Goes to War." *American History* (Vol. 34, no. 3, August 1999): pp. 30–37.

Coca-Cola Web Site. http://www.cocacola.com (accessed June 20, 2011).

Hays, Constance L. *The Real Thing: Truth and Power at the Coca-Cola Company.* 2nd ed. New York: Random House, 2005.

Isdell, Neville, and David Beasley. *Inside Coca-Cola: A CEO's Secrets on Building the World's Most Popular Brand.* New York: St. Martin's Press, 2011.

Pendergrast, Mark. *For God, Country and Coca-Cola: The Definitive History of the Great American Soft Drink and the Company That Makes It.* 2nd ed. New York: Basic Books, 2000.

Cracker Jack

Children love popcorn, especially when a caramel coating adds sweetness and flavor to each piece. Mix in some peanuts, and the result is a simple yet surefire taste treat. These three ingredients—popcorn, caramel, and peanuts—make up Cracker Jack, a snack that is an essential part of the American childhood experience. Adding to the fun of purchasing Cracker Jack is that included in each box is a small toy, made even more enticing by being labelled a "prize."

The origin of Cracker Jack dates to 1871, when a German immigrant named Frederick William Rueckheim (1846–1934) began selling a popcorn snack on a Chicago street corner. Customers loved his confection (sweet treat), but they were bothered by the stickiness of the caramel. This problem was resolved when Louis Rueckheim (1849–1927), Frederick's brother, invented a secret process that kept the caramel dry and crispy. Around this time, Louis offered the popcorn-peanuts-caramel mixture to a salesman, who declared, "That's a crackerjack" (a popular slang term meaning very good). The brothers liked the salesman's exclamation and named their product Cracker Jack. The new popcorn snack made its debut in 1893 at Chicago's Columbian Exposition, the city's first **World's Fair** (see entry under 1900s—The Way We Lived in volume 1).

In 1908, Cracker Jack was immortalized in a song that was to become a favorite of baseball fans. In "Take Me Out to the Ball Game," lyricist Jack Norworth (1879–1959) penned the line, "Buy me some peanuts and Cracker Jack." Then in 1912, small toys were added to each box. In ensuing decades, over twenty-three billion prizes have been "awarded" to Cracker Jack purchasers. The numerous Cracker Jack prizes offered across the years include miniature plates, puzzles, books, bookmarks, pinball games, plastic figurines, and self-adhesive stickers. The product's logo, consisting of an illustration of a boy named Sailor Jack and his dog Bingo, was introduced during World War I (1914–18).

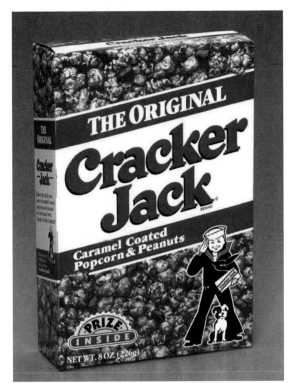

According to the jingle, "Candy-coated popcorn, peanuts, and a prize—that's what you get in Cracker Jack."
© AP IMAGES.

Over the years, Cracker Jack has been marketed in a Butter Toffee flavor and in a fat-free version. The Cracker Jack company also sells other products, including Checkers Popcorn, Campfire Marshmallows, and Angelus Marshmallows. Still, its first product, based on Frederick William Rueckheim's original formula, remains the company favorite.

Rob Edelman

For More Information

The Cracker Jack Box. http://members.cox.net/jeepers/CrackerJackBox.html (accessed June 20, 2011).

Jaramillo, Alex. *Cracker Jack Prizes.* New York: Abbeville Press, 1989.

White, Larry. *Cracker Jack Toys: The Complete, Unofficial Guide for Collectors.* Atglen, PA: Schiffer Publishing, 1997.

Diners

Before the dominance of national **fast food** chains (see entry under 1920s—Food and Drink in volume 2) in the 1950s, the diner was the most popular type of inexpensive restaurant for many Americans. Like

A typical roadside diner. © MICHAEL NEELON/ALAMY.

their fast food cousins, diners emerged as a response to the expanding automobile culture in the United States. Many diners were located along highways, where they offered short-order, home-style meals, complete with apple pie and coffee, to hungry travelers.

The diner itself evolved from horse-drawn lunch wagons, which were common during the late nineteenth century. These lunch wagons also served take-out meals in the downtowns of many cities after the restaurants had closed for the night. By the 1890s, stationary diners were being built. The stationary diners resembled lunch wagons, with counters, stools, and grills efficiently laid out in a compact, horizontal format. Simple dishes like hamburgers, hot dogs, eggs, soups, and desserts were served. These early diners were sometimes converted railroad or trolley cars, or were mass produced by such entrepreneurs as Thomas H. Buckley, who had planted them in more than 275 cities across the country. By the 1930s, diners took on a streamlined look, often clad in shiny, chrome-like materials and featuring Formica or stainless-steel counters, giving them a sleek Art moderne, or art deco, signature that emphasized cleanliness and efficiency (Art deco, also called art moderne, was an artistic movement of the 1920s and 1930s influenced by the machine age and characterized by geometric patterns and curving forms).

After the 1960s, as a response to the standardized look and menu of fast-food outlets such as **McDonald's** (see entry under 1940s—Food and Drink in volume 3) and **Burger King** (see entry under 1950s—Food and Drink in volume 3), many diners were expanded to include table service and also redesigned to express a unique atmosphere, such as Grecian, Mediterranean, colonial, Polynesian, or Googie (a futuristic, space-age decor that emerged in Los Angeles, named for a coffee shop of the same name built there in 1949).

From the 1970s, there has been a revival of interest in the diner as a center of American popular culture, where feisty, overworked employees "slung hash" for impatient customers. The 1982 film *Diner,* directed by Barry Levinson (1942–), helped perpetuate this image. So, too, did one of the most famous television commercials of all time, which featured a harried waitress easily mopping up spills in a New Jersey diner with Bounty paper towels (the "quicker picker-upper!"). The Henry Ford Museum in Dearborn, Michigan, includes a fully equipped 1946 diner as part of its collection of cultural artifacts.

Edward Moran

For More Information

Baeder, John. *Diners.* Rev. ed. New York: Harry N. Abrams, 1995.

Gutman, Richard J. S. *American Diner Then and Now.* New York: HarperCollins, 1993.

Hess, Alan. *Googie Redux: Ultramodern Roadside Architecture.* Rev. ed. San Francisco: Chronicle Books, 2004.

Witzel, Michael Karl. *The American Diner.* St. Paul, MN: MBI, 2006.

Hot Dogs

A hot dog is a sandwich that Americans by the millions enjoy at sporting events, picnics, and backyard cookouts. Along with a **hamburger** (see entry under 1950s—Food and Drink in volume 3) and **French fries** (see entry under 1950s—Food and Drink in volume 3), it is a simple,

Americans love hot dogs at picnics, ballgames, and barbeques. © D. HURST/ALAMY.

common, all-American food. In 2000, Americans consumed some twenty billion hot dogs.

A hot dog consists of a boiled or grilled frankfurter on a soft bun that is long and thin, to follow the shape of the frank. Most often, the sandwich is garnished with mustard or ketchup. Sauerkraut, onions, and pickle relish are often added, singly or in combination. Frankfurters (franks), also known as wieners (though franks often contain pork while wieners contain beef), are smoked sausages that have been enclosed in several-inch-long cylindrical casings. Their main ingredient is beef or a combination of beef and pork. The origin of the frankfurter is imprecise. Some say that, many centuries ago, the Babylonians devised such sausages by stuffing spiced meat into animal intestines. Others claim that it was invented in Frankfurt, Germany (the city from which the food derives its name), during the thirteenth century.

Frankfurters and buns supposedly were wedded when Charles Feltman (1841–1910), a German immigrant, concluded that visitors to the Brooklyn, New York, seaside community of **Coney Island** (see entry under 1900s—The Way We Lived in volume 1) might enjoy a hot sandwich they could hold in their hands while strolling about. In 1867, Feltman attached a small charcoal stove to a pushcart and began selling freshly cooked frankfurters on rolls. Feltman parlayed his profits into a restaurant, Feltman's German Beer Garden, which he opened in Coney Island. At Feltman's, seven grills prepared thousands of frankfurters each day, which were sold for ten cents apiece. In 1916, Nathan Handwerker (1892–1974), an ex-Feltman's employee, began selling "hot dogs" from a small building located at Surf and Stillwell Avenues in Coney Island, right by a subway station entrance. Handwerker priced his hot dogs at five cents. They proved so popular that his enterprise became a Coney Island landmark that exists to this day. The business eventually evolved into Nathan's Famous, a fast-food chain. Unlike **McDonald's** (see entry under 1940s—Food and Drink in volume 3), **Burger King** (see entry under 1950s—Food and Drink in volume 3), and Wendy's, where hamburger variations are the signature products, hot dogs still are spotlighted at Nathan's Famous. In the 1930s, the Oscar Mayer Company became the first company to sell frankfurters in supermarkets. Oscar Mayer also began targeting children in its marketing campaigns. Beginning in 1936, its iconic hot-dog shaped Weinermobile embarked on promotional cross-country trips.

The hot dog made its debut at sporting arenas just after the turn of the twentieth century. Harry Stevens (1855–1934), a concession-stand operator at New York's Polo Grounds, a ballpark located in upper Manhattan, was having difficulty selling ice cream and cold sodas during early-season New York Giants baseball games. On a whim, he replaced them with franks and buns. Legend has it that T. A. "Tad" Dorgan (1877–1929), a newspaper cartoonist, heard Stevens's vendors yelling, "Get your dachshund sausages while they're red hot!" He caricatured them as dachshund dogs, and from then on the sandwiches were known as hot dogs.

Rob Edelman

For More Information

Graulich, David. *The Hot Dog Companion: A Connoisseur's Guide to the Food We Love.* New York: Lebhar-Friedman Books, 1999.

" Hot Dog and Sausage Pop Culture." *National Hot Dog & Sausage Council.* http://www.hot-dog.org/ht/d/sp/i/38572/pid/38572 (accessed June 20, 2011).

Kraig, Bruce. *Hot Dog: A Global History.* London: Reaktion Books, 2009.

Sebak, Rick, writer and producer. *A Hot Dog Program* (video). Alexandria, VA: PBS Home Video, 1999.

Ice-cream Cone

One of the most popular American snacks, it is generally believed the ice-cream cone was initially popularized at the 1904 St. Louis **World's Fair** (see entry under 1900s—The Way We Lived in volume 1). At that time, Ernest Hamwi, a Syrian waffle vendor, created the "World's Fair Cornucopia" by taking portions of ice cream being dispensed by a fellow vendor who had run out of dishes and serving them up inside waffles that were folded into a cone-like shape. However, other sources, including the Library of Congress, claim that the ice-cream cone was invented on July 23, 1904, by Charles E. Menches of St. Louis and that it did not make its debut as a "walk-away" treat until later that year, at the St. Louis Exposition. A year earlier, a patent for a cone maker had been granted to Italo Marchiony (1868–1954), a New York pushcart vendor, who claimed to have been serving ice-cream cones (paper and later pastry) since 1896. But it was Hamwi who apparently popularized the concept through his Cornucopia Waffle Company and, later, his Missouri Cone Company.

Since the early 1900s, billions of these confectionery treats have been enjoyed all over the world (They are known as "cornets" in the United Kingdom). During the 1920s and 1930s, consumers enjoyed cones in a variety of shapes, including **skyscrapers** (see entry under 1930s—The Way We Lived in volume 2) and battleships. Since the 1940s, two kinds of cones have emerged as standards: "sugar" cones, which can be flat-bottomed or pointy, and "waffle" cones made from a large folded wafer. In recent years, cones have been increasingly likely to hold a broader variety of frozen treats, including creamy gelato and low-fat frozen yogurt. Hand-baked and hand-rolled waffle cones, often in a variety of flavors like chocolate, oat bran, or honey, have also become popular.

Edward Moran

For More Information

Damerow, Gail. *Ice Cream! The Whole Scoop.* Lakewood, CO: Glenbridge Publishing, 1995.

Dickson, Paul. *The Great American Ice Cream Book.* New York: Atheneum, 1972.

Funderburg, Anne. *Vanilla, Chocolate, and Strawberry: A History of American Ice Cream.* Bowling Green, OH: Bowling Green University Popular Press, 1995.

Gustaitis, John. "Who Invented the Ice Cream Cone?" *American History Illustrated* (Vol. 23, 1988): pp. 42-44.

Powell, Marilyn. *Ice Cream: The Delicious History.* Woodstock, NY: Overlook Press, 2005.

Jell-O

Jell-O is the brand name for a powdered, fruit-flavored gelatin dessert invented in 1897 and widely popularized after the 1920s. The gelatin itself is derived from the bones and hides of cows and pigs. The dessert first appealed to busy American housewives seeking low-cost, convenient dishes to serve to their families. Over the years, its makers took full advantage of new advertising and marketing strategies to promote the brand image of Jell-O, making it arguably the nation's most recognizable and popular dessert product.

Powdered gelatin was invented in 1845 by Peter Cooper (1791–1883), but the concept did not catch on until 1897, when Pearl B. Wait developed a fruit-flavored version that his wife named Jell-O. He sold the patent to Orator Francis Woodward in 1899 for $450, who began marketing the product in 1902 through the Genesee Pure Food Company of LeRoy, New York. At the time, gelatin desserts required much labor and time to prepare, making them available only to wealthier consumers who had the proper equipment. The advent of powdered Jell-O made these desserts available to the general public for the first time. Jell-O introduced its first pudding products in 1929.

Jell-O desserts have wiggled and wobbled their way onto U.S. tables since the early 1900s. © MICHAEL NEELON/ ALAMY.

From its earliest days, Jell-O's manufacturers were masters at promoting their product. They created recipe booklets and offered promotional items such as molded dishes to persuade house-wives to use the new product (They even handed out Jell-O molds to immigrants at Ellis Island). In 1903, Jell-O representatives promoted the product using a fictional-ized character called the Jell-O Girl. The character was refashioned in 1908 by Rose O'Neill (1874–1944), creator of the **Kewpie doll** (see entry under 1900s—Print Culture in volume 1). Through the 1920s, O'Neill's Kewpie dolls appeared in many advertisements for Jell-O. Artists like **Norman Rockwell** (1894–1978; see entry under 1910s—Print Culture in volume 1) and Maxfield Parrish (1870–1966) contributed illustrations to promote the brand. L. Frank Baum (1856–1919), author of ***The Wizard of Oz*** (see entry under 1930s—Film and Theater in volume 2), published an edition of his Oz books as a tie-in with Jell-O. In later years, the product was pro-moted on **radio** (see entry under 1920s—TV and Radio in volume 2) by **Jack Benny** (1894–1974; see entry under 1940s—TV and Radio in volume 3) and Kate Smith (1907–1986) and on television by Roy Rogers (1911–1998), **Andy Griffith** (1926–; see entry on *The Andy Griffith Show* under 1960s—TV and Radio in volume 4), and Ethel Barrymore (1879–1959). From the 1970s through the 1990s, **Bill Cosby** (1937– ; see entry under 1980s—TV and Radio in volume 5) was the chief spokesperson for Jell-O and Jell-O Pudding.

Sometimes sneered at by critics who see it as a low-class dessert suitable only for cafeterias and truck-stop diners, Jell-O, despite its wiggly texture, has become a symbol of colorful fun for millions of fans.

Edward Moran

For More Information

Armitage, Shelley. *Kewpies and Beyond: The World of Rose O'Neill.* Jackson: University Press of Mississippi, 1994.

Celebrating One Hundred Years of Jell-O. Lincolnwood, IL: Publications International, Ltd., 1997.

Kraft Foods. *Jell-O History.* http://www.kraftbrands.com/jello/explore/history/ (accessed June 20, 2011).

Wyman, Carolyn. *Jell-O: A Biography.* San Diego: Harcourt, 2001.

Soda Fountains

From the late 1800s through the 1950s, Americans gathered at drug store soda fountains to gossip, flirt, chat, and drink elaborate new concoctions of sugary syrup, ice cream, and carbonated water. In an era when drinking alcohol was being criticized more and more, the clean, ornate soda fountains provided a socially acceptable alternative to bars and saloons, and the frothy new "soda pop" they dispensed was thought to be the height of health and modernity. The invention of home refrigeration and bottled sodas, along with a population spread out in **suburbs** (see entry under 1950s—The Way We Lived in volume 3) instead of gathered in town centers, contributed to the end of the soda fountain's golden age. However, soda fountains still have a place in American culture, readily visible in films and television, from the 1919 film *True Heart Susie,* starring **Lillian Gish** (1883–1993; see entry under 1910s—Film and Theater in volume 1), to the 1970s television series about the 1950s, ***Happy Days*** (see entry under 1970s—TV and Radio in volume 4).

Philadelphia, Pennsylvania, became the birthplace of the soda fountain in 1825, when apothecary Elias Durand (1794–1873) opened the first modern drugstore there, selling the newly invented "soda water" by the glass. Soda water was supposed to have numerous health benefits, but soon people began to gather at Durand's shop as much to socialize as to drink the carbonated beverage. Soon, drugstores added cream and syrups flavored with sugars, herbs, and spices to create their own soda water recipes. They built elaborately decorated counters with seats for

A soda jerk serves a thirsty group of customers cherry colas and cream sodas at a soda fountain. © PETRIFIED COLLECTION/THE IMAGE BANK/GETTY IMAGES.

patrons and ornate faucets for serving their drinks. The people, mostly men, who worked behind the counters creating the delicious drinks were called "soda jerks," because they jerked the handles on the dispensers to spray foamy carbonation into the syrup. Formulas for chocolate, lemon, strawberry, and sarsaparilla (root beer–flavored) sodas as well as far more complex sodas were found in large recipe books behind the counter.

One day in 1874, another Philadelphian, Robert Green, ran out of cream for making sodas. When he added vanilla ice cream instead, he had created another mainstay of the soda fountain, the ice cream soda. Soon ice cream sundaes and milk-shakes joined sodas on the fountain menu. By 1910, there were over one hundred thousand soda fountains across the United States, many serving food as well as sodas and ice cream.

World War II (1939–45) brought severe rationing of many of the ingredients used at soda fountains as well as a shortage of men to work at them, resulting in a steep decline for the industry. After the war, the fountains revived briefly, receiving a boost from the **juke-box** rock music of the 1950s (see entry on juke boxes in 1930s—Music in volume 3), but they did not make enough money for their owners and soon disappeared. The closest thing to the once-trendy soda fountain in contemporary American life might be the increasingly popular coffee shops, especially **Starbucks** (see entry under 1990s—The Way We Lived in volume 5).

Tina Gianoulis

For More Information

"The Drug Store Soda Fountain." *Drugstore Museum.* http://www. drugstoremuseum.com/sections/level_info2.php?level_id=3&level=1 (accessed June 20, 2011).

Funderburg, Anne Cooper. *Sundae Best: A History of Soda Fountains.* Bowling Green, OH: Bowling Green State University Popular Press, 2002.

Pearce, Elizabeth R. "Brown Cows and Walking Sundaes: A Soda Fountain Memoir." *Gourmet* (Vol. 43, July 1983): pp. 20–28.

Rapoport, Roger. "Restored Soda Fountains of Yesteryear." *Americana* (Vol. 19, no. 3, July-August 1991): pp. 60–64.

Schwartz, David M. "Life Was Sweeter, and More Innocent, in Our Soda Days." *Smithsonian* (Vol. 1, July 1986): pp. 114–23.

1900s

Music

Music was an immensely popular form of entertainment in America in the first decade of the century, though not in the same way it is today. Americans did not buy prerecorded records or CDs and play them on stereo equipment. Instead, most American popular music was produced in the home, usually with a piano, from sheet music purchased from one of many sheet music companies.

Most music was produced by amateurs for small audiences of family and friends, but music was also a developing form of artistic expression in this decade. In fact, this was a decade of vibrant musical production. The sheet music publishing industry was centered in a district of New York City known as Tin Pan Alley, where skilled musicians composed popular music to sell to the masses. Between 1900 and 1909, nearly one hundred of the Tin Pan Alley songs had sold more than one million copies of sheet music. Ragtime music was one of the most popular forms of sheet music, and the king of ragtime was an African American named Scott Joplin (c. 1867–1917). African Americans as a whole fared better in the field of music than they did elsewhere in American popular culture during the decade. Bert Williams (1875–1922), George Walker (1873–1911), Bob Cole (1868–1911), and the Johnson Brothers (J. Rosamond, 1873–1954; James Weldon, 1871–1938) were among the most successful composers of the decade.

Two of the most important American musical forms trace their roots to this decade. Performers W. C. Handy (1873–1958) and Ma Rainey (1886–1939) published and performed the first songs recognized as the blues in this decade. Jazz originated in New Orleans, Louisiana, out of music that combined the rhythms of blues, ragtime, traditional African folk music, and other musical forms. Both blues and jazz emerged as uniquely American music forms in the 1920s, and some of the earliest and greatest practitioners of these forms were African Americans.

Thomas Edison (1847–1931) invented the phonograph in 1877, a device that could play music that had been recorded on a metal cylinder. Other phonographs, first called gramophones, played music recorded on a vinyl disc. The first recordings to be sold to a wide audience were recorded in 1902 by opera singer Enrico Caruso (1873–1921). Soon, other opera and concert singers began recording their songs. More popular singers began to record songs, but their recordings did not become a mass phenomena until the 1910s, when recording companies improved their manufacturing and marketing systems.

Jazz

Jazz music is one of the most original and innovative musical forms to develop in the United States. Throughout the twentieth century, jazz evolved to encompass a variety of complex styles and it produced some of the period's greatest composers and musicians.

Jazz originated in the early 1900s, mostly in the South, especially in New Orleans, Louisiana. Drawing from African American blues and ragtime music, jazz introduced complex rhythms and a wider range of tones to create a new style. As it developed in the 1910s and 1920s, a number of important early innovators took jazz in new directions, including Joseph "King" Oliver (1885–1938), Sidney Bechet (1897–1959), Jelly Roll Morton (1890–1941), and trumpeter Louis Armstrong (1901–1971). Armstrong was a phenomenal soloist, and he moved the solo instrument to the forefront of jazz. Jazz music often began with a single melody, and then various soloists would add their own touches to it until it became their own. While African American jazz artists such as Armstrong were creating new innovations in jazz, white musicians and band leaders, such as Paul Whiteman (1890–1967), brought a "softer" version of jazz to white audiences for **dancing** (see entry under 1900s—The Way We Lived in volume 1) in the 1920s.

In the 1930s and early 1940s, jazz moved into what is known as the "swing era." Bands got bigger and the music became more popular. Rather than consisting of small groups of five to seven musicians, now the **big bands** (see entry under 1930s—Music in volume 2) might be as large as twenty people, including four to five trumpet players, four to five saxophone players, a drummer, a bassist, and often vocalists. During this time, African American bands continued to be the most innovative. The band led by Fletcher Henderson (1897–1952) was extremely popular, as was the band of Count Basie (1904–1984). Both were known for their driving rhythms and great sound. Even more important was Duke Ellington (1899–1974), who led

Premier jazz composer and musician Duke Ellington in 1959. © EVERETT COLLECTION/ ALAMY.

his own band and gained widespread acclaim for his superb songwriting capabilities. Ellington wrote popular songs such as "Take the 'A' Train" and "It Don't Mean a Thing If It Ain't Got That Swing." He also extended jazz in a new direction by writing longer pieces of music that resembled classical music in their complexity. His composition "Black, Brown, and Beige," a musical history of African Americans, is a notable example of this development. Following these African American musical leaders, white band leaders such as Benny Goodman (1909–1986), Tommy Dorsey (1905–1956), and Glenn Miller (1904–1944) also made jazz music that excited dancers and listeners of all ethnicities.

Jazz's popularity—both as "swing" jazz and as "big band" jazz—music led younger black musicians in the mid-1940s to break out in a new direction. Feeling that popular jazz music was too simple and bland, musicians such as Charlie Parker (1920–1955), Dizzy Gillespie (1917–1993), Thelonious Monk (1917–1982), and Bud Powell (1924–1966) created a new style called "bebop." Bebop was not dance music. It had complex rhythms and lightning-fast solo note runs that favored innovation and personal expression over melody. Parker and Gillespie showcased this new style in such compositions such as "Ornithology," "Ko-Ko," and "Salt Peanuts." Both big bands and swing music faded in the 1950s as **rock and roll** (see entry under 1950s—Music in volume 3) became more popular, but jazz in the bebop style continued. Bebop did not draw the large crowds of dancing fans, but it continued to excite loyal listeners in jazz clubs and concert halls across the United States.

In the 1950s and 1960s, jazz moved in new directions again. Bebop continued, including a version called "hard bop," but the music also developed in other ways. "Cool jazz" emerged under the influence of trumpeter Miles Davis (1926–1991). This style was more introspective and subdued, evoking a wider range of moods than the fiery-fast bebop style. Davis' album *The Birth of the Cool* remains a landmark work in this style. This period also saw the rise of new and important jazz musicians. Bassist Charles Mingus (1922–1979) brought gospel and blues influences back into jazz. Mingus also wrote musical works that expressed political views and commented on the problems of racism in America. John Coltrane (1926–1967) emerged on the saxophone as one of the most impressive soloists in the history of jazz on albums such as *Blue Train, Giant Steps,* and *A Love Supreme.* This era also produced important white jazz musicians, including pianist and composer Dave Brubeck (1920–), who had hits with his songs "Take Five" and "Blue Rondo à la Turk," both of which used complex time signatures and rhythms, and saxophonist Stan Getz (1927–1991), who helped fuse Brazilian bossa nova styles with jazz in a way that became very popular in the early 1960s.

In the later 1960s and the 1970s, jazz continued to evolve. "Free" jazz or "avant-garde" jazz took bebop one step further in exciting but difficult compositions that moved away from the standard song and melody composition form. Musicians such as Ornette Coleman (1930–) and Cecil Taylor (1929–) experimented with new and often dissonant (lacking harmony) sounds in their music. In the 1970s, jazz fusion emerged as a way to combine jazz and rock styles. Musicians such as John McLaughlin (1942–), Chick Corea (1941–), and Herbie Hancock (1940–) used electric guitars and keyboards to extend jazz's sound.

In the 1980s, 1990s, and beyond, jazz music moved on a number of levels. Fusion merged into a lighter, more commercial, form of jazz that purists did not consider jazz at all. Young players continued to emerge, both in the traditional jazz styles and in new innovative ways. Among the most popular of the traditionalists was Wynton Marsalis (1961–). He was also instrumental in forming and leading the Lincoln Center Jazz Orchestra, a group dedicated to keeping the classics of jazz alive. Thus, at the beginning of the twenty-first century, jazz no longer had the popularity it did in the 1930s and 1940s, but it had maintained its loyal fan base and continued to attract new ones. Because jazz includes so many diverse styles and artists that there is something for everyone to enjoy, it retains its place as one of the most important American musical styles.

Timothy Berg

For More Information

Burns, Ken, writer and director. *Jazz* (video). PBS-TV, 2000.

Collier, James Lincoln. *The Making of Jazz: A Comprehensive History.* New York: Houghton Mifflin, 1978.

Giddins, Gary, and Scott Knowles DeVeaux. *Jazz.* New York: W. W. Norton, 2009.

Gioia, Ted. *The History of Jazz.* 2nd ed. New York: Oxford University Press, 2011.

Hentoff, Nat, and Nat Shapiro. *Hear Me Talkin' to Ya: An Oral History of Jazz.* New York: Dover, 1966.

Holmes, Thom. *Jazz.* 2nd ed. New York: Facts on File, 2011.

Lee, Jeanne. *Jam!: The Story of Jazz Music.* New York: Rosen, 1999.

Meltzer, David, ed. *Reading Jazz.* San Francisco: Mercury House, 1993.

Public Broadcasting System. *Jazz: A Film by Ken Burns.* http://www.pbs.org/jazz (accessed June 20, 2011).

Seymour, Gene. *Jazz: The Great American Art.* New York: Franklin Watts, 1995.

Scott Joplin (1868–1917)

When one thinks of ragtime, one thinks of Scott Joplin, a pioneering African American musician and composer. Ragtime is a lively, melodic style of music that, at the turn of the twentieth century, was acknowledged as fresh and uniquely American. At the time, it was labeled "the folk music of the American city," and Joplin was crowned the "King of Ragtime Writers."

While growing up in Texas amid a family of sharecroppers, Joplin heard—and was influenced by—African American work songs and spirituals as well as European waltzes and marches. He began playing the piano and studied music with a German-born teacher, from whom he learned the manner in which European musical compositions were structured. He blended all of these influences into his own rhythmically adventurous brand of music, which he began performing while still an adolescent. In the 1890s, he found himself in Sedalia, Missouri, where he took music courses at the George R. Smith College for Negroes and became a member of the Queen City Band, an all-black group that performed at public and private events. Joplin's compositions were soon published; during his lifetime, his most fabled work was "Maple Leaf Rag" (1899). It was followed by "Peacherine Rag" (1901), "Augustan Club Waltz" (1901), "A Breeze from Alabama" (1902), "Elite Syncopation" (1902), "The Entertainer" (1902), "The Strenuous Life" (1902), "Gladiolus Rag" (1907), "Pine Apple Rag" (1908), and "Solace—A Mexican Serenade" (1909).

Joplin earned his living from sheet music sales and by teaching and performing. He viewed himself not as a writer of popular music, however, but as a serious composer. His more important compositions—which, predictably, were not his most popular in the mass market—included *The Ragtime Dance* (1902), a ragtime ballet, and *The Guest of Honor* (1903), a ragtime opera. During the final decade of his life, he worked on *Treemonisha* (1911), a second ragtime opera, whose key theme was the desperate need for education within the African American community. Unfortunately, *Treemonisha* was performed only once during Joplin's lifetime, in 1915.

Scott Joplin was long forgotten by the public at the time of the release of *The Sting* (1973), a film whose score consisted of Joplin rags. The success of the film, which won many Academy Awards, initiated a ragtime renaissance in the United States.

Rob Edelman

For More Information

Argyle, Ray. *Scott Joplin and the Age of Ragtime.* Jefferson, NC: McFarland, 2009.

Berlin, Edward A. "A Biography of Scott Joplin." *The Scott Joplin International Ragtime Foundation.* http://www.scottjoplin.org/biography.htm (accessed July 11, 2011).

Berlin, Edward. *King of Ragtime: Scott Joplin and His Era.* New York: Oxford University Press, 1996.

Curtis, Susan. *Dancing to a Black Man's Tune: A Life of Scott Joplin.* Columbia: University of Missouri Press, 1994.

Hubbard-Brown, Janet. *Scott Joplin: Composer.* New York: Chelsea House, 2006.

Phonograph

The phonograph gave birth to the modern recording industry. Without it, there would not be records, cassette tapes, compact discs, or digital MP3s. Invented by Thomas Edison (1837–1931) in 1877, the phonograph proved to be one of the most influential technologies in history.

The phonograph revolutionized entertainment and the field of music throughout the twentieth century until cassette tapes began crowding out the medium in the 1970s and then **compact disc** (see entry under 1980s—Music in volume 5) technology replaced it in the 1990s. Recorded music has been revolutionized again in more recent years with the development of other digital technologies, such as the **iPod** (see entry under 2000s—Music in volume 6).

Edison's invention came from experiments in which he attempted to record and preserve phone conversations. When he discovered that a human voice could cut a signal into tinfoil, the origins of the modern phonograph were born. Edison improved the device using wax cylinders and later adopted a disc format developed by Emile Berliner (1851–1929). Although the phonograph did not take off as a way to record and preserve phone calls, it did find great popularity in the entertainment world, enabling the development of the modern recording industry in the 1910s. Before this time, people could only hear music performed live or make their own music, and most people heard only a limited amount and variety of music. The phonograph changed all that. As phonographs became less expensive to purchase, more people could afford them. Record companies responded by producing records of all sorts. There were **blues** (see entry under 1920s—Music in volume 2) and **jazz** (see entry under 1900s—Music in volume 1) records, **country music** (see entry under 1940s—Music in volume 3), **big band** (see entry under 1930s—Music in volume 2) music, ethnic songs, dance music, classical symphonies, speeches, and many more kinds of records. The phonograph was especially popular with people in rural areas and with poor and middle-class people. People in rural areas lived too far away to attend live music concerts, and poor and middle-class people could not afford to hear symphony orchestras very often, if at all.

The phonograph proved to be an instrument of social change as well. In the 1950s, **rock and roll** (see entry under 1950s—Music in volume 3) was successful largely because teenagers could afford to purchase rock-and-roll 45-rpm singles to play on their phonographs. (Singles were

A portable phonograph, or record player, from the 1950s.
© POODLES ROCK/CORBIS.

called 45s because the recordings were played at a speed of 45 revolutions of the turntable per minute.) Because they could choose the records rather than having adults on the **radio** (see entry under 1920s—TV and Radio in volume 2) determine what they would listen to, teenagers helped spur rock and roll on to great success, spawning a whole era of teen rebellion. In the 1960s, that tradition continued as the phonograph provided a means for **folk music** (see entry under 1960s—Music in volume 4) artists to have their protest songs heard. Rock music continued pushing the boundaries of social convention and bringing new insights to young people around the world.

Few mass technologies have had such an important social impact. Eventually, the phonograph was eclipsed by the development of cassette tapes in the 1970s, compact discs in the 1990s, and the many forms of digital media in recent years. These more recent technologies have been more durable, portable, and lightweight than phonographs (by now, also called turntables). Despite this, many enthusiasts still collect vinyl records and restore old phonographs, keeping the technology alive.

Timothy Berg

For More Information

Coleman, Mark. *Playback: From the Victrola to the Mp3; 100 Years of Music, Machines, and Money.* New York: Da Capo Press, 2003.

Eisenberg, Evan. *The Recording Angel.* New ed. New Haven, CT: Yale University Press, 2005.

Koenigsberg, Allen. *The Patent History of the Phonograph, 1877–1912.* Brooklyn, NY: APM Press, 1990.

Millard, Andre. *America on Record: A History of Recorded Sound.* 2nd ed. New York: Cambridge University Press, 2005.

1900s

Print Culture

In an age before radio and television claimed the attention of Americans, reading was one of the most popular leisure-time activities. American writers and publishers churned out a variety of reading material to suit the tastes of every reader, from comic strips to magazines to dime novels to literary classics.

The comic strip was created just before the turn of the century when Richard Outcault (1863–1928) created a character known as the Yellow Kid in a series known as *Hogan's Alley*. Later strips such as *The Katzenjammer Kids* and *Mutt & Jeff* made such characteristics as word balloons, a distinctive cast of characters, and the use of a series of panels the common conventions of the comic strip. Still, by 1908 there were only five newspapers that ran daily comic strips.

Although magazines—collections of fiction and nonfiction often published on a weekly or a monthly schedule—had been around for many years, the so-called "magazine revolution" of 1893 made it possible to produce massive numbers of magazines and sell them for very little money—sometimes as little as a nickel an issue—thanks to the financial support of advertisers. By 1900, magazines such as *Argosy, Cosmopolitan*, the *Ladies' Home Journal, McClure's, Munsey's*, the *Saturday Evening Post*, and others were read by millions of readers. American advertisers enthusiastically sought space in these magazines, for they provided the best possible way to reach the greatest number of potential consumers.

The same technological advances in printing that allowed for the mass-circulation magazine also spurred the sales of the dime novel, a cheaply produced paperback book that sold for a dime. Dime novels were usually written by unknown writers who worked from outlines provided by the publisher; the stories involved romance, mystery, and adventure. Westerns were one of the most popular forms. Although he did not write dime novels, Jack London (1876–1916) wrote adventure stories set at sea or in the West, and his books sold millions. London was considered by many at the time as a "hack" writer (a writer who writes solely to make money or who writes over and over in the same way, almost as if using a formula). Today, London is considered one of the greater American novelists and is read widely in schools.

Argosy

The cover of a 1933 Argosy *magazine.* © THE PROTECTED ART ARCHIVE/ALAMY.

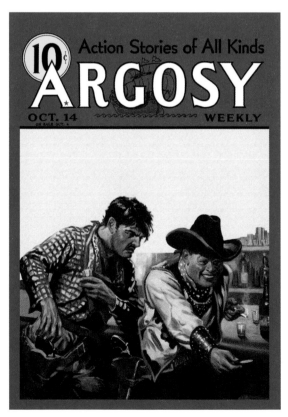

A popular men's magazine published in the United States from 1888 until 1979, *Argosy* was the first of the **"pulp" magazines** (see entry under 1930s—Print Culture in volume 2), so called because of the cheap, rough paper on which they were printed. It was also the first adult magazine to rely almost exclusively on fiction for its content, usually adventure, detective, science fiction, or western stories that were thought to appeal to a male readership.

Argosy traced its roots to *Golden Argosy: Freighted with Treasures for Boys and Girls,* a magazine created by Frank Munsey (1854–1925) in 1882 to appeal to young people. By 1886, Munsey was publishing adult stories in the magazine, whose name he changed to *Argosy* two years later. In 1896, he shifted to pulp paper and began publishing serial fiction (stories that were "serialized," or broken into sections across several issues) exclusively, with an emphasis on action, adventure, and mystery stories. By the time of Munsey's death in 1925, *Argosy* had helped popularize fictional characters like **Tarzan** (see entry under 1910s—Print Culture in volume 1), **Zorro** (see entry under 1910s—Print Culture in volume 1), **The Shadow** (see entry under 1930s—Print Culture in volume 2), and Sam Spade. It featured stories from some of the most noted authors of the day.

By 1907, *Argosy* had a circulation (the total number of copies sold) of five hundred thousand, but the magazine had a checkered history in the twentieth century. Circulation declined to forty thousand by 1940. The magazine was renamed *New Argosy* in 1942 but was banned from distribution through the mail because of its use of obscenity. Sold to Popular Publications, a major publishing company, the magazine was renamed *Argosy: The Complete Men's Magazine* in 1946 and became a "slick" periodical with four color layouts and better-quality adventure, sports, and humorous stories. By 1953, the circulation had increased to 1.25 million. Popular Publications was dissolved in 1972 and the magazine was sold to Blazing Publications, Inc. It finally folded in 1979, a victim of rising postal rates.

Edward Moran

For More Information

"The Argosy & Related Magazines." *Galactic Central.* http://www.philsp.com/mags/argosy.html (accessed June 20, 2011).

Moonan, Willard. "Argosy." In *American Mass-Market Magazine.* Edited by Alan and Barbara Nourie. Westport, CT: Greenwood Press, 1990.

Server, Lee. *Danger Is My Business: An Illustrated History of the Fabulous Pulp Magazines, 1896–1953.* New York: Chronicle, 1993.

A day at the races for Buster Brown, his dog Tige, and the Yellow Kid. © OLD PAPER STUDIOS/ALAMY.

Buster Brown

Though Buster Brown and his bulldog Tige are best known today as trademarks for a brand of clothing and shoes, they got their start as one of America's first comic strips. The beloved pair were created in 1902 by cartoonist Richard Felton Outcault (1863–1928), who also created the very first comic strip in the United States, *The Yellow Kid.* Buster Brown, dressed in his familiar red smock and bloomers, with blond bangs and an angelic face, was a mischievous little boy whose antics always got him into trouble. His loyal companion Tige was the first talking animal in a cartoon strip.

Buster Brown's popularity led manufacturers to pay to use his image on over two hundred products. Besides advertising such items as shoes and clothes, Buster and Tige appeared in books and **silent movies** (see entry under 1900s—Film and Theater in volume 1). Today, though few may remember Outcault's comic strip, which ended during the early 1920s, most Americans over the age of fifty remember Buster Brown shoes and clothes and know what a Buster Brown haircut looks like.

Tina Gianoulis

For More Information

Markstein, Donald D. "Buster Brown." *Don Markstein's Toonopedia.* http://www.toonopedia.com/buster.htm (accessed June 20, 2011).

Outcault, Richard Felton. *Buster Brown: A Complete Compilation, 1906.* Westport, CT: Hyperion Press, 1977.

Dime Novels

Dime novels captivated readers with sensational fictitious stories in the late nineteenth and early twentieth centuries. Called dime novels because the first editions cost just ten cents, dime novels were released at regular intervals and told exciting stories of adventure, mystery, and romance. Readers were encouraged to collect and read whole series of novels featuring a favorite hero or a type of adventure. Costs were kept down by printing the novels on low-quality paper, often with drawn illustrations. By 1900, several publishers had entered the market and in their heyday each title could sell millions of copies. The popularity of **pulp magazines** (see entry under 1930s—Print Culture in volume 2), **radio** (see entry under 1920s—TV and Radio in volume 2), and cinema squeezed dime novels out of the entertainment market by the 1920s. No original titles appeared after that decade.

The first dime novel was *Maleska, the Indian Wife of the White Hunter.* It was published in 1860 by Irwin P. Beadle (1821–1894) and was a romance set in the American West. Beadle's mass-market dime novels took advantage of the growing number of readers and cheaper printing technology. By the early 1900s, the range of settings for the stories was huge, although the plots were mostly the same. Dime novel

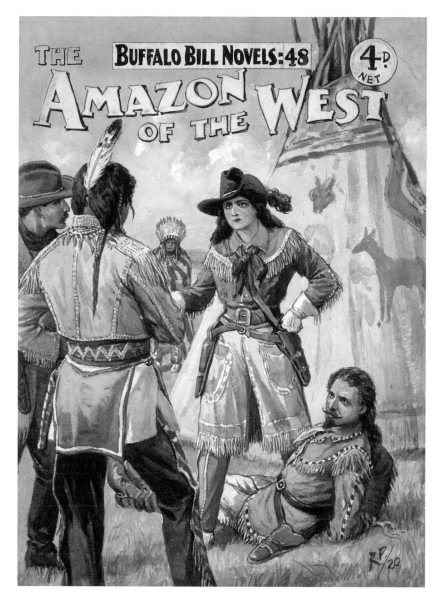

subjects included the American West, the Revolutionary War, Native Americans, the circus, the railroad, sports, science fiction, and detective mysteries. Polar exploration was also a common theme.

Dime novels were written to very strict guidelines, often by groups of writers working under the same name. Writers were instructed to make them exciting, entertaining, and moral. Even so, these tales of violence and passion were thought by some to be a corrupting influence on their young readers. Writers of dime novels included Edward Strate-meyer (1962–1930), who created the girl detective Nancy Drew, and Louisa May Alcott (1832–1888), the author of *Little Women.* Alcott wrote dime novels under the name A. M. Bernard to protect her reputation as a serious novelist.

Because they were printed on cheap paper and because they were seen as disposable, few dime novels exist outside of libraries in the twenty-first century. As literature, dime novels were considered by scholars to have little value. As historical artifacts, however, they reveal a great deal about American life in the late nineteenth and early twentieth centuries.

Chris Routledge

For More Information

Anderson, Vicki. *The Dime Novel in Children's Literature.* Jefferson, NC: McFarland, 2004.

Cox, J. Randolph. *The Dime Novel Companion: A Source Book.* Westport, CT: Greenwood Press, 2000.

Stanford University Special Collections. "Dime Novels and Penny Dreadfuls." http://www-sul.stanford.edu/depts/dp/pennies/home.html (accessed on June 20, 2011).

Sullivan, Larry E., and Lydia Cushman Schurman, eds. *Pioneers, Passionate Ladies, and Private Eyes: Dime Novels, Series Books, and Paperbacks.* New York: Haworth Press, 1996.

Gibson Girl

In the late 1800s, the socially restrained Victorian era was coming to an end, giving way to the more permissive modern era. In the last days of the Victorian age, a young American artist named Charles Dana Gibson (1867–1944) began to publish sketches of a new kind of American woman who was emerging in the new era. More women were going to work, and the money they earned gave them an unprecedented level of independence and confidence. Gibson was impressed with these dynamic young women, and he drew them over and over, at home, at work, and at play. Once women saw the romantic and elegant images of these "Gibson Girls"—which appeared in popular magazines like *Life* (see entry under 1930s—Print Culture in volume 2) *Harpers,* and *Collier's Weekly*—they began to imitate their style, creating a period of fashion that lasted from 1890 to 1910.

Gibson Girls were tall, athletic, and poised, with upswept hair and practical yet feminine clothes. At work, they might wear a tailored dress with long sleeves and a high collar with a necktie; at a party, a low-cut flowing dress with no sleeves was stylish. Their figures were trained into a fashionable "S" shape by a new kind of corset (an undergarment used to support and shape the waist, hips, and bust), called the "health corset" because it allowed the spine to remain straight. The "S" shape, formed by tightly corseted waists between a large bosom and large hips, was exaggerated further by wearing many layers of slips and underclothes. There was a Gibson Man as well. The men's fashion featured trimmed mustaches and jackets with padded shoulders.

The most important distinguishing feature of the Gibson Girl was that she was capable and adventurous as well as beautiful. By 1900, there were over five million working women in the United States, and across the country, women wanted to imitate the image and style of the Gibson Girl. Many new developments helped them follow the fashion, such as mass-circulation magazines and mail-order catalogs. Newly invented home sewing machines and pattern catalogs also helped women reproduce the clothes they admired in Gibson's magazine drawings.

Tina Gianoulis

"Gibson Girl in Repose," 1890. Artist Charles Dana Gibson sketched a new woman for a new era. © NORTH WIND PICTURES ARCHIVES.

For More Information

Emery, Josiah, writer, director, and producer. *Charles Dana Gibson: Portrait of an Illustrator* (video). Acre Island Productions, 1996.

Gibson, Charles Dana. *The Gibson Girl and Her America: The Best Drawings of Charles Dana Gibson.* New York: Dover, 1969, 2010.

"Gibson Girls." *Gibson Girls.* http://www.gibson-girls.com/index.html (accessed June 20, 2011).

Patterson, Martha. "Survival of the Best Fitted: Selling the American New Woman as Gibson Girl, 1895–1910." *ATQ (The American Transcendental Quarterly)* (Vol. 9, no. 2, June 1995): pp. 73–88.

Good Housekeeping

Good Housekeeping magazine was founded in 1885 in the United States by Clark W. Bryan, whose stated goal was the creation of "perfection … in the household." When the British version of the journal was launched in 1922, its advertising promised, "infinitely more than a magazine—a New Institution, destined to play an important part in the lives of thousands of women." For over a century, *Good Housekeeping* has been just such an institution. The magazine offers advice and advertises products to help homemakers run their homes, although some critics feel that the magazine is outdated because it assumes that only women do housework.

Good Housekeeping was part of a wave of women's magazines that emerged in the early twentieth century to glorify housework and to encourage women to stay in the home. Working-class women were leaving their jobs as household servants for factories, forcing middle-class women to learn to do their own housework. The makers of new "labor-saving" devices such as the electric iron (invented in 1914) and the vacuum cleaner (invented in 1917) needed somewhere to advertise their products. Magazines like *Good Housekeeping* served the dual purpose of instructing women about housework and turning them into consumers who would buy these new products.

From the first, *Good Housekeeping* took its commitment to its readers seriously. In 1900, the Good Housekeeping Institute was founded to evaluate household products. Only products that passed the Institute's tests could be advertised in the pages of the magazine. In 1909, *Good Housekeeping* introduced its famous "Seal of Approval," which guaranteed that if any product bearing the seal proved to be defective within two years of purchase, *Good Housekeeping* itself would refund the money to the consumer. The Good Housekeeping Institute has been responsible for many consumer reforms. An early example of this interest occurred in 1905 when the Institute began inspecting packaged foods and published a "Roll of Honor for Pure Food Products" listing approved foods. The passage by Congress of the 1906 Pure Food and Drug Act was a direct result of the Institute's work.

Tina Gianoulis

For More Information

Holzman, Paul, and Micki Siegel. "90 Years of the Good Housekeeping Institute." *Good Housekeeping* (February 1990): pp. 69–114.

Horwood, Catherine. "Housewives' Choice: Women as Consumers Between the Wars." *History Today* (Vol. 47, no. 3, March 1997): pp. 23–29.

Seneca, Tracy. "The History of Women's Magazines: Magazines as Virtual Communities." *Impact of New Technologies.* http://besser.tsoa.nyu.edu/impact/f93/students/tracy/tracy_hist.html (accessed June 20, 2011).

The Katzenjammer Kids

The Katzenjammer Kids is the longest-running comic strip in American history. The strip, which began appearing in newspapers in 1897, was created by cartoonist Rudolph Dirks (1877–1968). The comic strip revolves around the shenanigans of Hans and Fritz Katzenjammer, young twins who delight in creating chaos. The boys outwardly appear to be innocent children, but they are, in reality, destructive brats who constantly torment and abuse everyone around them. Their favorite target is the Captain, who can never convince Mama Katzenjammer her sons are incorrigible (beyond reform). The word *katzenjammer* literally translates as "the howling of cats" and is a German euphemism for "hangover."

The strip greatly popularized the emerging comic strip medium. Dirks was one of the first comic artists to employ word balloons containing his characters' speech. Much of the strip's humor resulted from the vaudeville German dialect the characters spoke. In 1912, a legal battle between Dirks and his publisher resulted in competing versions of the strip that ran for decades. *The Katzenjammer Kids* continues to appear in newspapers and holds the distinction of being the only comic strip from the nineteenth century to survive into the new millennium.

Charles Coletta

For More Information

Dirks, Rudolph. *Komical Katzenjammers—The Katzenjammer Kids Color.* New York: Dover Publications, 1974.

Markstein, Donald D. "The Katzenjammer Kids." *Don Markstein's Toonopedia.* http://www.toonopedia.com/katzen.htm (accessed June 20, 2011).

Horn, Maurice, ed. *100 Years of American Newspaper Comics.* New York: Gramercy Books, 1996.

Marschall, Richard. *America's Great Comic-Strip Artists: From the Yellow Kid to Peanuts.* New York: Stewart, Tabori & Chang, 1997.

Kewpie Dolls

Originally appearing in the form of magazine illustrations between 1905 and 1909, Kewpie dolls made their appearance in 1913 in a design patented by Rose Cecil O'Neill (1874–1944). During O'Neill's lifetime, the dolls were a popular novelty item, often associated with carnivals and country fairs, where they were given as prizes. The Kewpie doll is one of the earliest and most successful examples of a mass-marketed toy. It has since become a sought-after collectible and an enduring symbol of "cuteness."

O'Neill's earliest versions of the Kewpies began appearing in the pages of the *Ladies' Home Journal* between 1905 and 1909 and took the Kewpie name in 1909. In 1910, O'Neill moved her characters to the *Women's Home Companion.* Three years later, she designed a baby-like doll with its characteristic rotund shape and plume of wispy hair. The doll became

A collectible Kewpie doll.
© ASHLEY WHITWORTH/ALAMY.

an instant sensation and its sales made O'Neill a millionaire within a year. Just as **Barbie dolls** (see entry under 1950s—Commerce in volume 3) would later be dressed as a variety of characters, Kewpies came dressed as cowboys, farmers, bellboys, and firemen, and in the uniforms of U.S., British, French, and German soldiers. There was also a line of black Kewpies known as Hottentots. Besides the dolls, O'Neill created Kewpie images for a wide variety of products like chinaware, picture frames, clocks, greeting cards, wallpaper, and vases. O'Neill also wrote and illustrated a series of Kewpie books as well as a comic-strip version in the mid-1930s.

The Kewpie dolls were originally made of china or bisque (unglazed china). They were manufactured in Europe until World War I (1914–18), when U.S. firms like the Mutual Doll Company began making the Kewpies from a variety of materials, including fabric. To this day, Kewpie dolls remain a coveted item among doll and toy collectors.

Edward Moran

For More Information

Armitage, Shelley. *Kewpies and Beyond: The World of Rose O'Neill.* Jackson: University Press of Mississippi, 1994.

Brewster, Linda. *Rose O'Neill: The Girl Who Loved to Draw.* Princeton, IL: Boxing Day Books, 2009.

Formanek-Brunell, Miriam. *Made to Play House: Dolls and the Commercialization of American Girlhood, 1830–1930.* New Haven, CT: Yale University Press, 1993.

O'Neill, Rose Cecil. *The Story of Rose O'Neill: An Autobiography.* Columbia: University of Missouri Press, 1997.

"The Works of Rose O'Neill: Her Kewpies." *Rose O'Neill.org.* http://www .roseoneill.org/workskewpies.htm (accessed June 20, 2011).

Jack London (1876–1916)

One-time vagrant, gold miner, and socialist politician, Jack London is famous for his adventure stories and tales of the Yukon basin region in Alaska and Northwest Canada. Most famous of all are *The Call of the Wild* (1903) and *White Fang* (1906). Although often dismissed at the time as a writer of simple adventures, much of London's work has a tough, adult edge, with novels like *The Sea Wolf* (1904) exploring the savagery of the human soul.

Always ready for new experiences, London was a war correspondent in Japan, suffered scurvy (a disorder resulting from lack of Vitamin C) in the Klondike, and lived in wretched and filthy conditions in an English slum while conducting research for his work, *The People of the Abyss* (1903). Despite having no formal education, his writing entertained and informed millions of readers during his short working life. At one time, he was the best-selling author in the world. Even today, many stories and novels of Jack London remain favorites of young and old Americans alike and are still commonly assigned reading in high school classrooms.

Chris Routledge

For More Information

Dyer, Daniel. *Jack London: A Biography.* New York: Scholastic Press, 1997.

Haley, James L. *Wolf: The Lives of Jack London.* New York: Basic Books, 2010.

Kershaw, Alex. *Jack London: A Life.* New York: St. Martin's Press, 1997.

Labor, Earle, and Jeanne Campbell Reesman. *Jack London.* Rev. ed. New York: Twayne, 1994.

Lisandrelli, Elaine Slivinski. *Jack London: A Writer's Adventurous Life.* Berkeley Heights, NJ: Enslow, 1999.
Sonoma State University Library. *The Jack London Online Collection.* http://london.sonoma.edu/ (accessed June 20, 2011).

Mutt & Jeff

Mutt & Jeff, which appeared in American newspapers from 1907 to 1983, was the first successful daily comic strip. Created by Harry "Bud" Fisher (1885–1954), the strip revolved around the comedic misadventures of two mismatched friends—Augustus Mutt, who was tall and smart, and Jeff, who was short and simple minded. While earlier strips appeared only sporadically, *Mutt & Jeff* was the first feature to run six days a week, use the multiple panel format, and present a regular cast of characters. In 1911, the strip was seen in one of the first **comic books** (see entry under 1930s—Print Culture in volume 2).

Fisher's strip made its debut on the *San Francisco Chronicle* sports page on November 15, 1907. Initially, Mutt was the feature's solo star and its stories revolved around the born loser's hapless attempts to become wealthy. The focus of the strip changed forever on March 27, 1908, when Mutt encountered Jeff in an insane asylum. The little fellow was convinced he was the celebrated prizefighter Jim Jeffries (1875–1953). The pair became fast friends and behaved much like a stereotypical **vaudeville** (see entry under 1900s—Film and Theater in volume 1) team.

Mutt & Jeff, famous comic strip characters of the twentieth century. © THE PROTECTED ART ARCHIVE/ALAMY.

While the strip was crudely drawn and its humor simplistic, it was also innovative. It is credited with bringing topical humor (humor relating to current events) to the comics page. The pair trained with prizefighter Max Schmeling (1905–2005) and became friends with President Herbert Hoover (1874–1964) in 1929. The strip also poked fun at modern politics. In 1908, Mutt became the first comic strip character to run for president. Although he did not win the election, he ran for the office again in 1916 and 1932.

Fisher was known as a skilled businessman. In 1915, he won a $1,000-a-week guarantee plus 80 percent of the gross profits from his strip. He was the first cartoonist to copyright his strip and, thus, to own all rights to his characters. A flood of *Mutt & Jeff* merchandise further enhanced his income. The pair was featured on toys, books, cartoons, and even served as the inspiration for a ballet.

As early as the 1920s, Fisher delegated much of the work on the strip to ghostwriters and artists. Although the strip ran until 1983, its last decades saw a steadily declining readership and few creative highlights. Still, Mutt and Jeff are recalled as two of the comics' earliest superstars.

Charles Coletta

For More Information

Blackbeard, Bill, and Martin Williams. *The Smithsonian Collection of Newspaper Comics.* Washington, DC: Smithsonian Institution Press, 1977.

Fisher, Bud. *The Early Years of Mutt & Jeff.* New York: NBM, 2007.

Horn, Maurice, ed. *100 Years of American Newspaper Comics.* New York: Gramercy Books, 1996.

Markstein, Don. "Mutt & Jeff." *Don Markstein's Toonopedia.* http://www.toonopedia.com/muttjeff.htm (accessed June 20, 2011).

Robinson, Jerry. *The Comics: An Illustrated History of Comic Strip Art.* Rev. ed. Milwaukie, OR: 2006.

National Geographic

The National Geographic Society was founded at the end of the 1800s, a period of global change and discovery. Its monthly journal, *National Geographic,* reflects the thirst for travel, discovery, and new experiences that marked the move into the twentieth century. From its first issue in 1888, it was clear that *National Geographic* was not a boring scientific journal. Filled with color pictures of people and lands that were exotic and unusual to its American audience, the journal captured the imagination of readers of all ages.

In 1888, thirty-three members of the Cosmos Club, an elite Washington, D.C., club of professional men, joined together to form a society to learn and spread knowledge about the lands and peoples of the earth. The leaders of this National Geographic Society, whose early presidents included famed inventor Alexander Graham Bell (1847–1922), were determined that it should not be an exclusive organization, limited to scientists and scholars. Instead, they wished to attract a wide range of people who were interested in exploration, discovery, and the world around them.

The magazine became part of the plan to win a broad base of support for the Society. At a time when color photographs were rare, the magazine pioneered new photography techniques in order to give readers a truly vivid look at the wonders of the world. The Society also funded expeditions into unknown regions, such as the 1909 journey to the North Pole by Robert Peary (1856–1920) and Matthew Henson (1866–1955) and the many undersea explorations of Jacques Yves Cousteau (1910–1997). The stories of these adventures appeared in the pages of *National Geographic*.

Although the Society's journal has received high praise for its photography, maps, and wide range of subject matter, it has also received criticism for its strictly nonpolitical stance and its tendency to present a pristine view of the world. For example, a feature about Berlin published just before the start of World War II (1939–45) contained no criticism of the Nazi government and no mention of its anti-Jewish policies. Since the 1970s, the magazine has taken a more critical approach to its subjects. It has published articles about such political topics as apartheid (a-PAR-tayt; racial segregation) in South Africa and the French Canadian separatist movement.

The National Geographic Society has continued to grow and modernize. Its projects include a cable television channel, Web sites, and computer software and apps, along with the ever-popular magazine and maps.

Tina Gianoulis

For More Information

Bryan, C. D. B. *The National Geographic Society: 100 Years of Adventure and Discovery.* New York: Harry N. Abrams, 1987.

The Complete National Geographic: Every Issue Since 1888. Washington, DC: The Society, 2010. CD-ROM.

National Geographic. http://www.nationalgeographic.com (accessed June 20, 2011).

Patterson, Carolyn Bennett. *Of Lands, Legends, & Laughter: The Search for Adventure with National Geographic.* Golden, CO: Fulcrum Press, 1998.

New York Times

The *New York Times* was founded in 1851 as a four-page paper called the *New-York Daily Times*. It tried to provide objective, serious coverage of the daily news. In 1896, the *Times* was bought by Adolph S. Ochs (1858–1935) and began to establish itself as New York's premier newspaper and the nation's "newspaper of record." Since 1897, it has carried a front-page motto: "All the News That's Fit to Print." In 1905, the paper's name even graced one of the most famous areas in New York City—Times Square.

A famous front page from the May 7, 1937, edition of the New York Times *describes the* Hindenburg *airship disaster in New Jersey.* © BETTMANN/CORBIS.

Apart from being a news source for politicians around the world, the *Times* has also fought for freedom of the press and set the standard for investigative journalism. Among the best publications at reporting on federal government and international news, it won a Pulitzer Prize for reporting on World War I (1914–18) in 1918. In the 1960s, critics claimed that the paper had grown too friendly with the federal government. In 1971, however, the *Times* once again proved its commitment to free speech when it reported on the "Pentagon Papers." These documents revealed that many prominent public supporters of America's war in Vietnam had grave doubts about it in private. Agents of President Richard M. Nixon (1913–1994) tried to stop publication of the "Pentagon Papers." The *Times* and the *Washington Post* defended their constitutional right to publish without censorship and won their case in the U.S. Supreme Court.

Although famous for its news coverage, the *Times* became a powerful cultural force in other fields as well. Its critics can make or break the careers of writers, actors, and film and theater directors. Its stories on society, culture, and science are highly regarded. Although in many ways an old-fashioned, establishment-friendly newspaper, the *Times* has managed to maintain its reputation for quality journalism. Still published by Ochs's descendants, the paper has been awarded over one hundred Pulitzer Prizes, more than any other paper. The Pulitzer Prizes are America's most prestigious journalism awards. Like other newspapers, the *Times* is looking at ways to move forward as the newspaper industry continues to change amidst the emergence of the **Internet** (see entry under 1990s—The Way We Lived in volume 5).

Chris Routledge

For More Information

Diamond, Edwin. *Behind the Times: Inside the New New York Times.* New York: Villard Books, 1994.

Fireside, Harvey. *New York Times v. Sullivan: Affirming Freedom of the Press (Landmark Supreme Court Cases).* New York: Enslow, 1999.

Folkenflik, David. *Page One: Inside the New York Times and the Future of Journalism.* New York: PublicAffairs, 2011.

McGowan, William. *Gray Lady Down.* New York: Encounter Books, 2010.

The New York Times on the Web. http://www.nytimes.com (accessed June 20, 2011).

Page One: One Hundred Years of Headlines as Presented in the New York Times. New York: Galahad Books, 2000.

Saturday Evening Post

The *Saturday Evening Post* was one of the most influential and popular magazines in America from 1900 to 1930. With its mix of business news, nonfiction, romance stories, sports, humor, and illustrations, the *Post,* as it was known, set the standard for the weekly variety magazine. Although the *Post* remained in print for most of the twentieth century, its influence faded after the 1930s.

Publisher Cyrus H. K. Curtis (1850–1933) purchased the struggling *Saturday Evening Post* in 1897, hiring George Horace Lorimer (1867–1937) to edit his magazine. Lorimer believed in honesty, integrity, hard work, and self-reliance. He edited the magazine to promote these values, but he also knew that the purpose of a magazine was to entertain. He hired some of the best writers and illustrators in America.

Lorimer tried to provide the *Post*'s readers with a little bit of everything; he wanted to create a magazine for the entire family. Under Lorimer's guidance the *Post*'s circulation reached one million a week in 1908, two million in 1913, and three million in 1937. The contents of the magazine stayed roughly the same during these years and so did the price: Until 1942, an issue cost just five cents.

After Lorimer, the person most commonly associated with the magazine was illustrator **Norman Rockwell** (1894–1978; see entry under 1910s—Print Culture in volume 1). Rockwell, who began to paint covers for the *Post* in 1916, perfectly captured the tone of the magazine. He painted typical American scenes: a family sitting at a dinner table, a boy scout helping an older lady cross the street, a doctor listening to a doll's heartbeat. Many Americans clipped Rockwell's *Post* covers and framed them. Rockwell provided illustrations for the magazine for forty-seven years.

The *Post* began to fall out of touch with the mainstream in the 1930s. Editor Lorimer did not like the policies of Democratic president Franklin Delano Roosevelt (1882–1945), and he complained loudly about them. Soon the *Post* stopped seeming like the voice of American common sense and began to sound conservative and old fashioned. In the 1950s, advertisers moved their accounts to magazines popular with younger readers or to the new medium of television. The Curtis Company stopped publishing the failing magazine in 1969. In the years since

THE SATURDAY EVENING
POST

JUNE 3, 1950   15¢

Now We Have Plenty of Oil
By Arthur W. Baum

THAT GUY DUROCHER!
By Stanley Woodward

**WANT TO SEE EUROPE?
HERE'S HOW**

Humor in everyday life was just one of the themes of Saturday Evening Post *covers, this one from June 3, 1950.* © APIC/HULTON ARCHIVE/GETTY IMAGES.

that time, the *Post* has returned several times in one form or another, but never as a major magazine.

Tom Pendergast

For More Information

Cohn, Jan. *Creating America: George Horace Lorimer and the "Saturday Evening Post."* Pittsburgh: University of Pittsburgh Press, 1989.

Norman Rockwell Museum. http://www.nrm.org (accessed June 20, 2011).

Saturday Evening Post. http://www.saturdayeveningpost.com (accessed June 20, 2011).

Schwartz, Lew, and Doug Horton, eds. *Norman Rockwell and the Saturday Evening Post* (video). Video Arts Inc., 1986.

1900s

Sports and Games

Just as they are today, Americans were sports crazy in the first decade of the century. The sports of baseball, basketball, football, and boxing all expanded in popularity. The Olympics became an international spectacle of sports. Not content to remain spectators, Americans participated in bowling, golf, and lawn tennis.

Baseball had grown in popularity throughout the nineteenth century and was dominated at the beginning of the decade by the eight-team National League. The American League was formed in 1900 to challenge the National League. By 1903, the two leagues began to cooperate and play games against each other. Attendance at professional baseball games boomed during the decade, growing from 3.6 million in 1901 to 7.2 million in 1910. Fans across America became obsessed with the World Series, which pitted the American League and National League champions against each other. Until 1947, professional baseball was segregated, which meant that black players could not play in the major leagues. Undaunted, African Americans formed their own baseball leagues. Several of the Negro League players established reputations that rivaled those of white baseball greats like Ty Cobb (1886–1961).

College football was the second most popular sport in the nation. The University of Michigan was the dominant team of the decade, rolling up a 55–1–1 record between 1901 and 1905. Michigan defeated

Stanford at the first Rose Bowl game in 1902, setting the stage for major bowl contests between the top football teams. College football was controversial, however; its extreme violence sometimes led to the death of players, and some teams kept players on the roster (list of participants) even when they were not students. College football was reformed in 1906, setting the stage for the modern rules that still govern football today.

The most controversial sport of the decade was boxing. Often conducted without gloves, boxing matches could be bloody affairs. Boxing was outlawed in many states and reformed in most others. But the so-called "sport of gentlemen" had its fans, and professional boxing matches, especially in the heavyweight class, drew a great deal of attention. No boxer drew more attention than Jack Johnson (1878–1946), who became the first African American to hold the heavyweight title when he defeated Tommy Burns (1881–1955) in 1908. Racist white fight fans were outraged, and they searched ineffectually for a "Great White Hope" to defeat Johnson, who did not lose his title until 1915.

Invented in 1891, basketball was in its infancy in the first decade of the century. It was played first in YMCA clubs and Amateur Athletic Union (AAU) leagues and was soon taken up by colleges. By 1908, the University of Chicago played the University of Pennsylvania in the first collegiate national championship game. Professional basketball also existed, but it would be years before it drew much attention.

Baseball

Despite having to endure labor strikes, scandals, and the rising popularity of football and basketball, baseball (nicknamed "America's National Pastime") has managed to maintain its allure and produce an array of legendary larger-than-life heroes.

The origin of baseball has long been a subject of controversy. What is certain is that the game was initially played in the United States before the mid-nineteenth century; in the 1840s, the New York Knickerbockers, the first baseball team in the United States, played in Madison Square in Manhattan, New York, and at Elysian Fields in Hoboken, New Jersey. During the following decade, teams were established throughout the Northeast, and even in the Midwest and the Far West. After the Civil War (1861–65), teams started charging admission to games. In 1869, the Cincinnati Red Stockings became the first team to field a complete squad of salaried players.

Meanwhile, the rules of the game kept changing and evolving. In 1876, the eight-team National League came into being. The rival American League, also consisting of eight teams, was formed in 1901. At the conclusion of the 1903 season, the top team from each league began meeting each other in the World Series, marking the birth of the sport's modern era. Concrete ballparks that seated thousands of fans were constructed in the major league cities. Among the game's early, colorful personalities were outfielders **Ty Cobb** (1886–1961; see entry under 1900s—Sports and Games in volume 1) and Tris Speaker (1888–1958); second baseman Napoleon Lajoie (1874–1959); pitchers Cy Young (1867–1955), Christy Mathewson (1880–1925), and Walter Johnson (1887–1946); and managers Connie Mack (1862–1956) and John McGraw (1873–1934).

The public image of the game was almost destroyed in the wake of the 1919 World Series "Black Sox" scandal, in which eight members of the Chicago White Sox conspired to accept bribes and throw the series to their opponents, the Cincinnati Reds. The sport's savior was **Babe Ruth** (1895–1948; see entry under 1910s—Sports and Games in volume 1), affectionately dubbed the "Great Bambino" and the "Sultan of Swat," a home run–slugging pitcher-turned-outfielder who during the 1920s became baseball's most illustrious personality. A slew of celebrated ballplayers made the majors during the 1920s and 1930s and established impressive records. Rogers Hornsby (1896–1963) recorded three seasons with batting averages over .400, and in 1924 he compiled a record .424 batting average. New York Yankees first baseman Lou Gehrig (1903–1941) played in 2,130 straight games and earned the enduring affection of baseball fans. Ruth smashed 60 "round-trippers" (home runs) in 1927 and amassed a total of 714 during his career. The 1934 All-Star game saw pitcher Carl Hubbell (1903–1988) strike out Ruth, Gehrig, Jimmie Foxx (1907–1967), Al Simmons (1902–1956), and Joe Cronin (1906–1984) in succession. All were future Hall of Famers.

Two of the most famous players in baseball, New York Yankees teammates Lou Gehrig and Joe DiMaggio, 1936. © CSU ARCHIVES/EVERETT COLLECTION INC./ALAMY.

The Baseball Hall of Fame and Museum in Cooperstown, New York, a shrine to the game's greatest players, opened in 1939. The 1941 season was highlighted by two stellar accomplishments: Yankees outfielder Joe DiMaggio (1914–1999) hit in 56 straight games; and Boston Red Sox outfielder Ted Williams (1918–2002) became the last major leaguer to date to hit over .400.

Since the nineteenth century, African Americans had been banned from playing major and minor league baseball. Another milestone for the sport came in 1945, when Brooklyn Dodgers executive Branch Rickey (1881–1965) signed **Jackie Robinson** (1919–1972; see entry under 1940s—Sports and Games in volume 3) to a contract. Robinson debuted with the Dodgers two years later. The significance of this event transcended baseball, becoming one of the milestones in the evolution of the fight for equal rights for African Americans.

During the 1950s and 1960s, a new generation of baseball stars emerged, including slugging outfielders Willie Mays (1931–), Mickey Mantle (1931–1995), and Hank Aaron (1934–); outfielder Roberto Clemente (1934–1972), the first great Latin player; and fireballing pitcher Sandy Koufax (1935–). The 1950s also saw the first relocation of both National and American League franchises since 1903, with the Boston Braves, Philadelphia Athletics, and St. Louis Browns becoming, respectively, the Milwaukee Braves, Kansas City Athletics, and Baltimore Orioles. At that time, St. Louis was the westernmost major league city; the 1958 season saw the Brooklyn Dodgers and New York Giants resettle on the West Coast, in Los Angeles and San Francisco. Then, in 1961, the American League added two new franchises, the Los Angeles Angels (now known as the Los Angeles Angels of Anaheim) and Washington Senators, with the original Senators relocating to Minnesota as the Twins. The following year, the National League added the New York Mets and Houston Colt .45s (later Astros). In 1972, the "new" Washington Senators moved to Arlington, Texas, to become the Texas Rangers. Four teams were added to the major leagues in 1969; two in 1977; two in 1993; and two in 1998.

The adage "records are made to be broken" is ever the case in baseball. In 1961, slugger Roger Maris (1934–1985) hit 61 homers, breaking Babe Ruth's single-season mark. In 1974, steady Hank Aaron topped Ruth's career total of 714 homers, eventually retiring with 755 round-trippers. Pete Rose (1941–), nicknamed "Charlie Hustle," ended his career with 4,256 hits, topping Ty Cobb's 4,189. In 1973, sturdy pitcher

Nolan Ryan (1947–) struck out 383 batters, the single-season mark; during his twenty-seven-year career he amassed a record 5,714 strike-outs, and also pitched seven no-hitters.

Although these individual accomplishments were remarkable, baseball is a team sport. Of all major league baseball teams across the decades, the New York Yankees have been the most dominant by far. During the twentieth century, the Bronx Bombers won approximately one out of every four World Series played, including five in a row between 1949 and 1953, four in a row from 1936 to 1939, and three consecutively between 1998 and 2000.

The 1994 season saw the venerable sport suffer through another crisis: a player strike, which not only shut down the season in August but canceled the World Series. Inestimable numbers of fans lost interest in the game at the major league level. Two events helped rekindle its popularity. In 1995, "Iron Man" Cal Ripken (1960–) broke Lou Gehrig's consecutive games played streak; he voluntarily ended his streak three years later, at 2,632 straight games. Also in 1998, sluggers Mark McGwire (1963–) and Sammy Sosa (1968–) battled each other to break Roger Maris's season home-run record. Both of them did, with Sosa ending the year with 66 runs and McGwire topping him with 70. McGwire's record did not last long, as **Barry Bonds** (1964–) (see entry under 2000s—Sports and Games in volume 6) of the San Francisco Giants set his own record in 2001 with 73 homers. Although Bonds would go on to break Hank Aaron's record for career home runs as well, his achievements, and those of many of his contemporaries, would be called into doubt due to allegations of performance-enhancing drug use. The 1990s also saw the emergence of a new generation of baseball heroes, including Ken Griffey Jr. (1969–), Alex Rodriguez (1975–), Pedro Martinez (1968–), and Derek Jeter (1974–). Some of the stars of the 2000s included Albert Pujols (1980–), Ichiro Suzuki (1973–), and Miguel Cabrera (1983–).

Finally—and, perhaps, most tellingly—baseball is not played just at the professional level. Among the rites of childhood are the tossing, hitting, and catching of baseballs in sandlots and little leagues across America and around the world.

Rob Edelman

For More Information

Fleder, Rob. *The Baseball Book.* New York: Sports Illustrated Books, 2006.

Hernandez, Keith, and Mike Bryan. *Pure Baseball.* New York: HarperCollins, 1994.

"History of the Game: Doubleday to the Present Day." *MLB.com: History.* http://mlb.mlb.com/mlb/history/ (accessed June 20, 2011).

Neyer, Rob, and Eddie Epstein. *Baseball Dynasties: The Greatest Teams of All Time.* New York: Norton, 2000.

Pietrusza, David, Lloyd Johnson, and Bob Carroll. *The Total Baseball Catalog.* New York: Total Sports, 1998.

Pietrusza, David, Matthew Silverman, and Michael Gershman. *Baseball: The Biographical Encyclopedia.* Kingston, NY: Total Sports Illustrated, 2000.

Rader, Benjamin. *Baseball: A History of America's Game.* 3rd ed. Urbana: University of Illinois Press, 2008.

Thorn, John, Phil Birnbaum, Bill Deane, et al. *Total Baseball: The Ultimate Baseball Encyclopedia.* 8th ed. Wilmington, DE: Sport Media, 2004.

Vecsey, George. *Baseball: A History of America's Favorite Game.* New York: Modern Library, 2006.

Ty Cobb (1886–1961)

Ty Cobb in his Detroit Tigers uniform, 1915. © CORBIS.

Beginning in 1905, Tyrus Raymond Cobb—nicknamed the "Georgia Peach"—enjoyed a record-breaking twenty-four-year career as a major league **baseball** (see entry under 1900s—Sports and Games in volume 1) player. He compiled a lifetime batting average of .367, which has never been and may never be equaled. He hit over .300 for twenty-three consecutive seasons. Cobb led the American League in hitting an astounding twelve times. For decades, he held the major league record for the most hits—4,189, since eclipsed by Pete Rose (1941–)—and the modern-era stolen base record—892, later surpassed by Lou Brock (1939–) and Rickey Henderson (1958–). In 1936, he was the first player elected to the Baseball Hall of Fame.

However, Cobb's career and legacy have been tainted by his vicious temper and violent mode of play. He may have been brilliant and unrelentingly aggressive on the playing field, but he was despised by his fellow players—including his teammates—for his humorless demeanor, stiff

Southern formality, and inclination to slide into infielders spikes-first for no apparent reason.

Ty Cobb was an early advocate of unionizing ballplayers and was a vocal opponent of the Reserve Clause, which bound a player for life to the team that owned his contract. In his retirement, he also supported impoverished former ballplayers. But he continued squabbling with others in the game. Upon his death in 1961, no one representing Major League Baseball—and only three ballplayers of his era—bothered to attend his funeral.

Rob Edelman

For More Information

Bak, Richard. *Peach: Ty Cobb in His Time and Ours.* Ann Arbor, MI: Sports Media Group, 2005.

Holmes, Dan. *Ty Cobb: A Biography.* Westport, CT: Greenwood Press, 2004.

The Official Web Site of Ty Cobb. http://www.cmgww.com/baseball/cobb/index.html (accessed June 20, 2011).

Rhodes, Don. *Ty Cobb: Safe at Home.* Guilford, CT: Lyons Press, 2008.

Stump, Al. *Ty Cobb: A Biography.* Chapel Hill, NC: Algonquin Books of Chapel Hills, 1994.

James J. Corbett (1866–1933)

James J. "Gentleman Jim" Corbett is more than a boxing legend. He was the first of a new breed of modern-era boxers who approached the sport of boxing methodically. The fast, sleek Corbett believed in training for his fights and in employing speed and strategy rather than uncontrolled power to outsmart an opponent.

Through the late nineteenth century, professional boxing was not so much an organized sport as a barbaric fight-to-the-finish free-for-all in which bare-knuckled combatants wrestled and clawed their way to victory. Boxers were like hooligans who exuded a rough, crude manliness. The sport became more orderly with the institution of the Marquis of Queensberry rules (named after Sir John Sholto Douglas [1844–1900], the eighth Marquis of Queensberry, who helped draft the new boxing rules). Bouts consisted of three-minute rounds featuring minute-long rest periods in between, and to protect their hands boxers were required to wear five-ounce, padded gloves.

On September 7, 1892, the first modern-era heavyweight championship match was held with the Marquis of Queensberry rules in effect.

The reigning champion was John L. Sullivan (1858–1918), nicknamed "The Boston Strongboy," an old-style, bare-knuckle boxer. Corbett was the challenger. The smaller, quicker Corbett avoided Sullivan's bullish assaults and wore him down. He knocked out the exhausted champ in the twenty-first round to claim the heavyweight crown—and the modern era of boxing was born.

Unlike other boxers of his time, Corbett hailed from a middle-class family and attended college. While still the reigning champion, he performed on the stage and in **vaudeville** (see entry under 1900s—Film and Theater in volume 1), and he continued doing so after losing his title to Bob Fitzsimmons (1863–1918) in 1897.

Rob Edelman

For More Information

Fields, Armond. *James J. Corbett: A Biography of the Heavyweight Boxing Champ and Popular Theater Headliner.* Jefferson, NC: McFarland, 2001.

"'Gentleman' Jim Corbett." *The Cyber Boxing Zone.* http://cyberboxingzone.com/boxing/corbett.htm (accessed June 20, 2011).

Myler, Patrick. *Gentleman Jim Corbett: The Truth Behind a Boxing Legend.* London: Robson Books, 1998.

Jack Johnson (1878–1946)

Jack Johnson, a free-living, highly individualistic heavyweight boxing champion, was a black man who came of age and came to fame at a time when African Americans faced severe discrimination in American society. When Johnson earned his boxing title in 1908, African Americans faced many forms of racial bias. They were mostly consigned to second-class schools and menial jobs, and they almost always suffered ill-treatment at the hands of the police and the criminal justice system. They were regularly denied their right to vote. African American men who would not submit to white racism were often subjected to physical violence and even murder. In this era, Johnson, no lowly field worker or janitor, but the heavyweight champion of the world, threatened the myths of white superiority. Johnson showed no humility as he savored his fame. He drove expensive cars, hosted extravagant parties, and dated white women.

Johnson went on to defeat white opponent after white opponent. One of his most famous bouts, held in 1910, came against former

Heavyweight boxing champion Jack Johnson defeats former champ James J. Jeffries in Reno, Nevada, in 1910. © THE PROTECTED ART ARCHIVE/ALAMY.

champ James J. Jeffries (1875–1953). Their fight was advertised as a battle between "The Hope of the White Race vs. The Deliverer of the Negroes." Much to the shock of white America, Johnson pummeled the aging, overweight Jeffries to claim a resounding victory.

No "Great White Hope" boxer could stop Johnson in the ring, so the federal government stepped in. In 1912, he was convicted of violating the Mann Act, which prohibited the transportation of women across state lines for "immoral purposes." Johnson fled the country, lost his title to a six-foot, six-inch hulk named Jess Willard (1883–1968), and eventually faded into obscurity. But his athletic prowess, and his status as a black champion in a white-dominated world, can never be denied.

Rob Edelman

For More Information

Burns, Ken, writer and director. *Unforgivable Blackness: The Rise and Fall of Jack Johnson* (video). PBS-TV, 2005.

Jakoubek, Robert E. *Jack Johnson.* New York: Chelsea House, 1990.

Johnson, Jack. *My Life and Battles.* Edited by Christopher Rivers. Westport, CT: Greenwood, 2007.

Ward, Geoffrey C. *Unforgivable Blackness: The Rise and Fall of Jack Johnson.* New York: Knopf, 2004.

Kentucky Derby

The "Run for the Roses," otherwise known as the Kentucky Derby, is the world's most fabled horserace, as well as the oldest continual athletic competition held in the United States. It is the first of three annual races,

Jockey Ron Turcotte poses in the winner's circle with Secretariat, the first horse to run the Kentucky Derby in under two minutes, May 5, 1973. © AP IMAGES.

followed by the Preakness and Belmont Stakes, in which three-year-old thoroughbreds compete for the Triple Crown, which is earned by winning each event. Each spring, over one hundred thousand racing fans congregate at the Churchill Downs racetrack in Louisville, Kentucky, to witness what has come to be known as the "greatest two minutes in sports."

The race dates back to May 1875, when Colonel Meriwether Lewis Clark (1846–1899) staged the first Derby, which he modeled after the English Derby held at Epsom Downs in Surrey, England. The original Kentucky Derby course covered a mile and a half; eventually, it was reduced to a mile and a quarter. Aristides, a chestnut colt, was the first winner. Subsequent contests featured the top American thoroughbreds hailing from Kentucky and the Northeast. However, the Derby did not attain its status as racing's premiere event for another forty years.

At the turn of the twentieth century, Clark's racetrack was a failing enterprise. Between 1899 and 1914, the top northeastern stables bypassed Churchill Downs for the American Derby at Chicago's Washington Park, and the Kentucky Derby became a regional meet. Then, in 1915, financier, socialite, sportsman, and horse breeder Harry Payne Whitney (1872–1930) entered a filly (young female horse) named Regret, which became the lone female thoroughbred to win the Derby until the 1980s. This race signaled the beginning of the Derby's modern era. Matt Winn (1861–1949), a former Louisville tailor and Churchill Downs's longtime vice president and general manager, noted that Regret's victory "made the Kentucky Derby an American institution."

Isaac Murphy (1859–1896), an African American and the son of a former slave, was one of the most honored jockeys to compete in the early Kentucky Derby races, riding Buchanan, Riley, and Kingman to victory in 1884, 1890, and 1891. His three Derby triumphs were not duplicated until 1930, when Earl Sande (1898–1968) won his third race on Gallant Fox. The record was broken when Eddie Arcaro (1916–1997), who won a total of five Derbys, rode his fourth winner, Citation, in 1948. Bill Hartack (1932–2007) joined Arcaro as a five-time victor, while Willie Shoemaker (1931–2003) rode into the winner's circle on four occasions and Angel Cordero (1942–) won three times.

Among the legendary horses to have raced at Churchill Downs are Gallant Fox and Omaha, the only father-son combination to win the Triple Crown, in 1930 and 1935; Whirlaway, another Triple Crown victor, who set a record pace while winning the Derby in 1941; Citation, the 1948 Triple Crown winner and the first horse ever to earn $1 million in prize money; and Secretariat, the 1973 Triple Crown champion, the first horse to run the Derby in under two minutes.

Rob Edelman

For More Information

Bolus, Jim. *Derby Dreams.* Gretna, LA: Pelican, 1996.
Bolus, Jim. *Derby Fever.* Gretna, LA: Pelican, 1995.
Bolus, Jim. *Derby Magic.* Gretna, LA: Pelican, 1995.
Bolus, Jim. *Kentucky Derby Stories.* Gretna, LA: Pelican, 1993.
Bolus, Jim. *Remembering the Derby.* Gretna, LA: Pelican, 1993.
Brodowsky, Pamela K., and Tom Philbin. *Two Minutes to Glory: The Official History of the Kentucky Derby.* New York: Collins, 2007.
Chew, Peter. *The Kentucky Derby: The First Hundred Years.* Boston: Houghton Mifflin, 1974.
Churchill Downs Incorporated. *The Kentucky Derby.* http://www.kentuckyderby.com (accessed June 20, 2011).
Doolittle, Bill. *The Kentucky Derby: Run for the Roses.* New York: Time-Life Books, 1998.
Seggerman, Sheri, and Mary Tiegreen. *The Kentucky Derby: 101 Reasons to Love America's Favorite Horse Race.* New York: Stewart, Tabori & Chang, 2010.

Lionel Trains

For generations of Americans, gazing at a brand new Lionel train set as it chugged along loops of tracks laid out beneath a brightly lit Christmas tree is an extra-special childhood memory. Lionel trains are not the only electricity-powered toys marketed to American children and hobbyists, but of all electric train manufacturers, Lionel is by far the most famous, a status it earned for the quality, craftsmanship, and durability of its product.

Joshua Lionel Cowen (1877–1965), a young man who since childhood had been fascinated by trains and railroads, founded the Lionel Manufacturing Company in lower Manhattan, New York, in 1900. The story goes that, when he was seven, Cowen carved a small locomotive out of wood, which exploded upon his attempting to attach it to a miniature steam engine. Although Cowen did not invent the electric train—one had been displayed at the 1893 Chicago World's Fair—he was the first to produce miniature, electric trains as playthings. For his initial Lionel train, he hooked a small motor onto a red-stained wooden box with attached wheels, and added a gold-painted "Electric Express" to the side. He sold the car, along with thirty inches of track, for the then-hefty sum of $6. The product became a smash hit. Soon Cowen was manufacturing meticulously designed and painted miniature reproductions of diesel locomotives, steam engines, cabooses, and trolleys as well as coal, cattle, and passenger cars, all operated electrically. He produced his first accessory, a suspension bridge, in 1902, and eventually added tunnels and train stations. In 1915, he introduced smaller, less-expensive O-gauge trains. The term "gauge" refers to the width of the track, and O-gauge

Lionel trains captivated baby boomers and remain popular collectibles in the twenty-first century. © PICTORIAL PARADE/GETTY IMAGES.

models are designed to fit on tracks that are one and one-quarter inches between rails.

By the mid-1920s, Cowen's company completely dominated the model train business, selling over fifty million trains in the decades after its inception. Among the many Lionel classics were the 400E steam locomotive, first marketed in 1931; the 700E New York Central-Hudson steam locomotive, from 1937; and the F3 diesel locomotive, from 1948. In 1953, as parents by the thousands were buying Lionel trains for their **baby boomer** (see entry under 1940s—The Way We Lived in volume 3) offspring, Lionel recorded its highest profits ever. However, beginning in the late 1950s, Lionel trains—and all electric trains—went out of fashion, primarily because airplanes were replacing trains as the primary mode of cross-country travel.

Today, original Lionel trains are collector's items, highly coveted by vintage toy and train enthusiasts. They are especially beloved by baby boomers. In fact, in the 1990s, one celebrated baby boomer, rock musician Neil Young (1945–), even became a part owner in the company. In recent years, financial and legal problems have dogged the company but the 2004 release of trains based on the book and film *Polar Express* were a big hit with many train enthusiasts.

Rob Edelman

For More Information

Carp, Roger. *The World's Greatest Toy Train Maker: Insiders Remember Lionel.* Waukesha, WI: Kalmbach, 1997.

Hollander, Ron. *All Aboard! The Story of Joshua Lionel Cowen and His Lionel Train Company.* New York: Workman, 1981.

"Lionel Train History: Past and Present." *Lionel Trains.* http://www.lionel.com/CentralStation/LionelPastAndPresent (accessed June 20, 2011).

Osterhoff, Robert J. *Inside the Lionel Trains Fun Factory.* Winfield, IL: Project Roar, 2008.

Milton Bradley Company

The Milton Bradley Company is best known as the manufacturer of classic games, from **Scrabble** (see entry under 1940s—Sports and Games in volume 3) to **Twister** (see entry under 1960s—Sports and Games in volume 3), that have brought fun to players of all ages for over 140 years. The company was founded by Milton Bradley (1836–1911),

Milton Bradley's classic board game, The Game of Life. © CAMERASHOTS-CONCEPT/ALAMY.

who was working as a printer in Springfield, Massachusetts, when he produced a new family diversion called The Checkered Game of Life, a board game in which a player's goal was to lead a moral life and peaceful retirement.

Bradley continued to create games and publish educational materials for young children. By 1968, his company was the largest manufacturer of games in the United States. The popularity of Milton Bradley games such as Parcheesi, Yahtzee, Candy Land, Chutes and Ladders, Mouse-trap, and Go to the Head of the Class has spanned generations. Books published by Milton Bradley Publishing teach children about everything from numbers and letters to problem solving and computer skills.

The company became part of Hasbro Toys in 1984, but the Milton Bradley name is still used on its classic games. The Game of Life is still one of the most popular, though the goal has been updated. In the modern game, the player who retires with the most money wins.

Tina Gianoulis

For More Information

Lee, Laura. "Milton Bradley." *The Name's Familiar: Mr. Leotard, Barbie, and Chef Boy-ar-dee.* Gretna, LA: Pelican Publishing, 1999.

Miller, Raymond H. *Milton Bradley.* Detroit: KidHaven Press, 2004.

Negro Leagues

In 1947, **Jackie Robinson** (1919–1972; see entry under 1940s—Sports and Games in volume 3) became the first African American to play major league **baseball** (see entry under 1900s—Sports and Games in volume 1) in the twentieth century. Before the late 1940s, African American players were not permitted to pitch, hit, and field alongside such greats as **Babe Ruth** (1895–1948; see entry under 1910s—Sports and Games in volume 1), **Ty Cobb** (1886–1961; see entry under 1900s—Sports and Games in volume 1), Lou Gehrig (1903–1941), Walter Johnson (1887–1946), and other white baseball heroes, but that did not deter them from playing the game. The best black ballplayers swatted home runs, stole bases, and pitched shutouts in leagues of their own, all of which are informally known as the Negro Leagues.

Star pitcher Satchel Paige of the Negro League's Kansas City Monarchs, 1942.
© BETTMANN/CORBIS.

All-black baseball clubs existed in the nineteenth century and even took on white opponents on occasion. Back in 1869, the Pythian Baseball Club of Philadelphia, Pennsylvania, an all-black team, played—and beat—the all-white City Items. For several decades during this period, blacks and whites did play side by side, but integrated baseball ended in 1887 when Cap Anson (1852–1922), one of the most influential white ballplayers, declared that he never would play with or against black opponents. Anson's highly publicized declaration eventually evolved into a gentleman's agreement between the major league owners to exclude black players.

African Americans were thus restricted to playing on segregated teams. One of the top turn-of-the-twentieth-century teams was the Chicago American Giants, who put together an extraordinary 123-6 record one season while barnstorming cross-country. The Giants' star was pitcher-manager Andrew "Rube" Foster (1879–1930), who after World War I (1914–18) helped establish the eight-team Negro National League. Upon the league's success, a group of white owners formed the rival six-team Eastern Colored League. In 1924, each league's top team met in the first Black World Series.

The next two decades produced their share of legendary Negro League teams, beginning with the Kansas City Monarchs, Pittsburgh Crawfords, Homestead Grays, and Birmingham Black Barons. Among the top stars were gangly pitcher Leroy "Satchel" Paige (1906–1982), a master showman who was the league's biggest draw; James "Cool Papa" Bell (1903–1991), a lightning-fast base stealer; and brawny home-run hitter Josh Gibson (1911–1947), who may have belted close to one thousand home runs during his career. On occasion, Negro all-star teams would play similar squads composed of the top major leaguers. On these occasions, the African American ballplayers proved that the best of them could have been major league all-stars. Paige once struck out Hall of Famer Rogers Hornsby (1896–1963) five times in the same contest. New York Yankee legend Joe DiMaggio (1914–1999) called Paige "the best and fastest pitcher I've ever faced." Meanwhile, in these exhibitions, Gibson hit .412 against formidable major league pitching talent.

The integration of major league baseball signaled the beginning of the end of the Negro Leagues. Following integration, the very best African American prospects could be signed by the Brooklyn Dodgers, the Cleveland Indians, or the New York Giants. The could develop their skills in their team's farm systems and make it to the majors. Although the top pre-1947 African American players were not allowed to play alongside their Caucasian counterparts, they at least have joined them in the National Baseball Hall of Fame and Museum in Cooperstown, New York. Beginning with the 1971 induction of Satchel Paige, Negro Leaguers have been elected to the Hall of Fame. In addition, the Negro Leagues Baseball Museum in Kansas City, Missouri, honors African American baseball players.

Rob Edelman

For More Information

Black Baseball's Negro Baseball Leagues. http://www.blackbaseball.com (accessed June 20, 2011).

Hogan, Lawrence D. *Shades of Glory: The Negro Leagues and the Story of African-American Baseball.* Washington, DC: National Geographic, 2006.

Holway, John B. *Black Diamonds: Life in the Negro Leagues.* New York: Stadium Books, 1991.

McKissack, Patricia C., and Fredrick McKissack, Jr. *Black Diamond: The Story of the Negro Baseball Leagues.* New York: Scholastic, 1994.

Negro Leagues Baseball Museum. http://www.nlbm.com (accessed June 20, 2011).

Peterson, Robert. *Only the Ball Was White: A History of Legendary Black Players and All-Black Professional Teams.* New York: Oxford University Press, 1992.

Ward, Geoffrey C., and Ken Burns, with Jim O'Connor. *Shadow Ball: The History of the Negro Leagues.* New York: Knopf, 1994.

Olympics

The earliest Olympic games took place in ancient Greece, possibly as far back as the fourteenth century BCE. The ancient Olympics mixed sport with pagan religious festivities, and the Romans banned them in

The 1980 U.S. Olympic ice hockey team defeats Finland 4-2 in the final game, thus winning the gold medal in Lake Placid, New York. © BETTMANN/CORBIS.

393 CE. Baron Pierre de Coubertin (1862–1937) staged the first modern summer Olympic games for amateur athletes in Athens, Greece, in 1896. The first official winter games were held in 1928 in St. Moritz, Switzerland, though the events of the eleven-day "International Winter Sports Week" in Chamonix, France, are usually called the first winter games. In the 1960s, the first "Paralympics" allowed athletes with disabilities to compete on a world stage. Until 1994, both the summer and winter Olympics were held in different cities the same year, every four years; that changed, however, with the winter and summer Olympics alternating every two years.

The Olympics were started in a spirit of fair play and honor among nations, but they have always reflected their times. The Stockholm, Sweden, games of 1912 saw women compete for the first time, though they did not take their place in track and field events until 1928. In 1936, Nazi leader Adolf Hitler (1889–1945) hoped that the Berlin, Germany, Olympics would show the superiority of the "Aryan" race (non-Jewish Caucasians), but African American runner **Jesse Owens** (1913–1980; see entry under 1930s—Sports and Games in volume 2) had other ideas. He went on to win four gold medals.

Many Olympic competitions make household names of its stars. Swimmer Johnny Weissmuller (1904–1984) won four medals in 1924 and became famous as **Tarzan** (see entry under 1910s—Print Culture in volume 1) in a series of films; swimmer Mark Spitz (1950–) managed seven swimming golds in 1972. Boxer Cassius Clay, who later changed his name to **Muhammad Ali** (1942–; see entry under 1960s—Sports and Games in volume 4), went on to be one of the best-known sportsmen of all time. Track stars such as Carl Lewis (1961–) and Florence Griffith Joyner (1959–1998) thrilled spectators with breathtaking performances. As a team, members of the 1980 U.S. men's hockey team became instant Olympic legends when they defeated the highly favored Soviet hockey team, and then went on to win the gold medal.

In the late twentieth century, the influence of politics over the games grew stronger. The United States and the Soviet Union boycotted one another's games in the 1980s at the height of the **Cold War** (see entry under 1940s—The Way We Lived in volume 3). Terrorists disrupted the games in Munich, Germany, in 1972 and in Atlanta, Georgia, in 1996. In 1998, ten members of the International Olympic Committee were expelled for allegedly taking bribes from people seeking to hold the Olympics in Salt Lake City Utah. The Olympic Games have served as an opportunity for host nations to showcase their artistic, cultural, and political values. Since the 1980s, many of the athletes are well-paid professionals. Still, it is the courage, speed, and skill of the athletes that make the Olympics special. Politics, commercialization, drug abuse, and other scandals never quite manage to overshadow the spectacle of the games themselves.

Chris Routledge

For More Information

Anderson, Dave, and Carl Lewis. *The Story of the Olympics.* Rev. ed. New York: HarperCollins, 2000.

Chronicle of the Olympics. London: Dorling Kindersley, 1998.

Guttmann, Allen. *The Olympics: A History of the Modern Games.* 2nd ed. Urbana: University of Illinois Press, 2002.

International Olympic Committee. http://www.olympic.org/ (accessed June 20, 2011).

Miller, David. *The Official History of the Olympic Games and the IOC: Athens to Beijing, 1894–2008.* Edinburgh: Mainstream, 2008.

Pound, Richard W. *Inside the Olympics: A Behind-the-Scenes Look at the Politics, the Scandals, and the Glory of the Games.* Etobicoke, Ontario, Canada: Wiley Canada, 2004.

Ouija Boards
● ●

Invented in the late 1800s, the Ouija (WEE-jee) board was part of a fascination with spiritualism and the occult (supernatural phenomena) that swept the United States and Europe during the last half of the nineteenth century. What made the "talking board" special was that the average person could use it to try to contact the spirit world without the help of a psychic or a medium (someone said to be naturally sensitive to the spirit world and able to communicate with its spirits). Since its invention, the Ouija board has been marketed and sold as a toy. Both its fans and its critics, however, have often taken it much more seriously, viewing it as the key to an unseen world of spirits that some think is better left alone.

In 1848, two sisters, Kate Fox (1839–1892) and Margaret Fox (1833–1893) of Hydesville, New York, became famous when they said they had communicated with the spirit of a long-dead peddler. Soon, people all over the country were holding séances (meetings at which people attempt to communicate with spirits). Some séances included mediums who supposedly went into trances in which dead people could speak directly through them (a trance is a sleep-like condition in which the medium appears conscious but unable to move or act). For those without the special skills of a medium, several methods were used to enable the dead to speak. Table turning involved placing hands around a table, which would then rock and thump to indicate the presence of spirits. A *planchette* (a heart-shaped piece of wood with a pencil attached and wheels or sliders to allow it to glide across paper) would write a spirit message. Fascinated and thrilled by the frightening world of ghosts, most fans of spiritualism cheerfully ignored the likelihood that one of their own was pushing the table or the pencil around, consciously or unconsciously.

The Ouija board was a variation of the planchette. It eliminated the paper and substituted a board painted with the alphabet and a few common words like "yes," "no," and "maybe" to simplify the spirit writing process. The first Ouija board was invented in 1890 by toy manufacturer Charles Kennard (1856–1925), who named it for a word the board had

A Ouija board in action.
© JAMES PORTER/ALAMY.

told him meant "good luck" in Egyptian. In fact, "ouija" does not mean anything in either ancient Egyptian Arabic or, the language spoken in modern Egypt. When Kennard sold the patent to William Fuld (1870–1927) in 1892, Fuld explained the name by saying it was a combination of the French and German words for "yes," *oui,* and *ja.* The Ouija board was sold in novelty stores and toy shops, competing with other talking boards with names like "The Wireless Messenger" and "Mystic Tray."

In 1966, Fuld's children sold the Ouija board to Parker Brothers, a game company that continued to market the board as a harmless parlor game. Some people still feel it is better left alone. Others fear that playing with the board comes dangerously close to Satanism. Professional psychics worry that the board may unleash evil spirits. Some psychologists express concern that use of the board may further disturb a mentally unbalanced person. Nevertheless, Ouija board use continues to enchant mystics and enliven parties with its promise of access to the forbidden territory of the dead.

Tina Gianoulis

For More Information

Covina, Gina. *The Ouija Book.* New York: Simon and Schuster, 1979.

Hunt, Stoker. *Ouija: The Most Dangerous Game.* New York: Barnes and Noble, 1985.

Johnson, James P. "Ouija." *American Heritage* (Vol. 34, February–March 1983): pp. 24–27.

Museum of Talking Boards. http://www.museumoftalkingboards.com (accessed June 21, 2011).

"Ouija Board." *Skeptic's Dictionary.* http://www.skepdic.com/ouija.html (accessed June 21, 2011).

Rose Bowl

On and around every New Year's Day, the top college football teams face off in postseason "bowl games," one of which is the National Championship game. Of all the bowl games, the Rose Bowl, held in Pasadena, California, in early January—usually on January 1—is the oldest and the most fabled.

In 1902, business leaders in Pasadena sponsored a football game that would match a top West Coast team against one from back East. With eighty-five hundred fans looking on, the Michigan Wolverines smashed Stanford University 49–0. Disappointed in the loss by the local team, the Tournament of Roses committee did not follow through on a second contest. The next Rose Bowl was held fourteen years later, when Washington State bested Brown 14–0, after which the game would be played every year. Starting in 1924, contests have been held in the Rose Bowl stadium, with attendance often topping one hundred thousand. Since 1947, when Illinois trounced UCLA 45–14, the Rose Bowl opponents have been the champions of what today are known as the Big Ten and Pac-10 college football conferences. That tradition ended temporarily in 2002 when the Rose Bowl joined other bowl games in hosting the Bowl Championship Series' national championship game.

During the twentieth century, nineteen Rose Bowl winners were crowned national champions. The first was the Michigan team that won the original game. The popularity of the Rose Bowl resulted in the founding of other postseason college bowl games. During the 1930s, the Orange (1933), Sugar (1935), Sun (1936), and Cotton (1937) Bowls were established. Other bowls followed in subsequent decades.

Bowl games are usually preceded by elaborate parades through the streets of the host city. Not surprisingly, the most famous is the Rose Bowl's "Tournament of Roses" parade, which predated the football contest. The procession is famed for its ornately designed floats, each festooned with floral arrangements. Watching it on television is a New Year's Day ritual for football fans and nonfans alike.

Rob Edelman

For More Information

Hendrickson, Joe, with Maxwell Stiles. *The Tournament of Roses: A Pictorial History.* Los Angeles: Brooke House, 1971.

Hibner, John Charles. *The Rose Bowl, 1902–1929: A Game-by-Game History of Collegiate Football's Foremost Event, from Its Advent through Its Golden Era.* Jefferson, NC: McFarland, 1993.

Michelson, Herb, and Dave Newhouse. *Rose Bowl Football Since 1902.* New York: Stein and Day, 1977.

"Rose Bowl Game History." *The Tournament of Roses.* http://www .tournamentofroses.com/the-rose-bowl-game/history/historical-overview (accessed June 21, 2011).

Riffey, Michael K., and Laura A. Adams. *More Than a Parade: The Spirit and Passion Behind the Pasadena Tournament of Roses.* Las Vegas, NV: Stephens Press, 2007.

Turner, Michelle L. *The Rose Bowl.* Charleston, SC: Arcadia, 2010.

1900s

The Way We Lived

In the first decade of the century, Americans began to experience the first of the technological transformations that would make life in the twentieth century so dissimilar from life during its predecessor. Two technological innovations alone were responsible for a great deal of this change: electricity and the automobile. Electricity brought great changes to life in the home, from electric lighting that allowed life to go on while darkness descended outside to the development of electric appliances that made housework so much easier. The electric vacuum cleaner was invented in 1907, for example, although it was too expensive for most Americans.

The automobile had an even more revolutionary impact on the lifestyles of American citizens. Developed in the nineteenth century, automobiles began to see mass production in the 1900s by such companies as Ford and General Motors. With a car, Americans could travel farther than ever before. A variety of businesses serving travelers resulted, from diners to gas stations. The telephone, another nineteenth-century invention, likewise allowed people to close the distances between themselves. By the 1930s, most Americans had access to a telephone.

Americans spent their leisure time in a number of different ways during the 1900s. Religion was often the center of many people's lives. Evangelical religion enjoyed a boom in popularity, thanks in part to a number of charismatic traveling preachers. The most notable preacher of the decade was Billy Sunday (1862–1935), a former National League baseball player whose sermons drew great crowds. Americans also sought to improve themselves by attending Chautauqua events, which were traveling variety programs that stressed education and self-improvement. Other Americans enjoyed the escapism of amusement parks, where they rode the Ferris wheels and roller coasters that were becoming increasingly popular. The most famous American amusement park of the time was Coney Island, situated near New York City.

Avon

For more than a century the Avon Products company has been known for the direct-selling approach it uses to merchandise its cosmetics and personal-care products. In short, Avon employs women known as "Avon Ladies" to personally demonstrate items to customers in the privacy of their own homes. Avon's vintage television commercials typically opened with the sound of a chiming doorbell followed by the phrase, "Avon calling!"

Originally known as the California Perfume Company, the business was founded in 1886 by David McConnell (1858–1937), who later renamed it Avon to honor the birthplace of his favorite author, William Shakespeare (1564–1616). Avon's direct-selling method was pioneered by Mrs. P. F. E. Albee of Winchester, New Hampshire, who became the first Avon Lady soon after the company's establishment. In 2010, Avon was the world's largest direct-selling company, employing 6.5 million sales representatives in over 100 countries around the world (about 2 percent of whom are male), and with total sales revenues of $10.9 billion.

Avon suffered a decline in its fortunes in the 1970s and 1980s owing the changing lifestyles of its clientele. Many women began working outside the home, the arena where most of its demonstrations and sales had traditionally taken place. Also during this period, many salespeople left Avon to pursue more lucrative career opportunities. In the 1990s, the company redesigned its focus and advertising, upgraded its product line, and trained its sales force to make presentations in workplace settings, where 50 percent of sales now take place. Avon also considerably expanded its presence outside of the United States, especially in Brazil and other South American countries, China, and eastern Europe. With almost half of its top executives being female, the Avon Company is considered one of the most "women-friendly" enterprises.

Edward Moran

For More Information

Avon.com: The Company for Women. http://www.avoncompany.com (accessed July 13, 2011).

Hastin, Bud. *Bud Hastin's Avon Collector's Encyclopedia.* 18th ed. Paducah, KY: Collector Books, 2008.

Klepacki, Laura Ann. *Avon: Building the World's Premier Company for Women.* Hoboken, NJ: Wiley, 2006.

Morris, Betsy. "If Women Ran the World, It Would Look a Lot Like Avon." *Fortune* (July 21, 1997).

Reynolds, Patricia. "Ding Dong! Avon Lady Is Still Calling." *Minneapolis Star Tribune* (September 9, 1996).

Zajac, Jennifer. "Avon Finally Glowing Thanks to Global Sales—and New Lip-Shtick." *Money* (September 1997).

A reproduction page from the Sears homes catalog shows few changes to this Illinois mail-order house, originally purchased for $725 in 1909.
© AP IMAGES/FRED ZWICKY.

Catalog Houses

Most people are used to buying clothes and other specialty items from catalogs, but in the first half of the twentieth century, Americans could also use mail-order registers to purchase houses. As Americans began moving into cities and their **suburbs** (see entry under 1950s—The Way We Lived in volume 3) in increasing numbers after 1890, they needed affordable housing. Catalog houses offered Americans a unique way to solve their housing problems.

The catalog house industry began in earnest after 1907 with the founding of the Aladdin Company, which was soon joined by competitors, most notably **Sears, Roebuck and Co.** (see entry under 1900s—Commerce in volume 1). Sears sold catalog houses between 1908 and 1940. In every supplier's catalog, customers could select from a number of different housing styles, with bungalows and colonial revival homes being among the most popular models. When customers ordered a catalog house, they would receive the complete architectural plans, a complete construction manual, and often the building materials as well. These building materials came pre-cut and numbered for easy assembly. All the homeowner had to do was provide the land; the foundation materials, such as concrete or stone; the labor; and other amenities such as windows, doors, and plumbing. Sears and other companies provided guarantees of satisfaction and often easy payment credit plans to make the houses even more affordable.

As a cultural phenomenon, catalog houses became a common part of the American landscape, popping up in towns all over the United States. They even became the subject of films, most notably in the 1921 short comic film *One Week* by Buster Keaton (1895–1966). In the film, Keaton assembles his own catalog house incorrectly, which predictably results in all sorts of funny problems. *One Week* was one of the most popular comedies of 1921, an indication not only of Keaton's wide-spread adoration, but also of the popularity of catalog houses.

During the **Great Depression** (see entry under 1930s—The Way We Lived in volume 2) of the 1930s, catalog house sales decreased, as fewer people could afford to buy homes of any type. Although many examples still stand, the catalog house never rebounded in popularity after 1940.

Timothy Berg

For More Information

Clark, Clifford Edward, Jr. *The American Family Home*. Chapel Hill: University of North Carolina Press, 1986.

Jackson, Kenneth T. *Crabgrass Frontier: The Suburbanization of the United States*. New York: Oxford University Press, 1985.

McAlester, Virginia, and Lee McAlester. *A Field Guide to American Houses*. New York: Alfred A. Knopf, 1994.

Stevenson, Katherine Cole, and H. Ward Jandl. *Houses by Mail: A Guide to Houses from Sears, Roebuck and Company*. Washington, DC: Preservation Press, 1986.

Thornton, Rosemary Fuller. *The Houses That Sears Built*. 2nd ed. Alton, IL: Gentle Beam, 2004.

Chautauqua Movement

In the years between the 1870s and the 1920s, the name Chautauqua came to be synonymous with culture, learning, entertainment, and social activism. Originating at a New York religious institute, the

Porches overlook Chautauqua Lake at this historic western New York retreat. © BOB DOWNING/MCT/LANDOV.

Chautauqua movement, which focused on self-improvement through education, spread across small-town America. Today, the spirit of lifelong education endures thanks to the efforts of the Chautauqua Institution.

In 1873, in the little town of Chautauqua, New York, two Methodist ministers, John Heyl Vincent (1832–1920) and Lewis Miller (1829–1899), developed a unique program of study that combined various nonreligious educational subjects with typical Sunday school topics. By 1874, their idea had become reality and the Chautauqua Institution offered a nine-week summer session of adult education courses. As the word spread, more and more people were drawn to the unusual school. They studied politics, culture, literature, and science, and they attended lectures and performances by the most esteemed intellectuals of the day, including feminist Susan B. Anthony (1820–1906); inventors Alexander Graham Bell (1847–1922) and Henry Ford (1863–1947); Helen Keller (1880–1968); and nine presidents of the United States.

The leaders of Chautauqua soon became aware that only a few of those Americans who were hungry for learning and cultural dialogue lived within traveling distance of New York. They mailed courses of home study to interested students and sent speakers traveling on a circuit to over two hundred Chautauquas around the country. Soon the arrival of the Chautauqua circuit was greeted with as much enthusiasm as a traveling circus. Lecturers, entertainers, politicians, and preachers made the rounds, bringing much-needed information, intellectual stimulation, and diversion to communities that had little contact with urban cultures.

Two major developments of the 1920s brought an end to the era of the Chautauqua: the automobile, which ended the isolation of American small towns; and the motion picture, which provided entertainment nationwide. However, New York's Chautauqua Institution still offers its dynamic study sessions, drawing more than 170,000 visitors from all over the country in 2011.

Tina Gianoulis

For More Information

Case, V., and R. O. Case. *We Called It Culture: The Story of Chautauqua.* Garden City, NY: Doubleday, 1948.

Chautauqua Institution. http://www.ciweb.org/ (accessed June 21, 2011).

Gould, J. E. *The Chautauqua Movement: An Episode in the Continuing American Revolution.* Albany: State University of New York Press, 1961.

Kostyal, K. M. "An Enduring Tradition." *National Geographic Traveler.* (May–June 1993): pp. 28–32.

Schultz, James R. *The Romance of Small-Town Chautauquas.* Columbia: University of Missouri Press, 2002.

Schurr, Cathleen. "Chautauqua: Yesterday and Today." *American History Illustrated* (July–August, 1992): pp. 40–47.

Simpson, Jeffrey. *Chautauqua: An American Utopia.* New York: Harry N. Abrams, 1999.

Coney Island

For poor and working-class New York City dwellers in decades past, a luxury resort vacation was a fantasy, an indulgence available only to the

New Yorkers enjoy a day at Coney Island in the late 1930s. © WILLARD R. CULVER/NGS IMAGE COLLECTION/THE ART ARCHIVE/ART RESOURCE, NY.

wealthy. But almost any New Yorker could travel to Coney Island, a five-mile-long sandy strip in the southern part ofBrooklyn. Once there, they could frolic in the Atlantic Ocean and build sand castles, dine on **hot dogs** (see entry under 1900s—Food and Drink in volume 1), and ride on **roller coasters** (see entry under 1900s—The Way We Lived in volume 1) and carousels.

Actually, Coney Island had initially attracted well-to-do Manhattanites. In the 1840s, steamships began bringing visitors to its beach; two decades later, horse cars made excursions there. In the 1860s and 1870s, large luxurious resort hotels were built. Given its accessibility, however, Coney Island eventually became a desirable destination for all New Yorkers. Bridge construction between Manhattan and Brooklyn and the development of the New York City subway system in the late nineteenth and early twentieth centuries allowed urban dwellers from all walks of life easy access to Coney Island. Soon, it became a haven for the masses, with its beach becoming, on a sweltering summer day, the most densely populated strip in the world.

According to legend, Charles Feltman (1841–1910) invented the hot dog on Coney Island in 1867. Coney Island's delights included the construction of its first carousel in 1875 and of the first American roller coaster, the Switchback Railway, in 1884. By 1886, Coney Island could boast of three racetracks, making it a horse-racing center. Captain Paul Boyton (1848–1924) bought the land for Sea Lion Park in 1895. The park was the world's first outdoor, enclosed (fenced in) amusement park. It had the first Shoot-the-Chutes ride in America. It was remodeled into a state-of-the-art theme park in 1903 and renamed Luna Park. On opening day, Luna Park attracted forty-three thousand paying customers.

In 1897, the rival Steeplechase Park opened. Its centerpiece was the Steeplechase Race Course, on which couples raced one another atop wooden horses-on-wheels. Steeplechase Park burned down in 1907 but was rebuilt the following year and remained in operation until 1964. Meanwhile, Luna Park fell into decline. It burned down in 1944, and five years later its land became a parking lot. A third Coney Island amusement park, named Dreamland, opened in 1904 but burned to the ground in 1911.

In 1923, the first section of Coney Island's boardwalk opened. Four years later came the eighty-five-foot-high Cyclone, the area's most famous roller coaster. On July 4, 1955, a record 1.5 million bathers and fun seekers visited Coney Island, yet ten years later, Coney was in decline as an amusement area. In recent decades, while still attracting the newest wave of poor immigrant New Yorkers, the surrounding neighborhood became a crime-riddled slum. However, 2001 marked the opening of KeySpan Park (now MCU Park), built on the former site of Steeplechase Park: a seventy-five-hundred-seat baseball stadium that houses the minor league Brooklyn Cyclones, the first professional baseball team to play in Brooklyn since 1957. The arrival of KeySpan Park and the Cyclones led many to hope that Coney Island would be a community ripe for revival. Development plans in the 2000s were bountiful—including one that would have had Coney Island as a key site for the 2012 **Olympics** (see entry under 1900s—Sports and Games in volume 1)—but New York City lost its bid to London, England, and little progress has been made on Concy Island.

Rob Edelman

For More Information

Denson, Charles. *Coney Island: Lost and Found.* Berkeley, CA: Ten Speed Press, 2002.

Glueck, Grace, and Paul Gardner. *Brooklyn: People and Places, Past and Present.* New York: Harry Abrams, 1991.

Immerso, Michael. *Coney Island: The People's Playground.* New Brunswick, NJ: Rutgers University Press, 2002.

Kasson, John F. *Amusing the Million: Coney Island at the Turn of the Century.* New York: Hill and Wang, 1978.

McCullough, Edo. *Good Old Coney Island: A Sentimental Journey into the Past.* New York: Scribner, 1957.

Register, Woody. *The Kid of Coney Island: Fred Thompson and the Rise of American Amusements.* New York: Oxford University Press, 2001.

Stanton, Jeffrey. *Coney Island History Site.* http://www.westland.net/coneyisland/ (accessed June 21, 2011).

Dancing

Dancing—rhythmically moving the body, especially the feet, to the sound of music—is a long-treasured social activity and a significant aspect of cultures around the world. People of all ages dance for many reasons: as an act of celebration, at weddings and proms; as an act of recreation or as socialization linked to courtship, in dance halls, nightclubs, discos, and high school gyms; and as a religious or tribal rite, with participants occasionally garbed in elaborate costumes. In the United States,

Famous husband-and-wife dance team Vernon and Irene Castle in the early twentieth century. © BETTMANN/CORBIS.

dancing is primarily a social activity. As popular music, as well as popular culture, evolved through the decades, a range of dance styles and crazes have emerged.

Immigrants who came to the United States, from the nation's beginnings to the present day, brought with them native dances that remained a rich part of their cultures. Early popular dances included folk dances, most often done in groups, and ballroom dances such as the waltz, which was imported from Europe. All of these were formal dances, which depended upon learning a pattern of movements or steps. Some dances remain linked to their ethnic origins. For example, Polish Americans perform versions of the polka, a fast-paced dance developed in Bohemia during the early nineteenth century. Polka parties and competitions continue to flourish in Polish American communities to this very day. At the same time, as many early immigrant groups began to meet at social events, their dances became intermingled, leading to the creation of the American square dance. The square dance was a folk dance hybrid that became a common recreational activity for settlers as they headed west during the nineteenth century. Still other dances originated in North America. One was the cakewalk, created in the nineteenth century by plantation slaves. The cakewalk combined a straight, firm body and a quasi-shuffling movement with the legs.

Through the end of the nineteenth century, ballroom and square dances were the most popular forms of American dance. However, with the emergence of ragtime music in the 1890s came a new, less-formal style of dance, based more on freely moving one's body to the sound of the music. One dance employing this style was the one-step, so named because one quick walking step accompanied each beat of the music. The one-step generated other dance variations, including the turkey-trot, the grizzly bear, the bunny hug, and the Boston dip. The celebrated husband-and-wife dance team of Vernon (1887–1918) and Irene (1893–1969) Castle fashioned the one-step into the castle walk, which became popular across America. Another one-step offshoot was the two-step, which was accompanied by ragtime and, eventually, by swing music.

The most popular early twentieth-century dance, however, was the fox-trot, a one-step variation. The fox-trot became fashionable because it combined slow and quick steps, allowing for an increased diversity of dance-floor movement. With the Roaring Twenties, and America's distancing itself from the prudery (excessive attention to modesty or what is considered proper behavior) of the Victorian Era, came the popularity of the **Charleston** (see entry under 1920s—The Way We Lived in volume 2), an energetic dance distinguished by a twisting step. The Charleston is as much an artifact of 1920s American culture as **Prohibition** (the banning of alcohol; see entry under 1920s—The Way We Lived in volume 2) and speakeasies (places where alcohol was illegally sold). The Charleston, along with other dances of the period, including the shimmy and the black bottom, were variations of the fox-trot.

In the 1930s, swing music, which evolved from **jazz** (see entry under 1900s—Music in volume 1), came to the forefront of popular culture. At the time, America was a segregated society (one divided socially by race). Swing music was performed by dance-band orchestras (known as big bands) that were groundbreaking in that they occasionally brought together white and black musicians. Swing music is lively and danceable and, consequently, various dance crazes evolved in response to its popularity. The first was the lindy hop, an acrobatic dance that originated in Harlem during the late 1920s and was refined by dancers at Harlem's Savoy Ballroom. The jitterbug, an even more physically animated dance, grew out of the lindy hop, and was a favorite between the late 1930s and the end of World War II (1939–45). By the 1950s, the popularity of swing music had subsided, yet the jitterbug and its various offshoots still were embraced by teenagers, who danced them to the sounds of early **rock and roll** (see entry under 1950s—Music in volume 3), music that combined elements of **country music** and of **rhythm and blues** (see these entries under 1940s—Music in volume 3).

In the early 1960s, dancing in America was revolutionized by the twist. In 1960, singer Chubby Checker (1941–) recorded a song titled "The Twist," and a dance craze was born. In order to "do the twist," dancers stood in place and rotated shoulders and hips in opposite directions, often switching their weight from one foot to another. However, they did not touch. Before the twist, the act of dancing required a partner, whom you held in your arms while swaying across the dance floor or at least touched while twirling to the beat of the music. The appeal of the twist signaled a major evolution in dancing. Because of the lack of physical contact, dancing became more of an individual pursuit. Countless 1960s and post-1960s dances were performed by standing in place and moving one's upper body and arms, but not necessarily the feet. Although dance partners maintained eye contact, they hardly touched. The limbo rock, the mashed potato, the watusi, the pony, and the Bristol stomp were a few post-twist dances that, like the twist, won popularity with the emergence of a hit record.

Other favored twentieth-century dances have been Afro-Latin–based. The first was the tango, which created a sensation in 1913 and remained popular off and on through the century. Other Afro-Latin dances include the rumba, the samba, the mambo, the cha-cha, and salsa. In the 1970s, the hustle and disco (the latter not only a dance but an attitude, as well as a style of music and dress) emerged from New York City dance clubs and won widespread popularity. ***Saturday Night Fever*** (1977; see entry under 1970s—Film and Theater in volume 4), a smash-hit movie starring John Travolta (1954–), helped to popularize **disco** (see entry under 1970s—Music in volume 4). The film and disco itself are as closely linked to late-1970s American culture as the Charleston is to the 1920s.

In the 1980s and 1990s, the fashionableness of **rap and hip hop** (see entry under 1980s—Music in volume 5) music, which originally came forth in opposition to the increasing commercialization of rock music, resulted in the creation of a new dance style, known as break dancing. In break dancing, solo dancers performed dazzling gymnastic routines that derived from a combination of martial arts and the character of Robot on *Soul Train* (1971–2006), an African American music-and-dance-oriented television show. Break dancing quickly became mainstream, however, and was spotlighted in another hit movie, *Flashdance* (1983).

In the late 1990s, partner dancing and step-dancing enjoyed a revival with a renewed interest in **big band** (see entry under 1930s—Music in volume 2) music and swing dancing as well as in square dancing and line dancing. In recent years, hip-hop culture has continued to generate many new dancing styles, dominating popular dance, especially among teens.

Rob Edelman

For More Information

Cohen, Selma Jeanne, ed. *International Encyclopedia of Dance.* New York: Oxford University Press, 1998.

Erenberg, Lewis A. *Swingin' the Dream: Big Band Jazz and the Rebirth of American Culture.* Chicago: University of Chicago Press, 1998.

Hager, Steven. *Hip Hop: The Illustrated History of Break Dancing, Rap Music, and Graffiti.* New York: St. Martin's Press, 1984.

Stearns, Marshall, and Jean Stearns. *Jazz Dance: The Story of American Vernacular Dance.* New York: Macmillan, 1968.

Stowe, David. *Swing Changes.* Cambridge, MA: Harvard University Press, 1994.

Electric Appliances

Perhaps nothing has changed everyday life within the American household more than the invention of electric household appliances. Within the first few decades of the twentieth century, most homes in the United States gained access to electricity, and inventors created and improved many devices that used this new power. The aim of these new electric devices was to shorten the time and decrease the effort required to maintain the household.

Before the introduction of electricity and running water, household jobs such as cooking, cleaning, and laundry provided full-time work for the women and children of the family. Laundry required a full day of hauling water in washtubs, scrubbing clothes on ridged metal boards called washboards, and hanging clean clothes out to dry in the sun. Clothes were then ironed with heavy flatirons, which were heated on wood-burning stoves. Cooking, too, was a highly skilled and time-consuming operation, involving baking breads and cakes in wood-stove ovens, and canning and preserving foods for future use.

In 1879, Thomas A. Edison (1847–1931) invented the electric light bulb, and soon after he helped build the first electricity generating plant in New York City. As electricity began to find its way into American homes, inventors began to create new uses for it, and American consumers were ready to try these new inventions. In 1908, janitor James M. Spangler invented the first electric vacuum cleaner. By 1919, the Eureka Vacuum Company was producing two thousand vacuum machines per day. In 1913, the home **refrigerator** (see entry under 1910s—The Way We Lived in volume 1) was invented. By 1931, over one million refrigerators were manufactured and sold. Everyone wanted to own one of the new washing machines, invented in the 1920s, even though they had to be filled and emptied by hand and the clothes fed, piece by piece, into the wringer on top. The fully automatic washer was not developed until the 1940s. In the 1980s, electronic components such as microprocessors made electric appliances even "smarter," with programmable timers and more variety of features. For some, however, efficiency was more important than convenience. In the early 1990s, the Environmental Protection Agency created the Energy Star Program to help consumers identify energy-efficient appliances.

Although electric appliances changed the housewife's labor considerably, they did not necessarily decrease the amount of time she spent doing housework. In 1924, the average homemaker spent fifty-two hours a week doing housework, while in 1966, surrounded by laborsaving devices, she spent fifty-five hours per week. One reason for this is that, as appliances made cleaning easier, people began to expect more from those who kept the house. For example, whereas laundry was previously washed once a week and clothes worn several days before being laundered, modern housekeepers may do laundry every day because family members wear an item only once before washing it.

Tina Gianoulis

For More Information

"American-Made: Turn of the Century Household Items." *American Heritage* (Vol. 31, June–July 1980): pp. 50–58.

National Academy of Engineering. "Household Appliances." *Greatest Engineering Achievements of the 20th Century.* http://www.greatachievements. org/?id=2963 (accessed June 21, 2011).

Shapiro, Laura. "Household Appliances: How Appliances Have Changed Housework." *Newsweek* (Vol. 130, no. 24, Winter 1997/98): pp. 36–40.

Strasser, Susan. *Never Done: A History of American Housework.* New York: Henry Holt, 1982.

Evangelism
. . . .

Evangelism, or enthusiastic preaching of the Christian gospel, has always played an important role in U.S. Protestantism, as in the Great Awakening of colonial days or the Methodist camp meetings on the frontier in the nineteenth century. In the twentieth century, evangelism often took the form of elaborate crusades organized by such preachers as **Billy Sunday** (1862–1935; see entry under 1900s—The Way We Lived

Husband-and-wife televangelists Jim and Tammy Faye Bakker speak to their PTL Network television audience in 1986.
© AP IMAGES/LOU KRASY.

in volume 1), Oral Roberts (1918–2009), or Billy Graham (1918–), or, later, in the multimedia productions of "televangelists" like Pat Robertson (1930–) with his *700 Club,* Jim Bakker (1940–) and his wife, Tammy Faye Bakker (1942–2007), with their PTL Network, and Jerry Falwell (1933–2007) with his Moral Majority.

While most Christians, including mainstream Protestants, Roman Catholics, and Orthodox believers, affirm baptism as a prerequisite for church membership, many evangelicals demand a "born-again" experience in which an already baptized Christian undergoes a personal experience with Jesus Christ. To these believers, evangelism involves more than just bringing information about Christ and his teachings; it demands an ongoing process of keeping believers enthusiastic about their faith. Evangelical crusades in large stadiums or on television are viewed by their organizers as revival meetings, designed to give already baptized Christians a chance to reaffirm their faith and be reassured about their salvation.

As U.S. society became more urbanized and educated during the twentieth century, some religious leaders feared that it was becoming secularized as well, a phenomenon in which religious values lose their power to influence individuals and the culture at large. This motivated evangelists such as Sunday and Graham to organize tent meetings or crusades that moved from city to city with elaborate programs that included choirs and music, fellowship, personal counseling, and an "altar call" in which people were asked to come forward to reaffirm their faith publicly. The centerpiece of these crusades was always a rousing sermon preached with grand oratorical flourishes, often warning of hellfire and damnation, but also describing the joys of heavenly bliss.

Over the years, critics often charged that evangelism in its worst aspects bred a corrupt system that exploited sincere believers for money or power, as described by Sinclair Lewis (1885–1951) in his 1927 novel *Elmer Gantry*. In more recent years, revelations of sexual and financial misdeeds by some television evangelists, such as Bakker and Falwell, have confirmed these suspicions. Among U.S. evangelists of the twentieth and twenty-first centuries, Graham, consulted by U.S. presidents for spiritual advice—including President **Barack Obama** (1961–; see entry under 2000s—The Way We Lived in volume 6) in 2010)—remains evangelism's most prominent role model of moral and intellectual integrity.

Edward Moran

For More Information

Ahlstrom, Sidney. *A Religious History of the American People.* 2nd ed. New Haven, CT: Yale University Press, 2004.

Hardman, Keith. *Seasons of Refreshing: Evangelism and Revivals in America.* Grand Rapids, MI: Baker Books, 1994.

Ferris Wheel

Long a popular ride at state fairs and **amusement parks** (see entry under 1950s—The Way We Lived in volume 3), the Ferris wheel is a tall, upright wheel with seats suspended around its rim. Mounted on a fixed structure, the wheel rotates while the swinging seats remain basically parallel to the ground, allowing riders to enjoy panoramic views of the surrounding area. During the twentieth century, Ferris wheels dominated the midways at amusement parks and state fairs in small towns and rural areas throughout the United States as riders sought rare bird's-eye views of the surrounding landscapes.

The Ferris wheel is named for U.S. engineer George Washington Gale Ferris (1859–1896), who had installed the first ride at Chicago's Columbian Exposition in 1893. It was 250 feet (76 meters) high and weighed 4,800 tons. Its axis (the shaft around which the wheel spun) was the largest single piece of forged steel that had been made up to that time. Two 1,000-horsepower engines powered the wheel, which had thirty-six wooden cars capable of holding sixty people apiece, each of whom paid fifty cents for one ride. The device, which symbolized American engineering ingenuity, has been described as "Chicago's answer to the Eiffel Tower," a much taller structure that had been the focal point of the Paris Exposition of 1889. The Chicago Ferris wheel was moved to St. Louis, Missouri, for the 1904 exposition there, and was finally scrapped in 1906.

Since that time, Ferris wheel builders have competed to build the biggest and best Ferris wheel. The record so far goes to the "Singapore Flyer," a $180 million structure that took riders on a 30-minute "flight" 541 feet (163 meters) above Singapore's Marina Bay in 28 enclosed capsules when it was opened in 2008. As long as people enjoy the thrill of looking at the world from high above, there are sure to be Ferris wheels.

Edward Moran

A ride on the Ferris Wheel still makes for an enjoyable time at the fair. © MIKE GREENSLADE/ ALAMY.

For More Information

Anderson, Norman D., and Walter R. Brown. *Ferris Wheels: An Illustrated History.* New York: Pantheon Books, 1983.

"Chicago's Great Ferris Wheel of 1893." *Hyde Park Historical Society.* http:// www.hydeparkhistory.org/newsletter.html (accessed June 21, 2011).

Weingardt, Richard. *Circles in the Sky: The Life and Times of George Ferris.* Reston, VA: American Society of Civil Engineers, 2009.

"World's Top Ten Tallest Ferris Wheels." *Consumer Traveler.* http://www .consumertraveler.com/today/worlds-top-10-tallest-ferris-wheels/ (accessed June 21, 2011).

General Motors

General Motors (GM) was founded by Billy Durant (1861–1947) in 1908 with his merger of the Oldsmobile and Buick companies. He added Cadillac the next year and the company just kept on growing. GM was the first company to gross more than $1 billion in a year. It dominated the U.S. and world car markets for most of the twentieth century, while its management structure had a major influence on the way large corporations are run. Ford brought no-nonsense motoring to the masses, but GM made the automobile an international symbol of modern America. From finned Cadillacs to the iconic 1957 Chevy, from unwieldy muscle cars to **sport utility vehicles** (SUVs; see entry under 1980s—The Way We Lived in volume 5), GM has built many of the definitive American cars.

The 1912 Cadillac from General Motors. © CAR CULTURE/GETTY IMAGES.

Unlike Henry Ford (1863–1947), whose skill was in manufacturing, Durant was brilliant at striking deals. He started out with car manufacturers and soon added component suppliers so that he could control every aspect of the business. After Alfred Sloan (1875–1966) took over in 1920, GM's cars became statements about a person's social status, tastes, and desires. The Chevy was a cheap first car; then you worked your way up through Buick and Oldsmobile. A Cadillac was something to dream about. Until 1961, when television ads took over, road shows called "Motoramas" moved around the country selling GM cars and creating a "car culture." GM updated its models every year. They became more "space-age" and more powerful. But GM has sometimes gone too far in trying to sell its products. In 1949, along with several others, GM was convicted of criminal conspiracy to replace electric trams with GM buses in forty-five American cities.

The attack by consumer advocate Ralph Nader (1934–) on the unsafe Corvair in the 1960s began GM's slow decline. Emissions regulations, oil crises, and stiff competition all took their toll on GM's gas-guzzling model range. A sharply comic film *Roger and Me* (1989) by Michael Moore (c. 1954–) highlights the terrible human cost of GM's failure in the 1980s. In June 2009, GM was forced to file for bankruptcy and accept a multi-billion dollar bailout from the federal government. Although controversial at the time, the plan appeared to work after GM downsized, turned a profit again, and paid its debt to the government ahead of schedule. With interests in companies around the globe, in the twenty-first century GM remains one of the world's largest and most powerful auto manufacturers.

Chris Routledge

For More Information

General Motors. http://www.gm.com (accessed June 21, 2011).

Holstein, William J. *Why GM Matters: Inside the Race to Transform an American Icon.* New York: Walker, 2009.

Madsen, Axel. *The Deal Maker: How William C. Durant Made General Motors.* New York: Wiley, 1999.

Nader, Ralph, and Barbara Ehrenreich. *The Ralph Nader Reader.* New York: Seven Stories Press, 2000.

Pelfrey, William. *Billy, Alfred, and General Motors.* New York: AMACOM, 2006.

Sloan, Alfred P. *My Years with General Motors.* Garden City, NY: Doubleday, 1963.

Taylor, Alex. *Sixty to Zero: An Inside Look at the Collapse of General Motors—and the Detroit Auto Industry.* New Haven, CT: Yale University Press, 2010.

Hairstyles

The way that human beings wear their hair can have many meanings. Beyond conforming to the fashion of the day, a hairdo can be an expression of personal style as well as an indication of religious, cultural, and political beliefs. Because of this, society often has strict rules about how hair should be worn. Those who rebel against society often begin with what are considered outlandish hairstyles. It is no accident that institutions like armies and prisons often initiate new members by cutting off their hair, thus removing this means of individual self-expression and encouraging conformity. From the Biblical story of Samson, who lost his superhuman strength when his hair was cut, to the radical student movements of the 1970s, when men's long hair was considered a revolutionary statement, hair has often been given a far greater significance than any other bodily feature.

Preoccupation with the latest hairstyle is far from being only a modern concern. From earliest times, people have adorned their hair in a wide variety of ways for a wide variety of reasons. Hairstyle can indicate economic class and social status. For example, in the second century BCE, members of Egyptian nobility shaved their heads and wore wigs made from braided animal hair or palm fronds, often dyed in bright colors. Noble-women in eighteenth-century England wore powdered wigs that were up to four feet tall and elaborately decorated with stuffed birds and bowls of fruit. Hairstyles can also be practical. Like many modern men, Louis XIV (1638–1715) of France wore his large curled wig in the 1700s to hide his baldness.

The significance of hairstyles has changed through the ages. Short hair was considered a sign of power in ancient Rome, but by the middle ages, short hair had become a symbol of dishonor. In 1644, when the Manchus conquered China, they forced Chinese men to shave the tops of their heads and wear their hair in a long braid at the back, called a queue, as a sign of being a conquered people. By the 1900s, when the Manchus were ousted from power, the queue had become a symbol of Chinese cultural identity. Chinese men kept the queue even when they emigrated, and Chinese immigrants to the United States were often persecuted for wearing it.

In the United States, until the beginning of the twentieth century, most women wore their hair long and pinned up on their heads. With the suffrage movement of the early 1900s came the **flapper** (see entry under 1920s—Fashion in volume 2) style, and short, "bobbed" hair became the modern hairdo. Because caring for long hair is time consuming and identified with soft femininity, short hair has often become popular when women have been politically active. Although longer hair soon became popular again, and American soldiers during World War II (1939–45) sighed over pinups of actress Rita Hayworth (1918–1987) and her long, flowing curls, the working women of the 1940s wore shorter, more practical styles. After the war, as affluence returned and many longed for a return to "tradition," hairstyles became more elaborate. Many women wore curls held stiffly in place by permanents or hair spray or tall beehives held in place with bobby pins. There was a rebellious side to the 1950s, however, and while clean-cut American boys wore crew-cuts, the rebel in the leather jacket often sported a greased-back duck tail.

Soon, rebellion became revolution. From the **beatniks** (see entry under 1950s—Print Culture in volume 3) of the early 1960s to the **hippies** (see entry under 1960s—The Way We Lived in volume 4) of the late 1960s and 1970s, young people began to question society's values. Both men and women, especially those who identified with political movements for peace and justice, began to wear their hair long. At the same time, black Americans began to fight for **civil rights** (see entry under 1960s—The Way We Lived in volume 4) and an end to discrimination. Black people, who for decades had felt compelled to force their hair into styles meant for white European hair, began to let their hair grow naturally into a fluffy style they called the Afro. The **Broadway** (see entry under 1900s—Film and Theater in volume 1) musical *Hair* (see entry under 1960s—Film and Theater in volume 4), which debuted in 1968, made the connection between hairstyle and the challenges of an entire generation. This connection continued into the 1980s with the rise of the **punk** (see entry under 1970s—Music in volume 4) movement. Perhaps because the hippies of the 1960s had failed to revolutionize society, punks were less idealistic and angrier than the hippies had been, and their style was more extreme. Punks shaved parts of their hair off and dyed the rest in bright, unnatural reds, blues, and purples, using gel to shape it into spikes. The extreme style of the punks opened the door to a new freedom. While most people never adopted the punk look, hair fashions have continued to remain less conventional and more open to individual expression.

The importance of hair fashion has been dramatized in various films and plays, from the serious to the campy. The 1975 film *Shampoo,* directed by Hal Ashby (1936–1988), spoofs pretentious celebrity hair stylists. *Hairspray* (1988) by John Waters (1946–) humorously explores the often uncomfortable transition between the conservative 1950s and the radical 1960s. In the 1989 tearjerker *Steel Magnolias,* by Herbert Ross (1927–2001), Dolly Parton (1946–) plays the owner of a Southern beauty parlor, a time-honored institution of female bonding. In *Blow Dry* (2000), director Paddy Breathnach (1964–) documents the hilarious troubles of a Scottish hair-stylists competition.

Tina Gianoulis

For More Information

Coates, Simon. "Scissors or Swords: Social Aspects of Medieval Hair-styles." *History Today* (Vol. 49, no. 5, May 1999): pp. 7–15.

Doyle, Marian I. *An Illustrated History of Hairstyles, 1830–1930.* Atglen, PA: Schiffer, 2003.

Fiell, Charlotte. *Hairstyles: Ancient to Present.* London: Fiell, 2010.

"How Important Are Hairstyles in the Workplace?" *Jet* (Vol. 99, no. 26, June 11, 2001): pp. 36–39.

Lassieur, Allison. "Hair Time Line: Evolution of Hair Designs." *National Geographic World* (No. 278, October 1998): pp. 12–16.

Sherrow, Victoria. *Encyclopedia of Hair: A Cultural History.* Santa Barbara, CA: Greenwood, 2006.

Wilkinson, Brian. "Growing Dissent: The Politics of Hair." *Seventeen* (Vol. 49, no. 5, May 1990): pp. 98–100.

Postcards

The picture postcard, with a graphic image on one side and a blank space for a message and an address on the other, made its debut in the late nineteenth century. Before **telephones** (see entry under 1900s—The Way We Lived in volume 1) saw widespread use, the postcard provided a quick and inexpensive way of sending short messages, either for business or social purposes. For more than one hundred years, vacationers have typically mailed postcards of scenes from faraway destinations to impress the "folks back home," often accompanied with clichéd messages like "Having a wonderful time. Wish you were here." Another familiar phrase, "pretty as a postcard," has been used to describe a setting that is pretty enough to be featured on a postcard. Businesses have long used postcards for advertising purposes, and musicians or record labels commonly use them to promote new recordings or club appearances. Over the years, some artists and graphic designers have produced higher-quality images that are especially in demand by deltiologists, more commonly known as postcard collectors.

The government-issue "postcards" sold in post offices, with a stamp already printed on the address side and a blank side for a message, are technically known as "postal cards." Austria-Hungary issued the first one in 1869. It was not until 1898 that the United States permitted "private mailing cards" that could have an image on one side, with the other side reserved for the stamp and the address. Messages on such cards had to be written atop the picture until 1907, when the U.S. Post Office permitted the blank side to be divided into two sections: the left side for a message and the right side for the address and the stamp. This format is still the most commonly used.

Picture postcards were enormously popular during the first two decades of the twentieth century. It has been estimated that nearly a billion of them were produced in the United States during this period. Picture postcards offer a visual overview of American popular culture and a graphic archive of the institutions and tourist locations considered important in their day.

Edward Moran

For More Information

Carline, Richard. *Pictures in the Post: The Story of the Picture Postcard and Its Place in the History of Popular Art*. Philadelphia: Deltiologists of America, 1972.

Klamkin, Marian. *Picture Postcards*. New York: Dodd, Mead, 1974.

Morgan, Hal, and Andreas Brown. *Prairie Fires and Paper Moons: The American Photographic Postcard, 1900–1920*. Boston: David R. Godine, 1981.

O'Keeffe, Sara. "Postcard Types." *Smithsonian Libraries*. http://smithsonianlibraries.si.edu/smithsonianlibraries/2009/10/postcard-types.html (accessed June 20, 2011).

Ryan, Dorothy. *Picture Postcards in the United States, 1893–1918*. Updated ed. New York: Clarkson N. Potter, 1982.

Roller Coasters

Travelling at speeds of up to one hundred miles per hour, hundreds of feet up in the air, roller coasters are the most thrilling of all amusement

A bird's-eye view of a roller coaster at Six Flags Over Georgia. © JRC, INC./ALAMY.

rides. Whether strapped into a miniature "train," dangling chairlift style, or even standing up, roller coaster fans enjoy the sensation of not being in control. Besides being built for the enjoyment of enthusiasts, roller coasters are also objects of local pride. The famous wooden Coney Island Cyclone was a New York City landmark in the early twentieth century. In the 1920s, boardwalk roller coasters helped publicize beach resorts. In the twenty-first century, roller coasters are the centerpieces of all big amusement parks.

However intricate the twists, turns, and loops of the track might be, roller coasters are really very simple. The cars carry enough energy from the first big downhill to take them through the rest of the course. In the twenty-first century, the cars are often launched from the start, rather than climbing a slope, but the principle remains the same. With names like Cyclone, Fireball, Superman, and the Big One, roller-coaster design in the twenty-first century is a fusion of high-tech construction, computer control, and big talk. However, no modern roller coaster can match the scale or speed of the first American roller coaster. Built to carry coal from the mines in the mountains of Pennsylvania, the Mauch Chunk Switchback Railway became a tourist attraction in 1870 and operated safely until 1933. Passengers paid one dollar for the scenic twenty-mile ride up the mountain, where they could eat lunch at a hotel near the summit. On the terrifying return trip, the cars are reputed to have reached speeds of over one hundred miles per hour.

Although rickety wooden roller coasters are still in operation, steel roller coasters, pioneered by **Disney** (see entry under 1920s—Film and Theater in volume 2) in the 1950s, are the most common coasters today. They enable maneuvers such as "corkscrews," loops, and unsettling "inversions." Roller coasters will always be dangerous, because people instinctively react negatively to "negative Gs" (the feeling of weightlessness). Designers have pushed at the limits of safety, and mechanical failures occasionally happen. But part of the enjoyment of riding a "coaster" is being afraid while feeling just safe enough.

Chris Routledge

For More Information

Coker, Robert. *Roller Coasters: A Thrill Seeker's Guide to the Ultimate Scream Machines.* New York: Main Street, 2002.

RCDB: Roller Coaster Database. http://www.rcdb.com/ (accessed June 21, 2011).

Rutherford, Scott. *The American Roller Coaster.* Osceola, WI: Motorbooks International, 2000.

Throgmorton, Todd H. *Roller Coasters: United States and Canada.* 3rd ed. Jefferson, NC: McFarland, 2009.

Billy Sunday (1862–1935)

Billy Sunday was an early forerunner of the contemporary religious right. The most famous traveling **evangelist** (see entry on Evangelism under 1900s—The Way We Lived in volume 1) of his day, Sunday crusaded across the nation with performances that united fundamentalist religious teaching and conservative politics with good old-fashioned showmanship.

In his early career, Sunday was a womanizing professional **baseball** (see entry under 1900s—Sports and Games in volume 1) player who liked to drink and fight. However, after hearing the services of an

evangelistic group from the Pacific Garden Mission in Chicago, Illinois, in 1886, Sunday was converted. He gave up drinking, swearing, and womanizing and began offering inspirational talks to his young fans.

Sunday left baseball in 1891 and began a touring ministry four years later. Promoters hyped his appearances as if they were **vaudeville** (see entry under 1900s—Film and Theater in volume 1) shows. Musical entertainment was furnished by choirs and bands. Sunday—the star of the show—combined dramatic gestures and colorful language to preach against sin and for the need to right oneself with God. His preaching produced hundreds of thousands of converts. A staunch right-winger, he also brought politics into religion, advocating the outlawing of alcoholic beverages and the banning of teaching evolution in schools.

Rob Edelman

For More Information

Bruns, Roger. *Preacher: Billy Sunday and Big Time American Evangelism.* New York: W. W. Norton, 1992.

Dorsett, Lyle W. *Billy Sunday and the Redemption of Urban America.* New ed. Macon, GA: Mercer University Press, 2004.

Martin, Robert Francis. *Hero of the Heartland: Billy Sunday and the Transformation of American Society.* Bloomington: Indiana University Press, 2002.

Sunday, Billy. *The Sawdust Trail: Billy Sunday in His Own Words.* Iowa City: University of Iowa Press, 2005.

Telephone

Although there are others who claim to have done so first, the telephone was invented in 1875 by a Scot, Alexander Graham Bell (1847–1922). His invention allowed people to talk to one another across vast distances. Within twenty years, telephones were common in the homes of the wealthy in the United States and Europe. The laying of the first

Former pro ballplayer-turned-traveling-evangelist Billy Sunday in Boston in 1927. © THE ART ARCHIVE/CULVER PICTURES/ART RESOURCE, NY.

Alexander Graham Bell calls long distance to Chicago from New York with the newly invented telephone, October 12, 1893.
© THE ART ARCHIVE/CULVER PICTURES/ART RESOURCE, NY.

transatlantic telephone cable in 1956 began to create what is known as the "global village." In the twenty-first century, the principles of telephony invented by Bell are behind innovations such as fax machines and the **Internet** (see entry under 1990s—The Way We Lived in volume 5). Although telephone messages are now transmitted using satellites and digital signals, until recently the telephone remained much as Bell anticipated.

Like many other things, the telephone was invented partly by accident. In the 1870s, the telegraph was the quickest way of sending messages over a long distance. But Bell hoped to speed up the system by making it possible to send more than one message at a time. He created a device that could convert sounds into electrical pulses and transmit them down a wire. From there, it was a short step to developing a machine that could carry the human voice. He was issued patent number 174465 for his invention on March 7, 1876. Soon after, he made the first telephone call, commanding his assistant Thomas Augustus Watson (1854–1934), who was in the next room: "Mr. Watson, come here! I want you!"

Bell's invention transformed the way people thought about distance, travel, and their communities. The telephone opened the way for long-distance gossip in a way that was impossible by telegraph, the older method of sending messages, yet in many ways the changes brought by the telephone were subtle and gradual. For a start, it did not change much in the way of the physical environment. The device itself was always quite small, stuck out of the way in hallways and booths. Where the telephone had its greatest impact was on the structure of society itself. As home telephones became more affordable in the 1920s and 1930s, people began using them as part of their social lives. For some commentators, this marked the beginning of a trend towards people becoming more private and self-centered. For others, however, the telephone simply freed people from having to travel to deliver simple messages. Either way, the telephone changed the way people lived their lives.

The telephone led to the growth of a whole range of services never before available. Police and firefighters could be called by the public from special telephone boxes on the street. (As more and more people acquired telephones, this practice was replaced beginning in the 1960s by the 911 system of alerting emergency services.) Telephone companies began to offer "wake-up" calls and messaging services. "Cold calling," whereby a salesperson uses the phone book to find new customers, became a useful but hated way to find new business. In an effort to limit the number of sales calls to homes, consumers and the federal government created the

National Do-Not-Call List in 2003. The arts and the media also felt the effect. The TV or radio phone-in became a cheap way for broadcasters to fill airtime. The plots of **detective fiction** (see entry under 1930s—Print Culture in volume 2) of the 1930s and 1940s often rely on a well-timed telephone call. Comedy routines from the early days of film include telephone jokes. Even in the twenty-first century, the telephone is a source of humor in shows ranging from *The Simpsons* (see entry under 1980s—TV and Radio in volume 5) to *The Office*.

By the 1930s, most households in America at least had access to a telephone. People could be contacted more easily, and they in turn could make contact with the outside world. The trend continued throughout the twentieth century and into the twenty-first. By the 1980s, documents could be transmitted by fax while **personal computers** (see entry under 1970s—The Way We Lived in volume 4) "talked" to one another using modems that connected to telephone lines. Car telephones were available in the 1960s, but it was in the 1990s that hand-held mobile telephones became cheap enough for most people to own. They even became a fashion item. By the beginning of the twenty-first century, the video telephone had moved out of science fiction and into offices and some homes. **Cellular phones** (see entry under 1990s—The Way We Lived in volume 5), **satellite** (see entry under 1950s—The Way We Lived in volume 3) links, **smart phones** (see entry under 2000s—The Way We Lived in volume 6) and the Internet meant that in 2010 there were few places on earth where one could not be reached by telephone.

Voicemail, answering machines, automated information services, and a host of other systems have made the telephone the most powerful communication tool of the early twenty-first century. But perhaps the best measure of the telephone's importance is that it is taken for granted. Telephones work behind the scenes so that by 2002, more than half of all telephone calls took place between machines, with no human intervention. In the twenty-first century, not having access to a telephone is a serious form of deprivation, and the multibillion-dollar telecommunications industry is fundamental to the world economy. Whether for medical emergencies, high-powered business deals, or ordering **pizza** (see entry under 1940s—Food and Drink in volume 3), the telephone remains an essential part of twenty-first century life.

Chris Routledge

For More Information

Coe, Lewis. *Telephone and Its Several Inventors: A History.* Jefferson, NC: McFarland, 1995.

Fischer, Claude S. *America Calling: A Social History of the Telephone to 1940.* Berkeley: University of California Press, 1992.

Gearhart, Sarah. *The Telephone.* New York: Atheneum Books for Young Readers, 1999.

Mercer, David. *The Telephone: The Life Story of a Technology.* Westport, CT: Greenwood, 2006.

Shulman, Seth. *The Telephone Gambit: Chasing Alexander Graham Bell's Secret.* New York: W. W. Norton, 2008.

Stern, Ellen, and Emily Gwathmey. *Once Upon a Telephone: An Illustrated Social History.* New York: Harcourt Brace, 1994.

World's Fairs

During the nineteenth and twentieth centuries, a series of international exhibitions in major cities around the globe attracted millions of visitors to national and corporate pavilions that demonstrated their industrial and cultural achievements. Many products now in common use were first seen by the general public at world's fairs, such as the **telephone** (see entry under 1900s—The Way We Lived in volume 1), in Philadelphia, Pennsylvania (1876); the **phonograph** (see entry under 1900s—Music in volume 1), in Paris, France (1889); incandescent lights and the **Ferris wheel** (see entry under 1900s—The Way We Lived in volume 1), in Chicago, Illinois (1893); the **ice-cream cone** (see entry under 1900s— Food and Drink in volume 1), in St. Louis, Missouri (1904); **television** (see entry under 1940s—TV and Radio in volume 3), in New York (1939); and the **IBM** (see entry under 1980s—Commerce in volume 5) computer, in New York (1964).

The first modern world's fair was London's Crystal Palace Exhibition of 1851, organized under the leadership of Prince Albert (1819–1861). The first in the United States was Philadelphia's Centennial Exposition of 1876, which commemorated the one hundredth anniversary of national independence. Chicago's Columbian Exposition of 1893 marked the rebirth of the city after a fire destroyed much of it in 1871; it was famous for its "White City" that inspired the City Beautiful movement in architecture and city planning. In 1933, Chicago's Century of Progress fair celebrated the city's centennial. The 1958

Brussels World's Fair celebrated Europe's revival after World War II (1939–45).

With its "World of Tomorrow" theme, the New York's World's Fair that opened in 1939 offered an optimistic view of the future to Depression-weary visitors. The Futurama exhibit of **General Motors** (see entry under 1900s—The Way We Lived in volume 1) imagined the United States as it might appear in 1960, complete with television, an elaborate **highway system** (see entry under 1950s—The Way We Lived in volume 3), high-rise urban centers, **suburbs** (see entry under 1950s—The Way We Lived in volume 3), and modern farms. The fair's symbols were the Trylon and Perisphere, an obelisk next to a sphere that included a prototypical utopian city called "Democracity." Unlike earlier fairs, the New York World's Fair of 1964 had few national pavilions, with most of the exhibits instead constructed by U.S. corporations to promote their products and images.

World's fairs in the later twentieth century had far less of an impact on the general public, for whom television, the **Internet** (see entry under 1990s—The Way We Lived in volume 5), and theme parks already provided much of the information and entertainment once offered by international expositions.

Edward Moran

For More Information

"A Brief History of World's Fairs." *Time.com.* http://www.time.com/time/photogallery/0,29307,1986326,00.html (accessed June 20, 2011).

Allwood, John. *The Great Exhibitions: 150 Years.* 2nd ed. London: Exhibition Consultants, 2001.

Badger, Reid. *The Great American Fair: The World's Columbia Exposition and American Culture.* Chicago: Nelson-Hall, 1979.

Findling, John E. *Chicago's Great World's Fairs.* Manchester, England: Manchester University Press, 1994.

Findling, John E., and Kimberly D. Pelle. *Encyclopedia of World's Fairs and Expositions.* 2nd ed. Jefferson, NC: McFarland, 2008.

Harrison, Helen. *Dawn of a New Day: The New York World's Fair, 1939/40.* New York: New York University Press, 1980.

Rydell, Robert W. *Fair America: World's Fairs in the United States.* Washington, DC: Smithsonian Institution Press, 2000.

1910s

A Tumultuous Decade

The 1910s were a period of great tumult and change in the United States. The decade began at a time of peace and prosperity. America found itself the richest nation in the world, thanks largely to the growth of huge companies that sold goods all over the world. The president, William Howard Taft (1857–1930), had succeeded Theodore Roosevelt (1858–1919) as the leader of the Republican Party, which offered its support to American businesses. Many Americans enjoyed improved living standards, as more people owned cars and used electricity in their homes with every passing year.

Great disruptions soon came in politics, international affairs, and the economy, however. In the presidential elections of 1912, Roosevelt left the Republican Party to become the nominee of the Progressive Party, the first serious challenger to the two-party system in many years. He and Socialist Party candidate Eugene V. Debs (1855–1926) helped draw votes away from Taft, which in turn led to the election of Democratic candidate Woodrow Wilson (1856–1924), a champion of progressive political reforms. Wilson led government efforts to reform the federal banking system, regulate large businesses, provide aid to farmers, and enact a progressive income tax (which meant higher tax rates for those who earned more). During the decade, four constitutional amendments were also adopted, calling for direct election of U.S. senators, the

1910s At a Glance

WHAT WE SAID:
Slang was still a decade away from being a prominent part of popular culture. One slogan did, however, enter the American lexicon:

"When It Rains, It Pours" (1911): This advertising slogan let consumers know that Morton salt would not clump up and stick together, but it was made popular in a different way. The expression came to mean that misfortune is rarely manifested as a single event.

WHAT WE READ:
The Rosary (1909): The best-selling novel of 1910, this sentimental romance was written by an English woman named Florence Barclay. The novel was translated into eight languages and had sold over a million copies by 1921.

Books by Theodore Dreiser: Dreiser became the dominant American realist writer with several books published during the decade: *Jennie Gerhardt* (1911), *Sister Carrie* (1911 [first published in 1900 but suppressed by the publisher]), *The Financier* (1912), *The Titan* (1914), and *The "Genius"* (1915).

O Pioneers! (1913) and *My Antonia* (1918): Author Willa Cather gained fame for her portrayals of people trying to survive in the harsh settings of the American prairie.

Over the Top (1917): Written by Arthur Guy Empey, who served with the British army in the trenches on the Western Front, this war book introduced Americans to the horrors of World War I in Europe.

The Rise of David Levinsky (1917): Abraham Cahan's story told of a Jewish immigrant's experience breaking into the world of business in New York City.

The U.P. Trail (1918): Written by one of the most popular writers of the decade, Zane Grey, this Western tells the story of the creation of the transcontinental railroad. Grey also published such favorites as *Riders of the Purple Sage* (1912), *The Lone Star Ranger: A Romance of the Border* (1915), and *The Desert of Wheat* (1919).

Magazines: *Saturday Evening Post, Collier's Weekly, Cosmopolitan,* and *American Magazine* were among the most popular magazines of the decade.

WHAT WE WATCHED:
Vaudeville shows and musical revues: These forms of entertainment, which began in the 1900s, continued their popularity into the 1910s, despite the rise of movies. The annual *Ziegfeld Follies,* with its stage full of chorus girls, was one of the biggest draws in New York, while traveling vaudeville shows brought variety to American cities large and small.

progressive income tax, the right to vote for women, and Prohibition (a ban on the sale of alcoholic beverages).

American foreign policy, which had long been concerned with having the United States avoid "entanglement" in foreign conflicts, also changed dramatically during the decade. In 1914, most of Europe

***Queen Elizabeth* (1913):** The first four-reel (sixty-minute) film, starring Sarah Bernhardt, allowed moviemakers to tell a full-length dramatic story.

***The Adventures of Kathlyn* (1913):** The first in a thirteen-part serial—a series of movies about one character or set of characters—starred Kathlyn Williams, who was billed as "The Girl without Fear." The most popular serial of the decade was *The Perils of Pauline,* which was released in biweekly installments in 1914.

***Quo Vadis* (1913):** The first eight-reel (two-hour) film, made in Italy, was shown in the United States.

***Gertie the Dinosaur* (1914):** This animated silent film featuring a female dinosaur, created by comic strip artist Winsor McCay, is considered the forerunner to modern animated films, including Walt Disney's *Steamboat Willie* (1929).

***Tillie's Punctured Romance* (1914):** Directed by Mack Sennett, known as the father of film comedy, this six-reel comedy was one of the most popular films starring the Keystone Kops, a group of inept policeman. It starred stage actress Marie Dressler and featured Charlie Chaplin and Mabel Normand in supporting roles.

***The Birth of a Nation* (1915):** The decade's most controversial film, directed by D. W. Griffith, tells the story of the American Civil War (1861–65) and Reconstruction (1865–77), and presents favorable depictions of the racist group the Ku Klux Klan. The film caused great controversy and was banned from many theaters.

***Intolerance* (1916):** Directed by D. W. Griffith, this film is considered the first great American epic. Over three-and-one-half hours long and with a huge cast, the story tells of the impact of historical events on ordinary people.

Western films directed by Thomas Ince: His action-packed movies about cowboys and villains on the frontier incl uded *War on the Plains* (1912), *Custer's Last Raid* (1912), *The Bargain* (1914), *Hell's Hinges* (1916), and *The Gun Fighter* (1917).

Movies about World War I: Moviegoers enjoyed such films as *War Is Hell* (1914), *The War Bride's Secret* (1916), *The Fall of a Nation* (1916), *The Little American* (1917)—directed by Cecil B. DeMille and starring Mary Pickford—and *The Kaiser, Beast of Berlin* (1918).

WHAT WE LISTENED TO:

John Philip Sousa: The famed bandmaster toured the world with his one-hundred-piece marching band in 1910.

Tin Pan Alley music: Professional sheet music companies located in New York City's Tin Pan Alley produced some of the decade's most popular music, including Irving Berlin's "Alexander's Ragtime Band" (1911), George M. Cohan's war-themed "Over There" (1917), Richard Whiting's "Till We Meet Again" (1917), and George Gershwin's "Swanee" (1919).

● ● ● ● ➤

became involved in World War I (1914–18), a terrible conflict that would claim nearly nine million lives. The United States tried to stay neutral because it had economic ties to countries on both sides of the fight, but German attacks on U.S. shipping and the United States' historic friendship with England and France drew the Americans into the

1910s At a Glance (continued)

The Victrola: The Victor Talking Machine Company modified Thomas Edison's phonograph into the Victrola in 1915, which soon became the most popular American record player. The first Victrolas, with their large, trumpet-like megaphones, were quite expensive, however, and did not gain wide popularity until the 1920s.

The Dixieland Jazz Band: This ensemble toured the United States in 1916 and became the first musicians to make a jazz recording in 1917.

War-influenced music: In 1918, World War I influenced popular music, resulting in songs such as "Would You Rather Be a Colonel with an Eagle on Your Shoulder or a Private with a Chicken on Your Knee?," "I'd Like to See the Kaiser with a Lily in His Hand," and "General Pershing Will Cross the Rhine."

"Oh, How I Hate to Get Up in the Morning": Irving Berlin's lighthearted portrayal of military life was one of the most popular songs of 1919.

African American musical groups: Several toured the country, introducing Americans to new musical styles that would become jazz and the blues. These groups included the Superior Orchestra, the Onward Brass Band, Ma Rainey's Georgia Jazz Band, and a band led by Jelly Roll Morton.

WHO WE KNEW:
John Dewey (1859–1952): This American philosopher, educator, and psychologist is widely credited for shaping the school system that continues to educate American children today. Dewey believed that American democracy would work best if all students were given an education that balanced academic learning and vocational training. His book *Democracy and Education* (1916) is still hailed as a guide to educating students capable of contributing to a democratic society.

William C. "Billy" Durant (1861–1947): Billy Durant emerged as one of the best-known businessmen of the decade thanks to his ambitious leadership of the car manufacturer General Motors, for a time the world's largest industrial company. Durant formed General Motors in 1908, and by 1910 the growing company had swallowed up thirty smaller companies, including eleven automakers. After losing control of the company in 1911, Durant regained his position in 1915 and rebuilt the company to become an industry leader by 1919, when it was valued at $1 billion. Durant was known as a great innovator in the automobile industry.

Marcus Garvey (1877–1940): An important black leader during the 1910s and 1920s, Marcus Garvey was born in Jamaica and traveled widely before arriving in America in 1916. With the influence of black leaders Booker T. Washington and W. E. B. DuBois fading, Garvey encouraged African Americans to join together to build businesses or, if whites would not accept them, leave the country in a "Back to Africa" movement. Garvey formed the Universal

war against Germany in 1917. Two million American soldiers served overseas and one hundred thousand of them died, half of them from disease. Although President Wilson hoped that American involvement in the war would "make the world safe for democracy" and lead to more

Negro Improvement Association and published a leading African American weekly paper, the *Negro World.* Though Garvey's plans saw little success, he was later hailed by black cultural theorist Malcolm X as a visionary.

W. C. Handy (1873–1958): Known as the "Father of the Blues," this African American musician toured with a minstrel show before deciding to specialize in a new form of music known as the blues. In 1912, Handy published his first song, "Memphis Blues," and he followed that in 1914 with "St. Louis Blues," the most recorded song in musical history. Handy became the first black performer to play in New York's Carnegie Hall in 1928.

Shoeless Joe Jackson (1887–1951): One of the most tragic figures in the history of baseball, Jackson rose from humble beginnings in the rural South to become one of baseball's greatest hitters while playing for the Cleveland Indians and the Chicago White Sox. Only Babe Ruth was thought to be a better hitter. But Jackson's reputation was forever ruined when he was implicated in the "Black Sox" scandal in which eight Chicago White Sox players were paid to lose the 1919 World Series.

Mary Pickford (1892–1979): This popular actress, known as "America's Sweetheart," starred in such films as *The Poor Little Rich Girl* (1917) and *Rebecca of Sunnybrook Farm* (1917). The first American actress to achieve international stardom, she was mobbed by fans at public appearances and signed a $1 million contract in 1916. Along with husband Douglas Fairbanks, D. W. Griffith, and Charlie Chaplin, Pickford established the United Artists movie company.

Margaret Sanger (1879–1966): An outspoken proponent of the rights of women, Margaret Higgins Sanger was prevented from becoming a doctor because of her gender, but she went on to become a pioneer in birth control practices for women. As a nurse, Sanger was alarmed at how many women saw their health and welfare endangered by their failure to avoid unwanted pregnancies. In the 1910s, she lectured widely about sexual practices, published a magazine called *The Woman Rebel,* and opened the nation's first birth-control clinic in 1916. She founded the National Birth Control League in 1914 and later was involved in creating the Planned Parenthood Foundation of America. By the 1950s, Sanger was involved in the development of the first birth control pill.

Jim Thorpe (1888–1953): Frequently named as one of the greatest athletes of all time, Native American Jim Thorpe played a variety of sports in his long career. He first came to fame as a college football player at Carlisle University. In 1912, he set a world record in the decathlon at the Summer Olympic Games in Stockholm, Sweden. Thorpe then played professional baseball for the New York Giants, the Cincinnati Reds, and the Boston Braves, and professional football for the Canton Bulldogs and the New York Giants.

American engagement overseas, senators in Congress refused to ratify Wilson's peace treaty.

The war highlighted some of the economic and racial issues facing the country. American businesses were growing increasingly dependent on foreign trade (selling goods to foreign countries). War had threatened foreign trade, and some said that war was fought to keep foreign markets open to American business. American workers, especially those in labor unions, continued to fight for improved wages and working conditions, though strikes ended once America entered World War I. With many workers leaving to join the armed forces, black workers gained access to many jobs they had been barred from before. The existence of jobs in wartime industries in the North called forth a "great migration" of blacks from the South.

Once the war ended, labor unrest grew. In 1919, hundreds of thousands of American workers walked off their jobs in steel, coal mining, and other industries. Police went on strike in Boston, Massachusetts, and there was a general strike involving all of the workers in Seattle, Washington. Black workers were outraged at being thrown out of jobs they had recently gained. This wave of strikes and protests scared businessmen and politicians. Police cracked down on strikers, causing riots in several cities. In what was known as the Red Scare of 1919, thousands of people were arrested and hundreds deported in a crackdown on people thought to be Communists, Socialists, or other radicals. The decade closed in a flurry of riots, arrests, and hysteria.

The 1910s saw a real flowering of popular culture in a number of areas. The most notable development in arts and entertainment was the development of the movie industry. Many Americans still saw short films in nickelodeons (cheap store-front theaters), but the movie industry was changing dramatically. Movies were longer and more polished, and they starred actors who soon became household names, such as Lillian Gish (1893–1993) and Rudolph Valentino (1895–1926). These movies were shown in ornate movie palaces. By 1916, nearly twenty-five million Americans saw a movie on any given day. Movies thus joined magazines in their ability to entertain millions of Americans across the nation. Magazines continued to flourish, with old standards such as *Collier's,* the *American Magazine,* and the *Saturday Evening Post* achieving circulations in the millions, while magazines such as *True Story, Vanity Fair,* and *Vogue* emerged to provide different forms of reading material.

While movies and magazines provided entertainment to the great masses, other forms of culture also flourished. American artists and writers were thrilled by the Armory Show of European artists in 1913, which sparked a rebirth in American artistic and literary activity. Novelists Theodore Dreiser (1871–1945) and Willa Cather (1873–1947) published important works in the decade. Poet Carl Sandburg (1878–1967) published poems celebrating his home town of Chicago, Illinois. Perhaps the most popular artist of the day was actually a magazine illustrator, named Norman Rockwell (1894–1978).

In their daily lives, Americans enjoyed an ever-growing variety of amusements. The Ringling Bros. and Barnum & Bailey Circus was formed in this decade and boasted that it was the "Greatest Show on Earth." Sports fans thrilled or booed to the exploits of the New York Yankees. Hockey joined the ranks of professional sports in 1917 with the establishment of the National Hockey League. Two "crazes" swept the nation in this decade—the bridge craze, which saw millions of Americans playing the popular card game, and the crossword puzzle craze, with new word challenges offered each week in newspapers and magazines.

Americans fell in love with two new foods in the 1910s: Campbell's soup, which came in a convenient can, and Oreo cookies. Both products continue to this day to be among the most popular brand in their class. Homemakers also enjoyed the newest electrical appliance, the refrigerator, which allowed them to keep foods fresh longer and to not make so many trips to the grocery store.

1910s

Commerce

In American business, the 1910s were a decade of organization. Across the country, large corporations sought ways to make their production more efficient. They hired managers in great numbers, and it was the manager's job to get employees to increase production. Many of these managers followed the thinking of an engineer named Frederick W. Taylor (1865–1915), who preached the principles of "scientific management." These new management techniques emphasized efficiency and order and getting the most out of workers. Managers also looked to automation, as more and more American businesses used assembly-line processes to produce their goods. The Ford Motor Company was the shining example of what organization could do for a company; Henry Ford (1863–1947) and his car company boosted his company's automobile production to 730,041 units by 1917.

When President Woodrow Wilson (1856–1924) brought his progressive political ideas to the White House in 1913, critics feared that his pro-reform administration would be antibusiness. In fact, progressive legislation helped business operate more efficiently. Both the Clayton Antitrust Act of 1914 and the creation of the Federal Trade Commission (FTC) helped restore healthy competition to American business by eliminating monopolistic (single company dominance) and anticompetitive business practices. Other legislation increased exports by promoting free trade with other nations, helped provide farmers with low-interest loans, and protected workers' rights.

The American economy was boosted dramatically by World War I (1914–18). Before it entered the war in 1917, the United States provided food and other goods to all of the warring countries. Once America entered the war, it was also free to provide military weapons and heavy industrial goods to its allies, France and the United Kingdom. President Wilson's government helped American companies organize their activities to ship war goods; labor unions felt it was unpatriotic to strike; and the economy boomed. During the course of the decade, the value of goods and services produced in the United States rose from $35.3 billion in 1910 to $91.5 billion in 1920. Even more importantly, the United States was now exporting more goods than ever before. Exports exceeded imports by $273 million in 1910. By 1920, they exceeded imports by $2.88 billion.

By the end of the decade, the American economy was the undisputed leader of the world. The Ford Motor Company, General Motors, General Electric, Eastman Kodak, DuPont, and other companies grew to have values greater than many small nations. The American Telephone and Telegraph Company (AT&T) laid telephone lines from New York to San Francisco, paving the way for transcontinental telephone service—and for AT&T to become the world's largest company eventually.

Individual Americans also enjoyed the country's economic growth. The income of the average American rose from $580 in 1914 to more than $1,300 by the end of the decade. Advertisers and a growing retail industry persuaded Americans to spend some of their disposable income. Department stores such as Wanamaker in Philadelphia and grocery stores like Piggly Wiggly in Tennessee adopted scientific management techniques to sell people more goods. L. L. Bean (1872–1967) founded his outdoor goods company in 1912 and soon shipped goods across the country to people who had received his catalog.

AT&T
• •

An outgrowth of the original Bell Telephone Company founded by Alexander Graham Bell (1847–1922) in 1877, the American Telephone & Telegraph Company is one of the best-known companies in the United States. The company is commonly known by its corporate initials, AT&T, or by its familiar nickname, "Ma Bell." Incorporated in 1885, AT&T became the parent company of the Bell System in 1915. In 1915, AT&T also extended its New York–based network to San Francisco, California, permitting the first transcontinental **telephone** (see entry under 1900s—The Way We Lived in volume 1) calls. The company had a controlling interest in Western Electric, its manufacturing unit, and in Bell Labs (now the independent Lucent Technologies), which served as its research and development division. AT&T introduced the first commercial transatlantic telephone service between the United States and London, England, in 1927 and the first transpacific service to Hawaii in 1931 and to Tokyo, Japan, in 1934. AT&T's development of the Telstar I **satellite** (see entry under 1950s—The Way We Lived in volume 3), launched in 1962, opened a new era of global telecommunications from space.

For its first century, AT&T was a government-regulated monopoly (single company that controls the market for a particular good or service) that provided telecommunications services throughout the United States in exchange for its commitment to offer universal service at a low price to consumers. Thanks to AT&T, 50 percent of all households had telephone service by 1945; 70 percent, by 1955; and 90 percent, by 1969. In 1974, however, the U.S. government filed an antitrust suit against AT&T that led to its breakup into eight smaller companies in 1984: a shrunken AT&T, plus seven "baby Bells" that provided local telephone service. The breakup reduced AT&T's assets from $149.5 billion to $34 billion and its employees from 1,009,000 to 373,000. Its familiar logo of a bell within a circle was replaced by a stylized globe and the monogram AT&T. For the next twelve years, AT&T described itself as an "integrated telecommunications services and equipment company" that, along with MCI, Sprint, and other newcomers, was one of many long-distance carriers. Since 1996, AT&T has been reinventing itself as a company that provides businesses and consumers with voice, data, and digital services via wireless, data, and cable networks. It reported annual revenues of $124 billion in 2010.

Edward Moran

For More Information

"About AT&T." *AT&T.* http://www.att.com (accessed June 21, 2011).

Brooks, John. *Telephone: The First Hundred Years.* New York: Harper & Row, 1976.

Cauley, Leslie. *End of the Line: The Rise and Fall of AT&T.* New York: Simon & Schuster, 2005.

Coll, Steve. *The Deal of the Century: The Breakup of AT&T.* New York: Atheneum, 1986.

Kleinfield, Sonny. *The Biggest Company on Earth: A Profile of AT&T.* New York: Holt, Rinehart, and Winston, 1981.

Stone, Alan. *Wrong Number: The Breakup of AT&T.* New York: Basic Books, 1989.

L. L. Bean

L. L. Bean, based in Freeport, Maine, is a supplier of outdoor apparel, furnishings, and equipment. Since its inception in 1912, it has become renowned for its products and services and for the rustic, genteel lifestyle that it represents. With a largely unchanging mix of products that includes khaki pants, the famous "Bean boot," and camping equipment,

The L. L. Bean retail store in Freeport, Maine. © ANDRE JENNY/ALAMY.

L. L. Bean has virtually defined the outdoors-oriented retailing industry. In the 1980s, when the **"preppy"** (see entry under 1980s—Fashion in volume 5) look was in vogue, L. L. Bean was practically revered. In Lisa Birnbach's best-selling book *The Official Preppy Handbook,* she wrote of the preppy rite of passage of going to the Bean store in Freeport at midnight. The company's catalog has been a legend for decades. Until the 1990s, there was only one store, in Freeport, and all orders were made through the catalog. For most people, the catalog *was* L. L. Bean.

Leon Leonwood Bean (1873–1967) got started in the business because he was tired of coming home from outings in the Maine woods with cold, wet feet. He created a lightweight leather boot with rubber bottoms and sold them via mail order. Unfortunately, the stitching came out on most of them. This fault turned out to be a blessing, since he returned his customers' money and thereby established the famous Bean unconditional guarantee. Unsatisfied with the performance of his product, Bean went back to the drawing board. The improved "Maine hunting shoe" is still sold today as the "Bean boot" and is probably L. L. Bean's best-known product. They have also offered a "field coat" since 1924, the design of which was widely emulated in the 1990s. Other Bean innovations have included keeping the store open for twenty-four hours a day year round, running a fly-fishing school, and offering a variety of environmental programs.

By the late 1990s, L. L. Bean was considered by some to be overly traditional. In an effort to keep up with competition from companies like Lands' End and Recreational Equipment Incorporated (REI), the company expanded the number of stores and tried to be more market savvy. In 2000, for example, L. L. Bean signed a contract with Subaru and boosted its name recognition with "L. L. Bean Editions " of some Subaru models. Although today most of its products are now made overseas, L. L. Bean promotes itself as modern, traditional, and distinctly American.

Karl Rahder

For More Information

"About L. L. Bean." *L. L. Bean.* http://www.llbean.com/customerService/aboutLLBean/index.html?feat=gn (accessed June 21, 2011).

"Bean There, Done That." *Harper's* (December 2000): p. 260.

Birnbach, Lisa. *The Official Preppy Handbook.* New York: Workman Publishing, 1980.

Gorman, Leon. *L. L. Bean: The Making of an American Icon.* Cambridge, MA: Harvard Business Press, 2006.

Montgomery, M. R. *In Search of L. L. Bean.* Boston: Little, Brown, 1984.

Symonds, William C. "Paddling Harder at L. L. Bean." *Business Week* (December 7, 1998): pp. 72–73.

1910s

Fashion

Fashion in the 1910s bore little resemblance to fashion in the twenty-first century. There were few, if any, famous designers or popular brands of clothes and few fashion magazines to publicize the latest clothing styles. The very idea of style would have seemed laughable to most people, whose highest hopes for their clothing were that it might be durable. Many Americans still wore clothes that were made at home; those who did not make their own clothes bought them at general stores or department stores based on price and durability, and not on whether the clothes were in style.

Only the wealthiest Americans had the luxury of thinking about the cut and style of their apparel. Wealthy men might have their suits hand-made in London, England, while rich women traveled to Paris, France, to view the latest in female fashions. Beginning in 1914, Americans could consult the magazine *Vanity Fair* for advice on stylish attire. This magazine was one of the first to promote stylish clothes for men in its articles and advertisements. The Arrow Collar Man, a stylishly handsome illustrated figure used to sell shirt collars, became the most famous fashion symbol of the decade thanks to his appearance in countless magazine advertisements.

In general, popular clothing during the decade trended towards greater simplicity and ease of use. Both men and women were beginning to enjoy more active lives—bicycling, golfing, and dancing were all becoming very popular—and their clothing changed to suit those lifestyles. Women gave up wearing the cumbersome corset (a heavy, tight undergarment) and began wearing the more comfortable brassiere, or bra, that was invented in 1913. Similarly, men gave up their thick woolen union suits in favor of the light cotton T-shirt that became popular among soldiers fighting in World War I (1914–18). Active people of both sexes also looked for lightweight footwear. Beginning in 1917, they could purchase Converse All Star tennis shoes, with their light uppers and no-skid rubber bottom.

Arrow Collar Man

Appearing in hundreds of print advertisements between 1905 and 1930, the Arrow Collar Man presented an iconic image—the ideal representation of a handsome, athletic, self-confident male. Even President Theodore Roosevelt (1858–1919) described him as a superb portrait of the "common man." The image of the Arrow Collar Man was used to advertise more than four hundred varieties of detachable collars. In the early decades of the twentieth century, most men's shirts still had detachable collars, often made of celluloid (Celluloid was the first synthetic **plastic** [see entry under 1900s—Commerce in volume 1]. Made from cellulose and camphor, other plastics replaced celluloid because it was highly flammable). The Arrow Collar achieved widespread brand recognition and become an advertising icon; if a man wore an Arrow Collar, the reasoning went, he must be like that handsome, athletic, self-confident Arrow Collar Man. The Arrow Collar Man was created by J. C. Leyendecker (1874–1951) for its manufacturer, Cluett, Peabody & Company. During the 1920s, the Arrow Collar Man served as an advertising model for Arrow Shirts with their newfangled attached collars.

Leyendecker, who preferred to work from live models, drew the Arrow Collar Man as a

An early 1920s advertisement for formal Arrow collars and shirts. © JOSEPH CHRISTIAN LEYENDECKER/CORBIS ART/ CORBIS.

polished, Anglo-Saxon figure. The portraits were designed to suggest an ideal image of the American male. He used several prominent actors for models, his favorite being Charles Beach (1886–1952), Leyendecker's business manager and companion for half a century. It has been reported that the fictional image received more fan mail than movie stars of the period, including **Rudolph Valentino** (1895–1926; see entry under 1920s—Film and Theater in volume 2). At the height of the Arrow Collar Man's popularity in 1920, he was receiving seventeen thousand love letters a week. He was also the subject of a **Broadway** (see entry under 1900s—Film and Theater in volume 1) show and several popular songs and poems.

After the campaigns featuring the Arrow Collar Man ended in 1930, Leyendecker continued his career as a magazine illustrator for the *Saturday Evening Post* (see entry under 1900s—Print Culture in volume 1) and other national publications. He was also said to be a prominent influence on another of America's greatest illustrators, **Norman Rockwell** (see entry under 1910s—Print Culture in volume 1).

Edward Moran

For More Information

Cutler, Laurence S., and Judy Goffman Cutler. *J. C. Leyendecker.* New York: Abrams, 2008.

"J. C. Leyendecker: A Retrospective." *The Norman Rockwell Museum.* http://www.tfaoi.com/newsmu/nmus21b.htm (accessed June 21, 2011).

"Joseph Christian Leyendecker." *National Museum of American Illustration.* http://www.americanillustration.org/artists/leyendecker_jc/leyendecker.html (accessed June 21, 2011).

Schau, Michael. *J. C. Leyendecker.* New York: Watson-Guptill, 1974.

Bra

• •

Few items of clothing have attracted as much attention—both positive and negative—as the brassiere, or bra. Worn by women to support and protect their breasts, the bra has become a symbol of femininity, female sexuality, and womanhood. So closely is the bra equated with the role of women in society that acceptance or rejection of the bra can be a political statement as well as a fashion decision.

The bra was invented in 1913 by New York City socialite Caresse Crosby (1892–1970). Rebelling against the confinement and unattractive lines of the corsets (a restrictive undergarment) that the fashion of the day dictated, Crosby directed a servant to sew together two handkerchiefs with ribbons to make a garment to wear over her breasts. Crosby was not the first to think of such a device, but she patented her invention and therefore was able to claim the rights to it. She sold the patent to Warners, a corset manufacturer, for $1500.

Bras have been used throughout the years to help women make their bodies look fashionable. In the 1920s, the bra was a tight band that allowed women to achieve a slim, boyish figure; by the 1930s, bras pushed women's breasts up and in to exhibit their cleavage (the visual line between the breasts). In 1935, Warners introduced the cup design, with different sized cups for a better individual fit. The 1940s and 1950s featured sturdy bras made of cotton and elastic. Big breasts became fashionable, and the 1950s saw the introduction of the padded bra and "falsies," small foam pads placed in the bra to enlarge the bustline.

In the 1960s, as women began to question their role in male-dominated society, men's obsession with women's breasts became a source of anger and dissent. The women's liberation movement accused men of viewing women mainly as objects of sexual desire, and made the bra a symbol of women's confinement to the expectations of men. At the 1968 **Miss America Pageant** (see entry under 1920s—The Way We Lived in volume 2), feminists protested male beauty standards by throwing curlers, makeup, and bras into a garbage can. Although no bras were burned, the media exaggerated the event and "bra-burner" became a synonym for feminist.

Since then, women have continued to wear bras, whether to address social conventions or a need for a supportive garment for their breasts. With forty-three separate component parts, the modern bra is an engineering marvel, and manufacturers are constantly working to improve the design. Sports bras have been introduced that can be worn under a shirt or alone by female athletes. During the technological boom of the 1990s, bras were even designed to contain heart monitors, global positioning system locators, cellular phones, and cancer warning sensors. The lingerie company Victoria's Secret scored a marketing triumph with its sophisticated Wonderbra in the 1990s. Regardless of manufacturer or design, the bra continues to reflect the tastes and conventions of American society in every era.

Tina Gianoulis

For More Information

Dowling, Claudia Glenn. "Ooh-la-la! The Bra." *Life.* (June 1989): pp. 88–96.

Fontanel, Béatrice. *Support and Seduction: The History of Corsets and Bras.* New York: Abradale, 1997.

Hawthorne, Rosemary, and Mary Want. *From Busk to Bra: A Survey of Women's Corsetry.* Cincinnati: Seven Hills Book Distributors, 1987.

Lindsay, David. *House of Invention: The Secret Life of Everyday Products.* New York: Lyons Press, 1999.

Walsh, John. "A Social History of the Bra." *AlterNet.* http://www.alternet.org/story/59877 (accessed June 21, 2011).

Tennis Shoes

The tennis shoe has been called the only new style of shoe to be invented in the past three hundred years. The athletic shoe was first introduced in the 1860s as the plimsoll, a lightweight canvas shoe with a rubber sole for playing lawn croquet. The athletic shoe has since evolved into not only a high-tech piece of sports equipment but also a sign of status and an expression of individual personality. Often called "tennies" or "sneakers," tennis shoes are no longer just for sports. They are a major part of the modern American wardrobe.

In 1916, a shoe company called Keds produced a lightweight canvas and rubber shoe that remained the basic pattern of the tennis shoe for the next fifty years. In the late 1960s, the customized athletic shoe first appeared, when University of Oregon track coach Bill Bowerman (1911–1999) began experimenting with new designs for a lightweight shoe with improved traction. He created a new type of sole by pouring latex rubber into a waffle iron. The odd-looking but efficient shoe he created by attaching his new sole to a nylon upper was dubbed the "moon shoe."

Bowerman became one of the founders of the **Nike** (see entry under 1960s—Commerce in volume 4) shoe company. Nike, along with athletic equipment company Spalding and German company Adidas, continued to improve the design of the running shoe during the 1970s. The **aerobics** (see entry under 1970s—Sports and Games in volume 4) craze of the 1970s and 1980s sparked more experimentation in specific shoe design for different sports. In the 1990s, shoes with technical accessories, such as built-in air pumps to customize fit, became popular.

Red sneakers, manufactured by the first tennis shoe company, Keds. © MICHAEL DWYER/ALAMY.

Modern athletic shoes can cost from $40 to $250 a pair. Manufacturing athletic shoes has become a $17 billion-a-year industry. The most popular sports shoes are often endorsed by well-known athletes, who receive millions of dollars in exchange for the use of their likenesses. The teenage boys who identify with those athletes are often drawn to the expensive brand-name shoes that their heroes endorse. Poor youth, some of whom see success in sports as a way out of poverty, want to own the "best" sneakers, even though the price tag may be out of reach. As a result, there have been rare but highly publicized tragedies in which young men were assaulted, a few even killed, by attackers who only wanted their athletic shoes.

Tina Gianoulis

For More Information

Cardona, Melissa. *The Sneaker Book: 50 Years of Sport Shoe Design.* Atglen, PA: Schiffer, 2005.

Smit, Barbara. *Sneaker Wars*. New York: Ecco, 2008.

Telander, Rick, and Mirko Ilic. "Senseless: In America's Cities, Kids Are Killing Kids over Sneakers and Other Sports Apparel Favored by Drug Dealers; Who's to Blame?" *Sports Illustrated* (Vol. 72, no. 20, May 14, 1990): pp. 36–43.

Wolkomir, Richard. "The Race to Make a 'Perfect' Shoe Starts in the Laboratory." *Smithsonian* (Vol. 20, no. 6, September 1989): pp. 94–103.

Unorthodox Styles. *Sneakers: The Complete Collectors' Guide*. London: Thames & Hudson, 2005.

Vanderbilt, Tom. *The Sneaker Book: Anatomy of an Industry and an Icon*. New York: New Press, 1998.

T-shirt

The T-shirt is one of the most popular examples of American casual fashion. Popularized by U.S. Navy sailors during the first two world wars, the T-shirt has become an essential element of the American wardrobe.

In 1913, the U.S. Navy issued short-sleeved, white cotton crewneck undershirts to sailors. Sailors returning from World War I (1914–18) had grown to prefer the T-shirt to the woolen undershirt that had been the typical undergarment since 1880. By World War II (1939–45), twelve million men were wearing the shirts. News photographs and newsreels showed sailors and soldiers working in only pants and T-shirts. Underwear was exposed to the public for the first time. America had become quite used to the display of American muscle under a thin layer of white T-shirt by the war's end.

Although the military persuaded America to embrace the T-shirt as an essential element of a man's wardrobe, films turned the T-shirt into an American cultural phenomenon. In 1951, the sculpted muscles of Marlon Brando (1924–2004) bulged under his T-shirt in *A Streetcar Named Desire*; his character Stanley Kowalski's powerful masculinity was reflected in Brando's physique and perfectly displayed beneath his T-shirt. In 1955, **James Dean** (see entry

Actor Marlon Brando (shown here with Vivien Leigh) portrayed a T-shirt-wearing tough guy in the 1951 film A Streetcar Named Desire, *helping to make the undershirt popular fashion garb.* © SUNSET BOULEVARD/CORBIS.

under 1950s—Film and Theater in volume 3) brought a youthful, anti-establishment attitude to the T-shirt in *Rebel Without a Cause*. This anti-establishment theme continued into the 1960s with Peter Fonda (1939–) in *Easy Rider* (1966). The sexual and rebellious characters that actors portrayed in films translated into the behavior of American youths. T-shirts became associated with youthful, American attitudes.

Women made T-shirts their own symbol of youth and rebellion during the **sexual revolution** (see entry under 1960s—The Way We Lived in volume 4) of the 1960s and 1970s. The teasingly revealing anatomy of a T-shirt–clad Jacqueline Bisset (1944–) in *The Deep* (1977) is perhaps the most famous illustration of women's adoption of the T-shirt in its day.

Soon T-shirts displayed attitudes in type. Although some T-shirts carried printed messages before the 1960s, in the 1970s they became personal billboards for individual expression. Anything from "Have a Nice Day" to profanity could be found on T-shirts. By the beginning of the twenty-first century, many T-shirts were platforms for advertising, especially for clothing companies such as **Abercrombie & Fitch** (see entry under 1990s—Fashion in volume 5) or tourist destinations like the Hard Rock Cafe chain. Because of their low cost and versatility, T-shirts were a staple garment of Americans and many others around the world. Offered in a variety of colors, styles, and with unlimited messages, the T-shirt can still be seen adorning young and old alike.

Sara Pendergast

For More Information
Brunel, Charlotte. *The T-Shirt Book.* New York: Assouline, 2002.
Nelson, Robin. *From Cotton to a T-Shirt.* Minneapolis: Lerner, 2003.

Zipper

Zippers provide easy opening and secure fastening for items such as luggage, clothing, and even plastic bags. Although zippers are contemporarily found in many everyday items, the device did not immediately interest people when it was first invented.

Elias Howe (1819–1867), inventor of the sewing machine, patented the first zipper in 1851. He called it an "automatic, continuous clothing closure." Howe never marketed his invention, though. Whitcomb

Judson patented his "clasp locker" in 1893. After its introduction at the **World's Fair** (see entry under 1900s—The Way We Lived in volume 1) in Chicago, Illinois, and the successful marking of his product through his Universal Fastener Company, he became known as the "Inventor of the Zipper."

Judson's invention laid the groundwork for modern zippers. Gideon Sundback, an employee of Universal Fastener Company, designed a zipper in 1913 that is similar to the zippers found today. Sundback's "separable fastener" received a patent in 1917. The Universal Fastener Company started producing hundreds of feet of the product a day.

The B. F. Goodrich Company put Sundback's fastener on its rubber boots and called the device a "zipper." The name stuck, but it took several years for the zipper to become popular. For the first twenty years of its existence, the device was only used to close boots and tobacco pouches. Other uses seemed impractical; the zipper was expensive and prone to rusting, and it sometimes broke open. However, when designers started using zippers in children's clothing in the 1930s, it did not take long for them to replace buttons in the flies of men's trousers. Soon, zippers were the preferred fastener for trousers, jackets, and all sorts of other items. By the beginning of the new millennium, zippers came in thousands of different styles and hundreds of different colors.

The zipper—a simple, yet vital, part of everyday life—has been around since the nineteenth century. © ARTPARTNER-IMAGES.COM/ALAMY.

Sara Pendergast

For More Information

Friedel, Robert. *Zipper: An Exploration in Novelty.* New York: W. W. Norton, 1994.

"The History of the Zipper." *About.com.* http://inventors.about.com/library/weekly/aa082497.htm (accessed June 21, 2011).

"A History of the Zipper, from Novelty to Ubiquity." *Random History.* http://www.randomhistory.com/zipper-history.html (accessed June 21, 2011).

1910s

Film and Theater

One of many amusements in the 1900s, movies began to compete seriously with books and magazines for people's leisure time in the 1910s. By 1916, twenty-five million Americans attended the movies every single day. Advances in technology and in the art of filmmaking helped to make movies an important part of American popular culture. Technologically, films could now be longer and could be shown on a bigger screen. Artistically, directors had developed the art of telling a story on film. They used rising "stars"—actors and actresses loved by their audience—to craft dramatic stories.

Nickelodeons, which showed short, one-reel films (films that fit on a single reel and were generally ten to twelve minutes long) in cramped spaces, faded in popularity during this decade. Soon the little nickelodeons were replaced by large, ornate theaters in many big cities. These "movie palaces," which seated hundreds of viewers in splendid and elaborate atmospheres, made going to the movies a special treat. Filmmakers soon made two-, three-, eight-, and even twelve-reel movies. These movies, called features, were long enough to tell a detailed story. Movies were still silent, of course, for sound would not come to films until the late 1920s.

Film production, which had once been centered in New York, relocated westward, settling in an area near Los Angeles, California, known as Hollywood. Open space and good weather allowed movie studios to make better movies in higher volume. The most notable directors soon became famous. The best-known director of the day was D. W. Griffith (c. 1875–1948), director of the famous *Birth of a Nation* (1915) and *Intolerance* (1916). Cecil B. DeMille (1881–1959) soon built a solid reputation. Griffith, DeMille, and other directors also turned to stars to help draw viewers to their movies. Among the best known stars of this early era of film-making were "America's Sweetheart" Mary Pickford (1893–1979), "Latin Lover" Rudolph Valentino (1895–1926), Charlie Chaplin (1889–1977), Lillian Gish (1893–1993), Douglas Fairbanks (1883–1939), Tom Mix (1880–1940), and many others.

On the stage, vaudeville was still the most popular form of live entertainment. A form of variety theater that included a range of acts, vaudeville shows were performed all across the nation in towns of every size. In many cities outside the South, African Americans participated in mixed-race vaudeville performances and toured with vaudeville shows of their own. Many of the most famous vaudeville performers of the day—including Chaplin, the Marx Brothers (Harpo, 1888–1964; Groucho, 1890–1977; Chico, 1886–1961; and Zeppo, 1901–1979), George Burns (1896–1996), and Jack Benny (1894–1974)—went on to star in movies and, several decades later, television. Large cities often had ornate theaters to house their vaudeville shows, and these theaters also showed movies.

Musicals and musical revues also gained in popularity during the decade. The most famous musical revue was the annual Ziegfeld Follies, which ran from 1907 to 1931 but was most popular during the 1910s. Though Broadway was still struggling to develop a successful theatrical tradition, a trend called the Little Theatre Movement saw the birth of local theater companies across the country. Eugene O'Neill (1888–1953), who would become one of America's most famous playwrights, had his first play performed by the Provincetown Players in New York City in 1916.

The Birth of a Nation

The Birth of a Nation was a groundbreaking 1915 silent film. Directed by D. W. Griffith (1875–1948), the film is set during the American Civil War (1861–65) and Reconstruction period (1865–1877). *The Birth of a Nation* depicts the era through the fictional stories of two white families caught up in the conflict, the Stonemans from the North and the slave-owning Camerons from the South. The film popularized the acting

A controversial scene with the Ku Klux Klan from the 1915 blockbuster silent film The Birth of a Nation, *starring Lillian Gish.*
© EPOCH/THE KOBAL COLLECTION/ART RESOURCE, NY.

careers of **Lillian Gish** (1893–1993; see entry in 1910s—Film and Theater in volume 1) and her younger sister, Dorothy (1898–1968). The sisters became two of the most familiar stars of the **silent movie** (see entry under 1900s—Film and Theater in volume 1) era. *The Birth of a Nation* introduced many technical and artistic advances in the new medium of film, although it remains controversial to this day because of its biased interpretation of the historical events it portrayed.

Based on *The Clansman,* a 1905 play written by Thomas Dixon Jr. (1864–1946), *The Birth of a Nation* sympathized with defeated Southern slaveholders. It portrayed the Confederacy and the **Ku Klux Klan** (see entry under 1910s—The Way We Lived in volume 1) in a generally favorable light, while painting a negative picture of Southern blacks during the period. The film depicted the Cameron plantation before the war as a happy place where slaves and masters lived together in harmony until Northern abolitionists disturbed the balance. After the war, Austin Stoneman sends a friend of mixed race, Silas Lynch, to encourage the emancipated slaves to vote and run for public office, provoking a horrified Ben Cameron to organize the Ku Klux Klan as an organ of white resistance. The narrative is personalized when romantic attachments develop between members of the two families, but these scenes are overshadowed by unflattering depictions of black characters, who are portrayed as uncouth and prone to violence. Not surprisingly, protests greeted *The Birth of a Nation* when the film opened in many cities in the spring of 1915. Among those criticizing the film were the National Association for the Advancement of Colored People (NAACP) and prominent African American educators Booker T. Washington (1856–1915) and W. E. B. DuBois (1868–1963).

Despite these controversies, *The Birth of a Nation* remains a milestone in the history of the early film industry. It was heavily promoted and advertised nationwide, making it the prototype for the modern "blockbuster." In the **nickelodeon** (see entry under 1900s—Film and Theater in volume 1) era, *The Birth of a Nation* was the first film for which a two-dollar admission was charged, proving that mass audiences would support serious movies. It also pioneered a number of production techniques still used by filmmakers. These techniques include the use of creative camera angles, such as close-ups and panoramic shots, and of artificial lighting for filming at night. Writer and film critic James Agee (1909–1955) declared that *The Birth of a Nation* was full of "tremendous magical images" that could be compared to Abraham Lincoln's speeches, Walt Whitman's poems, and Mathew Brady's photographs in evoking the sentiments of the Civil War era.

Edward Moran

For More Information

Dirks, Tim. "Birth of a Nation (1915)." *AMC Filmsite.* http://www.filmsite.org/birt.html (accessed June 21, 2011).

"Birth of a Nation and Black Protest." *Roy Rosenzweig Center for History New Media.* http://chnm.gmu.edu/episodes/the-birth-of-a-nation-and-black-protest/ (accessed June 21, 2011).

Hurwitz, Michael R. *D. W. Griffith's "The Birth of a Nation": The Film That Transformed America.* Charleston, SC: BookSurge, 2006.

Silva, Fred, ed. *Focus on "The Birth of a Nation."* Englewood Cliffs, NJ: Prentice Hall, 1971.

Stokes, Melvyn. *D. W. Griffith's "The Birth of a Nation": A History of the Most Controversial Picture of All Time.* New York: Oxford University Press, 2007.

Charlie Chaplin (1887–1977)

Charlie Chaplin was a brilliant mime artist and a key comic actor and director during Hollywood's **silent movie** (see entry under 1900s—Film and Theater in volume 1) era. Hired by the Keystone Film Company in 1913 for $150 a week, Chaplin quickly rose to superstar stature. Just four years later, First National paid him $1 million to make eight films. He once said that all he needed to make a comedy was a park, a policeman, and a pretty girl. Despite Chaplin's flippancy, much of the popularity of his films was attributable to his ability to combine wild visual jokes with pointed commentary on serious issues such as immigration and unemployment. The image of the man in the bowler hat with turned-out feet, a character frequently portrayed by Chaplin known as the "Little Tramp," is still famous the world over.

Silent movie comic actor Charlie Chaplin as the "Little Tramp," around 1920. © THE KOBAL COLLECTION/ART RESOURCE, NY.

The English-born Chaplin never became an American citizen and left the United States in 1952. In 1972, a special Oscar honored him as one of the most distinguished figures in Hollywood's history. He was knighted Sir Charles Chaplin by the British government in 1975.

Chris Routledge

For More Information

Charlie Chaplin. http://www.charliechaplin.com/ (accessed June 22, 2011).

Cook, David A. *A History of Narrative Film.* 4th ed. New York: W. W. Norton, 2004.

Epstein, Jerry. *Remembering Charlie: A Pictorial Biography.* New York: Doubleday, 1988.

Fleischman, Sid. *Sir Charlie Chaplin: The Funniest Man in the World.* New York: Greenwillow, 2010.

Mitchell, Glenn. *The Charlie Chaplin Encyclopedia.* London: Batsford, 1997.

Vance, Jeffrey. *Chaplin: Genius of the Cinema.* New York: Abrams, 2003.

Felix the Cat

• •

A comic-book and animated-cartoon character created around 1920 by
Otto Messmer (1892–1983) and Pat Sullivan (1885–1933), Felix the
Cat first appeared (without a name) in a 1919 animated cartoon called
Feline Follies. Felix the Cat was a lively, clever character who overcame
difficulties through the use of inventive solutions such as morphing his
body parts into tools. During the next decade, the black-and-white,
wide-eyed cat starred in more than 150 short animated cartoons. In
1923, he began appearing in a comic strip distributed by King Features.
Felix was the first important animal character to star in his own cartoon series, and also the first major cartoon character whose image was
licensed for use by toy companies and other businesses for depiction

Felix the Cat in a 1960 cartoon caper. © AF ARCHIVE/ALAMY.

on retail products. In 1927, Felix was the first character to appear on balloons in the **Macy's Thanksgiving Day Parade** (see entry under 1920s—Commerce in volume 2).

Through a series of favorable arrangements between the Messmer-Sullivan team and film distributors, Felix became a familiar presence in movie theaters around the country. Despite the character's popularity in silent films, his creators were unable to adapt their character when movies gained sound in the late 1920s. Competitor **Walt Disney** (see Disney entry under 1920s—Film and Theater in volume 2) soon emerged as the major film animator with another animal character: Mickey Mouse.

After an unsuccessful film revival in 1936, Felix the Cat continued to appear in newspaper comic strips and Dell comic books. In 1959, and again in 1982, Joe Oriolo (1913–1985) created a Felix the Cat cartoon series for television, adding such supporting characters as the Professor and Poindexter. His son, Don Oriolo, continued the tradition by producing *Felix the Cat: The Movie* in the 1980s and developing the "Baby Felix" character. Through such revivals, Felix the Cat remained a durable fixture of twentieth-century popular culture.

Edward Moran

For More Information

Canemaker, John. *Felix: The Twisted Tale of the World's Most Famous Cat.* New York: Pantheon, 1991.

FelixtheCat.com. http://www.felixthecat.com/ (accessed June 22, 2011).

Gerstein, David. *Classic Felix the Cat Page.* http://felix.goldenagecartoons.com/ (accessed June 22, 2011).

Messmer, Otto. *Nine Lives to Live: A Classic Felix Celebration.* Seattle: Fantagraphic Books, 1996.

Gertie the Dinosaur

Gertie the Dinosaur (1914) may not be the first animated cartoon ever created, but it easily is the most famous—and the most influential—of its day. The title character is a real charmer: a cuddly, sweetly mischievous prehistoric creature who not only was an audience favorite but also the first-ever animated movie star.

Gertie was the creation of Winsor McCay (1871–1934), a newspaper cartoonist and comic strip artist-turned-pioneering animator.

A lobby poster for Winsor McCay's 1914 animated film Gertie the Dinosaur. © MCCAY/THE KOBAL COLLECTION/ART RESOURCE. NY.

McCay's first animated cartoon was *Little Nemo* (1911), based on his comic-strip creation. *Little Nemo* consisted of four thousand drawings. *Gertie the Dinosaur* was his most celebrated follow-up animation. To create it, McCay used ten thousand drawings, each one representing an individual frame of film. All the drawings were inked on rice paper and mounted on cardboard.

McCay first presented his films as part of an act he performed in **vaudeville** (see entry under 1900s—Film and Theater in volume 1), in which he announced to the audience that he could make his drawings come to life. When presenting *Gertie the Dinosaur*, McCay portrayed the creature's trainer. As his film was projected, he synchronized his movements with those presented on-screen. McCay thus "talked" to Gertie, interacting with her and giving her commands to which she responded. At the finale, McCay "walked" into the movie, becoming an animated figure that Gertie would carry away on her back. He promoted the routine as "The Greatest Animal Act in the World!!!"

What is most astonishing about Gertie, however, was her fluid, detailed movement. She swayed back and forth and, as she breathed, her body would expand and contract. McCay also included a groundbreaking sense of realism in his animation. For example, as Gertie was shown uprooting a tree trunk and chomping away on it, bits of dirt could be seen falling to earth.

The film *Gertie the Dinosaur* (which has variously been called *Gertie, Gertie the Dinosaurus,* and *Gertie the Trained Dinosaur*) was released to movie theaters in an expanded, one-reel version. McCay surrounded the animation with a live-action story, which involved the animator agreeing to a bet with another cartoonist, George McManus (1884–1954), that he could make Gertie come alive. After the animated portion of the film, McCay and McManus were pictured at a dinner party, with McManus having lost the bet and paying for the meal.

Rob Edelman

For More Information

Maltin, Leonard. *Of Mice and Magic: A History of American Animated Cartoons.* New York: Penguin Books, 1980.

Markstein, Donald D. "Gertie the Dinosaur." *Don Markstein's Toonopedia.* http://www.toonopedia.com/gertie.htm (accessed June 22, 2011).

Lillian Gish (1896–1993)

Nicknamed the "First Lady of the Silver Screen," Lillian Gish is still considered the best serious film actress of her time. She brought a sense of realism to film acting that had not been seen before. Lillian appeared in many classic films, including **The Birth of a Nation** (see entry under 1910s—Film and Theater in volume 1) (1915) and *Way Down East* (1920).

Born Lillan de Guiche, Gish made her screen debut in 1912 along with her sister Dorothy (1898–1968) in *An Uneasy Enemy*. Both sisters would have successful film careers. Dorothy was a comedienne, whereas Lillian appeared in melodramas and in literary classics. Lillian had a much longer career and is more highly regarded today, but Dorothy actually appeared in more movies. Lillian's career ended after seventy-five years when she appeared in her last film, *The Whales of August,* in 1987.

Jill Gregg Clever

For More Information

Affron, Charles. *Lillian Gish: Her Legend, Her Life.* New York: Scribner, 2001.

Estate of Lillian Gish. *The Official Website of Lillian Gish.* http://www.lilliangish.com/ (accessed January 15, 2002).

Gish, Lillian, and Ann Pinchot. *The Movies, Mr. Griffith and Me.* Denver, Prentice-Hall, 1969.

"Lillian Gish." *American Masters.* http://www.pbs.org/wnet/americanmasters/tag/lillian-gish/ (accessed June 22, 2011).

Oderman, Stuart. *Lillian Gish: A Life on Stage and Screen.* Jefferson, NC: McFarland, 2000.

Keystone Kops

During the first two decades of the twentieth century, comedy was the favorite genre of moviegoers, and no moviemaker was more adept at tickling the funnybones of audiences than Mack Sennett (1880–1960). One of the most famous and enduring of his contributions to screen comedy was the Keystone Kops, a fictional gang of well-meaning but hilariously inept policemen. The Keystone Kops have long been synonymous with onscreen slapstick and bungling, chases filled with horseplay, and overall comic chaos.

Sennett served as a mentor for some of the era's most famous screen comedians, including **Charlie Chaplin** (1889–1977; see entry under

A publicity still for a Keystone Kops film, around 1915. © FPG/ARCHIVE PHOTOS/GETTY IMAGES.

1910s—Film and Theater in volume 1) and Mabel Normand (1894–1930). He also worked with dozens of other comic actors, including Ford Sterling (1883–1939), Chester Conklin (1888–1971), Hank Mann (1887–1971), Fred Mace (1878–1917), Edgar Kennedy (1890–1948), and Roscoe "Fatty" Arbuckle (1887–1933), all of whom at one time or another were members of the Keystone Kops. The head of this band of comic lunatics was a character named police chief Teeheezel, who was first portrayed by Mann, and then by Sterling.

The Kops were named for the Keystone studio, the film production company founded in 1912 by Sennett. They first appeared on screen in the Sennett-directed slapstick *Hoffmeyer's Legacy* (1912), but their popularity soared with the release of *The Bangville Police* (1913). Approximately five hundred short Keystone Kops comedies followed. The Kops also had a prominent role in *Tillie's Punctured Romance* (1914), a film that starred Chaplin, Normand, and comedienne Marie Dressler (1869–1934). *Tillie's Punctured Romance* was the first-ever feature-length film comedy.

The Kops wore handlebar moustaches and ill-fitting suits. During the course of their films, they would be tossed out of moving cars, or fall under moving cars, or be thrown over cliffs. Visual humor prevailed, because the films in which they appeared were silent.

The Keystone Kops' stardom began to fade as other screen comics—most notably Chaplin in 1914—began receiving the bulk of the attention at the Keystone studio, although they did keep appearing in Sennett slapsticks and were paid homage decades later in a sound-film farce featuring **Abbott and Costello** (see entry under 1940s—Film and Theater in volume 3) (Bud Abbott [1895–1974] and Lou Costello [1906–1959] were a popular comedy duo in the 1940s and 1950s). The film was titled *Abbott and Costello Meet the Keystone Kops* (1954). Furthermore, all sound-film comedy masters who rely on physical humor, from Abbott and Costello and the **Three Stooges** (see entry under 1930s—Film and Theater in volume 2) to latter-day entertainers Jerry Lewis (1926–) and Jim Carrey (1962–), owe a debt to Mack Sennett and his Keystone Kops.

Audrey Kupferberg

For More Information

Lahue, Kalton C., and Terry Brewer. *Kops and Custards: The Legend of Keystone Films.* Norman: University of Oklahoma Press, 1968.

Louvish, Simon. *Keystone: The Life and Clowns of Mack Sennett.* New York: Faber and Faber, 2004.

Sennett, Mack. *King of Comedy.* San Francisco: Mercury House, 1990.

Walker, Brent. *Mack Sennett's Fun Factory.* Jefferson, NC: McFarland, 2010.

Movie Palaces

From the early days of film until the 1950s, movie theaters closely resembled palaces. As going to the movies became a popular American activity, movie theaters grew from the original store-front **nickelodeons** (see entry under 1900s—Film and Theater in volume 1) into huge, ornate theaters such as the Regent (New York City, built 1913), the Million Dollar (Los Angeles, built 1918), and Radio City Music Hall (New York City, built in 1932). Unfortunately, after the emergence of **television** (see entry under 1940s—TV & Radio in volume 3) and growth of **suburbia** (see entry under 1950s—The Way We Lived in volume 3) in the 1950s, movie palaces began to disappear. Today there are still motion picture theaters, but they no longer play the major role they did during the first half of the twentieth century. During the **Great Depression** (see entry under 1930s—The Way We Lived in volume 2), movie palaces helped audiences forget their troubles for a while. The theaters even helped modern architecture find wider acceptance than it had previously.

The Strand in New York, although not the first movie palace, began the movie palace era, opening in 1914. The theaters held promotions such as free china, lotteries, and other prizes. Each theater had a different design theme and many boasted velvet ropes and crystal chandeliers. Moviegoers received a royal welcome from the doormen and ushers who staffed the theaters. Many theaters provided childcare, and one even boasted a miniature golf course.

By the late 1920s, audiences were becoming financially jaded, and after the Great Depression began in 1929 attendance declined drastically, although audiences were later lured back, enticed by the promise of low prices. The movie palaces experienced their peak during the late 1940s. Until then, motion picture studios owned the theaters also. A Supreme Court decision in 1948 made studios sell off the theaters.

During the 1950s, the decline of the movie palace began with the advent of television. Between 1947 and 1957, 90 percent of American households acquired a television. The theaters and studios tried to fight this development with movie spectaculars filmed with new techniques such as Widescreen, **3-D** (see entry under 1950s—Film and Theater in volume 3), and Cinerama. Unfortunately for their owners, theater audiences began to move away from the suburbs and, thus, away from the major theaters. Smaller neighborhood theaters began to appear, after which movie palaces all but disappeared.

A few palaces have been renovated and reopened, but most either stand empty and dilapidated or were torn down years ago. The lavish theater experience that movie palaces once offered audiences is now only a memory in American cinematic culture.

Jill Gregg Clever

For More Information

Hall, Ben. *The Best Remaining Seats: The Story of the Golden Age of the Movie Palace.* Rev. ed. New York: Da Capo Press, 1988.

Halnon, Mary. *Some Enchanted Evenings: American Picture Palaces.* http://xroads.virginia.edu/~cap/palace/home.html (accessed June 22, 2011).

Margolies, John, and Emily Gwathmey. *Ticket to Paradise: American Movie Theaters and How We Had Fun.* Boston: Little, Brown, 1991.

Melnick, Ross, and Andreas Fuch. *Cinema Treasures: A New Look at Classic Movie Theaters.* St. Paul, MN: MBI, 2004.

Valentine, Maggie. *The Show Starts on the Sidewalk: An Architectural History of the Movie Theatre.* New Haven, CT: Yale University Press, 1994.

Will Rogers (1879–1935)

Humorist Will Rogers was one of the most famous and beloved Americans of his time. His persona was that of a simple Everyman who employed common sense and clever good humor to view and comment on politics, lifestyles, and the American cultural scene.

Rogers, who was of Irish and Cherokee descent, was born in the Colagah Indian Territory, which is now Oklahoma. He quit school in 1891, became a cowboy in the Texas Panhandle, and performed with a traveling Wild West Circus. He first appeared on the New York stage in 1905 and became a full-fledged star on **Broadway** (see entry under 1900s—Film and Theater in volume 1) in the ***Ziegfeld Follies*** (see entry under 1900s—Film and Theater in volume 1) of 1916. Rogers soon appeared in motion pictures, debuting in *Laughing Bill Hyde* (1918). His popularity grew with the introduction of sound films in the late 1920s, which allowed him to entertain moviegoers with his unique brand of verbal humor. He quickly became a top box office star.

Rogers was a lifelong Democrat, and his support helped elect Franklin D. Roosevelt (1882–1945) to the U.S. presidency in 1932. Rogers was not above poking fun at his party's sometimes erratic behavior, however. On one occasion, he noted, "No, I'm not a member of an organized political party—I'm a Democrat." Upon his introduction to Republican president Calvin Coolidge (1871–1933), he quipped, "Didn't catch the name," the first of many times the humorist made the often dour (stern or gloomy) chief executive smile. Rogers was killed in a plane crash in 1935, sending the American populace into a period of mourning over the loss of a beloved comic institution.

Audrey Kupferberg

For More Information

Carter, Joseph H. *Never Met a Man I Didn't Like: The Life and Writings of Will Rogers.* New York: Avon Books, 1991.

Malone, Mary. *Will Rogers: Cowboy Philosopher.* Springfield, NJ: Enslow, 1996.

Rogers, Will. *Autobiography.* Boston: Houghton Mifflin, 1949. Reprint, New Brunswick, NJ: Transaction Publishers, 1998.

Sonneborn, Liz. *Will Rogers, Cherokee Entertainer.* New York: Chelsea House, 1993.

White, Richard D. *Will Rogers: A Political Life.* Lubbock: Texas Tech University Press, 2011.

Will Rogers Home Page. http://www.willrogers.org (accessed June 22, 2011).

Yagoda, Ben. *Will Rogers: A Biography.* New York: Knopf, 1993.

1910s

Food and Drink

Housework continued to become easier in the 1910s, thanks to the continuing spread of electricity and running water, the invention of new appliances, and the increased availability of pre-prepared food and drink. Vacuum cleaners, invented in 1908, made cleaning easier. Refrigerators, first made for home use in 1913, helped cut down on trips to the grocery store. The electric toaster, invented in 1919, made warming bread a snap. Real modern efficiency had not yet come to the home in the 1910s, however. Homemakers still had to wash clothes by hand and hang them on a line to dry. The high cost of many appliances made them difficult to afford for most people. For example, a refrigerator in 1920 cost about $600, nearly half of the average person's annual income.

Buying and preparing food certainly became easier in the 1910s, continuing a trend started in the previous decade. Grocery stores grew in size, carrying thousands of items to help make home life easier. Food producers kept inventing new ways to package food, hoping to earn money by making cooking quick and easy. Two famous products are good examples of the trend toward efficiency in American food preparation. Campbell's Soups—condensed soups that could be mixed with water to make a meal—became a national brand in 1911. Condensed soups allowed cooks to avoid the long preparation time involved in making homemade soup. In 1920, Americans bought more than one million cans of the twenty-one varieties of soup. Oreo cookies, invented in 1912, soon became America's favorite packaged cookie. Both items were helped along by carefully constructed advertising campaigns, and both remain among the leading brands in their respective product categories.

Campbell's Soup

For more than a century, the Campbell Soup Company has helped revolutionize eating habits around the world by offering a line of convenient and inexpensive canned soups. To prepare a serving of the condensed foodstuff, all consumers need do is add a can of water to the soup before heating it. Based in Camden, New Jersey, the firm developed as an outgrowth of the Joseph A. Campbell Preserve Company. The company had been started in 1869 by Joseph A. Campbell (1817–1900), a fruit merchant, and Abraham Anderson (1829–1915), a manufacturer of iceboxes. In 1897, general manager Arthur Dorrance (1893–1946) reluctantly hired his nephew, John T. Dorrance (1873–1930), a twenty-four-year-old chemist. John Dorrance invented a process for making the condensed soup by eliminating water from the cans, thus reducing company costs related to packaging, shipping, and storage. This breakthrough allowed the company to reduce the price of a can of soup from thirty cents to a dime. The company introduced its soups on the national market in 1912 and officially changed its name to the Campbell Soup Company in 1922.

Twenty-one flavors, including perennial favorites such as tomato and vegetable, were promoted in the company's first magazine ads in the early 1900s. Chicken noodle and cream-of-mushroom varieties made their debut in 1934, and other recipes were introduced over the following years. The Campbell Kids, a pair of rosy-cheeked cartoon characters, began appearing in ads in 1904. In the 1990s, the Campbell Kids were still promoting the soups by dancing to rap songs in television commercials. Campbell's familiar jingle—"M'm! M'm! Good! M'm! M'm! Good! That's what Campbell's soups are! M'm! M'm! Good!"—was first heard in **radio** (see entry under 1920s—TV and Radio in volume 2) commercials in the 1930s. Generations of Americans were introduced to Campbell's products via celebrity endorsements and through its sponsorship of the *Campbell Playhouse* on radio, as well as on popular **television** (see entry under 1940s—TV and Radio in volume 3) programs such as *Lassie* (see entry under 1940s—Film and Theater in volume 3) and *Peter Pan*.

Always a favorite—warm Campbell's tomato soup on a cold day. © MICHAEL NEELON/ALAMY.

The familiar Campbell's soup can was inspired by the red-and-white uniforms of the Cornell University football team, which had impressed a company executive with their brilliance and visibility. In the 1960s, pop artist Andy Warhol (1928?–1987) transformed the image into an icon by creating paintings and serigraphs featuring the cans as a focal subject.

In the latter decades of the twentieth century, Campbell's added several new lines of soup products. The new products included the Chunky line, a heartier soup that did not require the addition of water, and a line of Healthy Request soups with less sodium, cholesterol, fat, and calories. Campbell's is also the parent company of other familiar brand names such as Pepperidge Farm, V8, Prego, Pace, and Swanson. In 2010, the company reported net worldwide sales of $7.7 billion and controlled approximately 80 percent of the U.S. soup market.

Edward Moran

For More Information

"Campbell Soup Company: History." *Campbell's Community*. http://careers. campbellsoupcompany.com/History.aspx (accessed June 22, 2011).

Collins, Douglas. *America's Favorite Food: The Story of Campbell Soup Company*. New York: Abrams, 1994.

Parkin, Katherine. "Campbell's Soup and the Long Shelf Life of Traditional Gender Roles." In *Kitchen Culture in America: Popular Representations of Food, Gender, and Race*. Edited by Sherrie A. Inness. Phladelphia: University of Pennsylvania Press, 2001.

World's Greatest Brands: An International Review. New York: John Wiley & Sons, 1992.

Oreo Cookies

Since their introduction on March 6, 1912, Nabisco's Oreo cookies have become the most popular commercial cookie product in the United States. More than 362 billion Oreos have been consumed over the years. According to their manufacturer, that number is equivalent to a pile that would stretch five times the distance from the Earth to the moon. Known officially as Oreo Chocolate Sandwich Cookies, a single Oreo consists of two intricately patterned chocolate-colored wafers with a cream filling in between.

Introduced in 1912, Oreos are still the top-selling sandwich cookie. © AP IMAGES/RICHARD DREW.

Nabisco does not offer a definitive conclusion about the origins of the name "Oreo," but cites several theories: it might have been suggested by *or,* the French word for gold, which was the most prominent color on the original packaging; it might have come from a Greek word for mountain, since early prototypes were mound-shaped; or it might have been invented by surrounding "RE" (two letters in the word "cream") with two "O"s from the word "chocolate." Although Nabisco does make Oreos with chocolate filling, the traditional cream filling (Nabisco spells it "creme") is white in color.

Over the years, consumers of Oreos have entered into a great debate over how best to eat the cookies. Citing research it performed in the 1990s on the eating habits of Oreo consumers, Nabisco claims that 35 percent of respondents to one survey twist their cookies apart before eating them, 30 percent dunk them in milk, and 10 percent nibble them.

Over the years, some variations have been introduced to the standard Oreo. These variations include Double Stuf, an Oreo with a double portion of cream filling; Fudge Covered Oreo Sandwich Cookies; Oreo Golden Fudge Cremes snack cookies; and seasonal Oreos, such as those with orange cream sold at Halloween.

Edward Moran

For More Information

Oreo: Milk's Favorite Cookie. http://www.nabiscoworld.com/oreo/ (accessed June 22, 2011).
World's Greatest Brands: An International Review. New York: John Wiley & Sons, 1992.

1910s

Print Culture

Although going to the movies became an increasingly popular way to spend leisure time during the 1910s, books and magazines still constituted the core entertainment of most Americans. In this decade, the gulf widened between American high literature (writing concerned with philosophic ideas) and American popular literature (writing designed to inform and entertain). Some of the finest literary artists of the century published important works in this decade, including novelists Willa Cather (1873–1947), Theodore Dreiser (1871–1945), and Sherwood Anderson (1876–1941); and poets Gertrude Stein (1874–1946), Vachel Lindsay (1879–1931), T. S. Eliot (1888 1965), William Carlos Williams (1883–1963), and Ezra Pound (1885–1972). These writers, and many others, were discussed in small-circulation "little magazines" that were dedicated to the arts. They were also talked about in more general magazines such as *The Atlantic Monthly, The Smart Set, Vanity Fair,* and *The Seven Arts.* These artists, however, had few readers compared with the enormous audiences enjoyed by popular novelists and contributors to the popular magazines.

American magazines continued to prosper during the decade, thanks largely to the eagerness of advertisers to promote their products to the millions of Americans who read popular magazines. The most popular magazines, including the *Saturday Evening Post,* the *American Magazine,*

Collier's, Ladies' Home Journal, and *Good Housekeeping,* often devoted half of each issue's pages to advertisements. The advertising industry grew dramatically to encourage Americans to purchase an increasingly vast array of consumer goods. Several new magazines attracted attention in this decade, including *True Story,* a racy confession magazine for working-class readers, and *Vogue,* one of the first magazines devoted to fashion.

Beginning in 1912, the magazine *Publishers Weekly* began to use the term "best-seller" to describe the most popular fiction and nonfiction in America. This magazine and several others tracked those books that sold best, and their publicity helped drive sales even higher. Gene Stratton Porter (1868–1924), Zane Grey (1875–1939), Harold Bell Wright (1872–1944), Mary Roberts Rinehart (1876–1958), and Winston Churchill (1874–1965) all had several titles on the best-seller list in the decade. During the World War I (1914–18) years, there was a separate list of best-sellers dedicated solely to publications about the war. The *Tom Swift* series of adventure books for boys was one of the publishing sensations of the decade. The *Tom Swift* books set the stage for the *Hardy Boys* and the *Nancy Drew* series that would become so popular during the 1920s. Another surprise hit of the decade was the *World Book Encyclopedia,* whose goal was to provide the accumulated wisdom of the Western world in an easy-to-read format.

Fu Manchu

"Imagine a person, tall, lean and feline, high-shouldered, with a brow like Shakespeare and a face like Satan, a close-shaven skull, and long, magnetic eyes of the true cat green. Invest him with all the cruel cunning of an entire Eastern race … and you will have a mental picture of Dr. Fu Manchu, the yellow peril incarnate in one man." This is how mystery writer Sax Rohmer introduced the villain to readers in his first novel featuring the character. The shadowy, sinister Fu Manchu is one of the best-known antagonists ever featured in Western literature. More than just an evil outlaw, the Fu Manchu character embodied the racism and xenophobia (fear of foreigners) that pervaded Western culture a century ago.

Fu Manchu was the creation of Sax Rohmer, the pen name of British writer Arthur Henry Sarsfield Ward (1883–1959). His first accounts of

Fu Manchu appeared as a series of stories published in a British magazine between 1912 and 1913. These accounts were published in 1913 as a novel, *The Mystery of Dr. Fu Manchu,* which was soon followed by *The Devil Doctor* (1916) and *The Si-Fan Mysteries* (1917). In each of these stories, Fu Manchu is the head of a secret society, the Si-Fan, which carries out sinister plots for the Chinese government. He is opposed in each book by Denis Nayland Smith, a bold and fearless British secret agent.

After the third book, Rohmer left the evil doctor, but he returned to the character in 1931 with *The Daughter of Fu Manchu.* He then produced *The Mask of Fu Manchu* (1932), *Fu Manchu's Bride* (1933), and *The Trail of Fu Manchu* (1934). After a shorter break, Rohmer brought Fu Manchu and his nemesis, Nayland Smith, back in *President Fu Manchu* (1936). The characters reappeared in 1939 in *The Drums of Fu Manchu* and in 1941 in *The Island of Fu Manchu.* Rohmer again abandoned his character for a time but then featured him in three more books: *The Shadow of Fu Manchu* (1948), *Re-Enter Fu Manchu* (1957), and *Emperor Fu Manchu* (1959), Rohmer's last novel.

Five of the novels were adapted into films between 1920 and 1966. Three different versions of *Fu Manchu* dramas were produced for **radio** (see entry under 1920s—TV and Radio in volume 2) during the 1930s, with another appearing during World War II (1939–45). An American **television** (see entry under 1940s—TV and Radio in volume 3) series based on the character was broadcast from 1956 to 1957.

Justin Gustainis

English actor Boris Karloff as Dr. Fu Manchu in the 1932 film The Mask of Fu Manchu.
© AF ARCHIVE/ALAMY.

For More Information

Knapp, Lawrence J. *The Page of Fu Manchu.* http://mlb.mlb.com/mlb/history/ (accessed June 22, 2011).

Nevins, Francis M. *The Mystery Writer's Art.* Bowling Green, OH: Bowling Green State University Popular Press, 1971.

Van Ash, Cay, and Elizabeth Sax Rohmer. *Master of Villainy: A Biography of Sax Rohmer.* Bowling Green, OH: Bowling Green State University Popular Press, 1972.

Krazy Kat

Krazy Kat, which appeared in newspapers from 1910 until 1944, is widely regarded as the most significant comic strip in American history. Created by George Herriman (1880–1944), the strip revolved around the misadventures of the androgynous (not clearly male or female) Krazy Kat and his (or her) love for Ignatz Mouse. Ignatz despised this unwanted affection and responded by continually hitting Krazy with an endless supply of bricks. Offisa Bull Pupp, a third character, served as the strip's symbol of law and order. Pupp also completed the strip's central love triangle since he adored Krazy and felt obligated to place the violent Ignatz in jail. Herriman's strip was noted for its unique blend of poetry, wordplay, bold colors, and surrealism (Surrealism was a twentieth-century movement that involved representing the subconscious mind in pictures and words, often in disconnected or dreamlike ways. The melting watches of artist Salvador Dali (1904–1989) are an example of surrealism).

Krazy Kat evolved from an earlier Herriman strip titled *The Dingbat Family* (1910–16), part of which highlighted the family's pets. In 1913, the animals were given their own feature that grew increasingly inventive and bizarre. M. Thomas Inge writes in *Comics as Culture* that "the world of *Krazy Kat* is a world of fantasy set against the surreal and abstract landscapes of Herriman's imaginative approximations of the real Coconino County in the state of Arizona." Krazy's world was a place where anything could happen. Landscapes mutated constantly. The characters spoke in a pun-filled dialect that contained elements of Latin, Greek, Old English, Yiddish, Navajo, and African American speech. The strip blended broad slapstick with sophisticated, philosophical thoughts on the absurdities of life. Intellectuals were especially devoted to the strip and proclaimed Herriman a cartooning genius. President Woodrow Wilson (1856–1924) was an avid admirer and read *Krazy Kat* at cabinet meetings. The strip has also been the focus of intense academic examination as to its "true meaning." In *America's Great Comic-Strip Artists,* Richard Marschall states, "It has been portrayed as a variation on the eternal triangle of tragic romances; as a grand statement on freedom versus authority; as an allegory on innocence meeting reality; and, of course, as a comic cacophony of obsessions."

Although the strip was critically acclaimed, it was never a financial success. Only the admiration of publisher William Randolph Hearst

(1863–1951) kept *Krazy Kat* in newspapers for decades. When Herriman died in 1944, the strip ended, and the comics page lost a small bit of its luster.

Charles Coletta

For More Information

Herriman, George. *The Komplete Kolor Krazy Kat.* 2 vols. Princeton, NJ: Remco/ Kitchen Sink, 1990–91.

Inge, M. Thomas. *Comics as Culture.* Jackson: University Press of Mississippi, 1990.

Markstein, Donald D. "Krazy Kat." *Don Markstein's Toonopedia.* http://www .toonopedia.com/krazy.htm (accessed June 22, 2011).

Marschall, Richard. *America's Great Comic-Strip Artists.* New York: Abbeville Press, 1989.

Yoe, Craig. *Krazy Kat and the Art of George Herriman.* New York: Abrams ComicArts, 2010.

Triple Self-Portrait of artist Norman Rockwell for the cover of the February 13, 1960, issue of the Saturday Evening Post.
© ALBERT KNAPP/ALAMY.

Norman Rockwell (1894–1978)

Norman Rockwell is famous for his illustrative paintings that capture everyday American life in the twentieth century. Rockwell began studying art during his freshman year of high school. He quit school when he was fifteen to attend the National Academy of Design, eventually enrolling in the Art Students League. Rockwell was interested in accurately capturing the minutest detail of his subjects and their settings. This technique allowed him to tell their stories and reveal their personalities via their facial expressions and body language.

In 1913, Rockwell was hired as contributing art director of *Boy's Life* magazine. However, it was not until 1916, when he began his association with the **Saturday Evening Post** (see entry under 1900s—Print Culture in volume 1), that he arrived as an artist. The *Saturday Evening Post* was then a popular mass-market magazine. For the next forty-seven years, Rockwell was the

Post's most famous and prolific cover illustrator. Additionally, he illustrated everything from Boy Scout calendars to reprints of *The Adventures of Tom Sawyer* and *Huckleberry Finn* to advertisements for the Massachusetts Mutual Life Insurance Company.

After leaving the *Post* in 1963, Rockwell's art became more issue-oriented. Among his most famous works of the period is his 1964 *Look* magazine cover depicting the integration of an all-white elementary school. During and after his lifetime, Rockwell was the subject of controversy in relation to the very nature and meaning of art. To some, Rockwell is one of America's greatest artists. Others view him as an overly sentimental illustrator whose concerns were strictly commercial and who depicted a narrow and stereotypical segment of American society.

Rob Edelman

For More Information

Claridge, Laura P. *Norman Rockwell: A Life.* New York: Random House, 2001.

Durrett, Deanne. *Norman Rockwell.* San Diego: Lucent Books, 1997.

Gherman, Beverly. *Norman Rockwell: Storyteller with a Brush.* New York: Atheneum Books for Young Readers, 2000.

The Norman Rockwell Musem. http://www.nrm.org/ (accessed June 22, 2011).

Rockwell, Norman. *My Adventures as an Illustrator, by Norman Rockwell, as told to Thomas Rockwell.* Garden City, NY: Doubleday, 1960.

Schick, Ron. *Norman Rockwell: Behind the Camera.* New York: Little Brown, 2009.

Tarzan

Tarzan, the Lord of the Jungle, has been one of the most enduring heroic figures in American popular culture ever since its creation. Created by writer Edgar Rice Burroughs (1875–1950) in 1912, the Tarzan character first appeared in the pulp fiction *All-Story Magazine* (**Pulp magazines** [see entry under 1930s—Print Culture in volume 2] of the era consisted of sensational stories printed on low-quality—that is, pulp—paper). Tarzan has appeared in more than twenty novels, forty films, several **television** (see entry under 1940s—TV and Radio in volume 3) programs, **radio** (see entry under 1920s—TV and Radio in volume 2) serials, comic strips, cartoons, **comic books** (see entry under 1930s—Print Culture in volume 2), toys, and thousands of items of merchandise.

The character's stories have been translated into more than fifty languages. He is one of the most famous men who never actually lived.

Burroughs had failed at nearly every endeavor he attempted before he devised Tarzan. In the initial tale of the "Lord of the Apes," Burroughs reveals his animalistic jungle man to be, in actuality, John Clayton, the future Lord Greystoke. As a child, Clayton's parents die while on tour of Africa. A female ape named Kala, who calls him Tarzan ("white-skin" in ape language), adopts him. Raised among the apes, he learns to communicate with all the wild beasts. As an adult, Tarzan encounters African natives as well as white people visiting the continent. His most significant relationship is with Jane Porter, an English woman on expedition with her father. A romance blossoms between the jungle man and the civilized lady. The two face many obstacles in both Africa and England, where Tarzan eventually claims his family's inheritance.

Tarzan was an immediate hit with the public, who were thrilled by his jungle adventures filled with lost cities, fierce animals, evil poachers, and tribal warfare. Tarzan achieved even greater popularity through his many film appearances. In 1918, Elmo Lincoln (1889–1952) was the first movie Tarzan in *Tarzan of the Apes*. Numerous muscular actors would also don the hero's signature loincloth over the years. The performer most associated with the role was Johnny Weissmuller (1904–1984), a former five-time gold medal winner in swimming from the 1924 and 1928 **Olympics** (see entry under 1900s—Sports and Games in volume 1). His powerful physique and great athletic abilities served him well in a dozen Tarzan movies filmed between 1932 and 1948. In film, Tarzan is usually played as a much less well-spoken figure than Burroughs' original character. The famous line of dialogue, "Me Tarzan, You Jane," never appeared in a Burroughs tale. The film most closely capturing Burroughs's conception of the character is 1984's *Greystoke: The Legend of Tarzan, Lord of the Apes,* starring Christopher Lambert (1957–) as Tarzan. A new generation of fans encountered the jungle hero in a 1999 animated **Disney** (see entry under 1920s—Film and Theater in volume 2) feature film.

When Burne Hogarth (1911–1996), writer of the *Tarzan* comic strip, was asked in *Comics: Between the Panels* to account for the jungle man's lasting popularity, he stated: "He is energy, grace, and virtue. He symbolizes the inevitable life source, the earth, the seed, the rain, the harvest, achievement, the triumph of adversity and death."

Charles Coletta

For More Information

Duin, Steve, and Mike Richardson. *Comics: Between the Panels*. Milwaukie, OR: Dark Horse Comics, 1998.

Edward Rice Burroughs, Inc. *Edgar Rice Burroughs: Creator of Tarzan*. http://www.tarzan.org (accessed June 22, 2011).

Foster, Hal. *Tarzan in Color*. New York: Flying Buttress, 1992.

Horn, Maurice, ed. *100 Years of American Newspaper Comics*. New York: Random House, 1996.

Taliaferro, John. *Tarzan Forever: The Life of Edgar Rice Burroughs, Creator of Tarzan*. New York: Scribner, 1999.

Tom Swift Series

The *Tom Swift* series included more than forty novels for boys published by the Grosset & Dunlap Company between 1910 and 1941. Although most of the books in the series were published under the pen name "Victor Appleton," they were really written by writers working for the Stratemeyer Syndicate. The Stratemeyer Syndicate was a book packager that created juvenile literature under the supervision of its founder, Edward Stratemeyer (1862–1930). The writer responsible for most of the *Tom Swift* series was Howard Roger Garis (1873–1962). Over the years, the *Tom Swift* series sold some six million copies.

Tom Swift, the hero of the series, was an ingenious, plucky lad who used modern technologies like electricity and steam power to outwit his rivals by creating new devices. In so doing, Tom Swift became a symbol of American creativity in an era that admired scientists and inventors like Thomas Edison (1847–1931) and the Wright Brothers (Wilbur, 1867–1912; Orville, 1871–1948). In an advertisement for the first set of *Tom Swift* books, Stratemeyer wrote: "It is the purpose of these spirited tales to convey in a realistic way the wonderful advances in land and sea locomotion and to interest the boy of the present in the hope that he may be a factor in aiding the marvelous development that is coming in the future."

In the earliest books in the series, all published in 1910, Tom Swift helps his father, Barton Swift ("the aged inventor"), build or improve airships and submarines. Tom goes on to invent a sky racer (1911), a telephone with photographic capability (1914), a transcontinental air-express service (1926), and "talking pictures" (1928). A regular cast of characters populates the *Tom Swift* series, including Tom's buddy Ned

Newton, an eccentric older friend, Wakefield Damon, and their rival, Andy Foger.

In the 1950s, the Stratemeyer Syndicate introduced a series of books about Tom Swift Jr., written under the pseudonym of Victor Appleton II, but the books never achieved the popularity of the originals. In the 1980s, Simon & Schuster published several *Tom Swift* books in a science-fiction format. In 1991, Simon & Schuster returned to the "inventions" format with several volumes published under its Archway imprint.

Edward Moran

For More Information

Cooper, Johnathan K. *The Complete Tom Swift Sr. Home Page.* http://www .tomswift.info/homepage/oldindex.html (accessed June 22, 2011).

Dizer, John T., Jr. *Tom Swift and Company: "Boy's Books" by Stratemeyer and Others.* Jefferson, NC: McFarland, 1982.

Heitman, Danny. "Tom Swift Turns 100." *Smithsonian.com.* http://www .smithsonianmag.com/arts-culture/Tom-Swift-Turns-100.html (accessed June 22, 2011).

Johnson, Deidre. *Edward Stratemeyer and the Stratemeyer Syndicate.* New York: Twayne, 1993.

True Story

A popular "confessional" magazine, first published by Bernarr Macfadden (1868–1955) in 1919, *True Story* was enormously popular during the 1920s and 1930s. Its largely working-class readership devoured its sensational and often tawdry tales of sin, sex, and redemption. By challenging mainstream publishing norms and presenting scoundrels as heroes and heroines, *True Story* outraged conventional society with its depictions of vice and undesirable behavior.

Macfadden, the eccentric publisher of *Physical Culture* magazine, got the idea for *True Story* from the personal letters of "confessions" he received from his readers about their own involvement with illegitimacy, premarital sex, adultery, and criminal activities. During the magazine's heyday, it was dismissed by serious critics, one of whom complained that it allowed millions of readers to "wallow in the filth of … politely dressed confessions." *True Story* was the forerunner of many of the supermarket tabloids that emerged in later years, with their tales of sordid gossip and bizarre occurrences.

By the 1930s, Macfadden succeeded in transforming the publication into a somewhat tamer women's romance magazine. Altered in design and style over the years, the periodical survived into the twenty-first century billed as "a modern woman's guide to love and life." Its first-person stories reflected more contemporary concerns, such as "I'm Going to Blow Up My School," "I'll Be Wife #5," and "War and Hunger." Yet, like hundreds of other magazines, *True Story* was compelled to suspend publication in recent years because of declining sales.

Edward Moran

For More Information

Adams, Mark. *Mr. America: How Muscular Millionaire Bernarr Macfadden Transformed the Nation Through Sex, Salad, and the Ultimate Starvation Diet.* New York: Harper, 2009.

Ernst, Robert. *Weakness Is a Crime: The Life of Bernarr Macfadden.* New York: Syracuse University Press, 1991.

"A Publishing Empire." *Bernarr Macfadden: The Father of Physical Culture.* http://www.bernarrmacfadden.com/macfadden5.html (accessed June 22, 2011).

Vogue

Vogue is one of the world's most influential lifestyle magazines about women's fashion and beauty. Founded as a weekly society paper in 1892 and purchased by Condé Nast in 1909, *Vogue* was the first magazine of its kind to use lavish photographic spreads and colorful graphics to highlight the latest fashion trends. The magazine became so influential that the phrase "Vogue model" became a synonym for the highest standards in beauty, composure, and sophistication.

Under editor-in-chief Edna Woolman Chase (1877–1957) and art director Mehemed Gehmy Agha (1896–1978), *Vogue* published the work of leading photographers like Edward Steichen (1879–1973), Sir Cecil Beaton (1904–1980), and Baron de Meyer (1868–1949). These photographers presented their models in glamorous settings that reflected the elaborate **Hollywood** (see entry under 1930s—Film and Theater in volume 2) movies of the period. During World War II (1939–45), *Vogue* concentrated more on affordable, ready-to-wear lines of clothing but continued to emphasize quality and style.

In the postwar era, editor-in-chief Jessica Davies collaborated with art director Alexander Liberman (1912–1999) to reform the magazine using simpler, more contemporary graphics. Together with photographers Irving Penn (1917–2009) and Richard Avedon (1923–2004), they reinvented the fashion magazine with images that used starker lighting and put a stronger focus on the model. *Vogue* also upgraded its coverage of contemporary events by including more serious commentaries on art, film, and theater and articles on the lives of celebrities and entertainers.

Editor-in-chief Diana Vreeland (1906–1989), credited with coining the term "youthquake," brought an edgier tone to the magazine by highlighting the colorful and revealing fashions and accessories that were representative of the "swinging sixties." Models such as Twiggy (1949–), Penelope Tree (1950–), and Verushka (1939–) became celebrities in their own right via photo shoots that showed them in action-filled, "real life" poses outside the studio. Vreeland's successor, Grace Mirabella (1929–), guided the magazine through the second-wave feminist era of the 1970s, when women wanted to be taken seriously in the workplace without sacrificing elegance and good taste. During this period, *Vogue* itself shrank in size from a large-format magazine and became a monthly. Mirabella was succeeded as editor-in-chief by Anna Wintour (1949–), who promoted fashion trends by new designers.

Edward Moran

A woman models green fashion in this February 1955 cover of Vogue. © JEFF MORGAN 15/ ALAMY.

For More Information

Devlin, Polly. *Vogue Book of Fashion Photography.* London: Thames and Hudson, 1979.

Kazanjian, Dodie, and Calvin Tomkins. *Alex: The Life of Alexander Liberman.* New York: Alfred A. Knopf, 1993.

Lloyd, Valerie. *The Art of Vogue Photographic Covers: Fifty Years of Fashion and Design.* New York: Harmony Books, 1986.

Vogue Magazine. http://www.vogue.com/ (accessed June 22, 2011).

World Book Encyclopedia

Published since 1917, the *World Book Encyclopedia* is a general reference work. The encyclopedia deliberately uses nontechnical language and abundant graphics to make it especially accessible to students and general readers without sacrificing depth and accuracy. The editors of the first edition emphasized the use of "everyday, simple language" in the eight-volume set.

In 1919, *World Book* began the practice of printing annual revisions of its encyclopedia, which has been followed every year since except for 1920, 1924, and 1932. *World Book*'s first major revision took place in 1929, when the set was expanded to thirteen volumes. In 1931, *World Book* adopted the unit-letter system of arrangement, in which each volume was a different-sized book that contained all the entries for one or more letters of the alphabet. The set was expanded to nineteen volumes in 1933, to twenty volumes in 1960, and to twenty-two volumes in 1972. The final volume in the set is a research guide and an index.

World Book has traditionally worked with educators in an attempt to keep its product in line with current teaching practices. In 1936, it created an editorial advisory board of distinguished educators and established a curriculum-analysis program to ensure that the encyclopedia would be especially useful to its student readers. In 1955, *World Book* launched a classroom research program designed to monitor exactly which subjects typical students were looking up in the reference work.

World Book entered the digital age in 1990 with the publication of *Information Finder,* its first CD-ROM encyclopedia, which included the full text of both the encyclopedia and a dictionary. In 1996, *World Book* partnered with IBM to produce a line of electronic reference works and learning products, and with Tiger Electronics to create the *World Book* Learning Center, an electronic learning aid. *World Book Online* was launched in 1998, with an interactive Web site that delivers articles, maps, pictures, sounds, and video to registered subscribers.

World Book has also created other reference products, including *Childcraft,* a resource library for preschool and elementary-school children, first published in 1934, the *World Book Dictionary* (1963), the *World Book Atlas* (1964), *Early World of Learning* (1987), plus annual volumes about science, health, and medicine. The *World Book Student Discovery Encyclopedia,* an introductory general reference set, appeared in

1999. Adapting to the times, the *World Book Encyclopedia* is also available online and includes video and other multimedia features.

Edward Moran

For More Information

Hancock, Susan, ed. A Guide to Children's Reference Books and Multimedia Material. Brookfield, VT: Ashgate, 1998.
World Book Online. http://www.worldbook.com/ (accessed June 22, 2011).

Zorro

Spanish actor Antonio Banderas resurrected the character of the dashing Zorro on screen in the 1998 film The Mask of Zorro. © MOVIESTORE COLLECTION LTD./ALAMY.

Zorro, the masked avenger of the Old Southwest, has been one of the most popular heroic figures of the twentieth century. The character, created by Johnston McCulley (1883–1958) in 1919, first appeared in a story titled "The Curse of Capistrano" in the pulp magazine *All-Story Weekly.* El Zorro ("The Fox") dressed completely in black and wore a mask and a wide-brimmed hat to conceal his identity as he fought evildoers in nineteenth-century California. He rode a jet-black horse named Tornado and was a master with both sword and whip. His trademark was to carve a "Z" with his blade upon his enemies. Without his costume, Zorro was the wealthy Spanish count Don Diego, who assumed a foppish manner to conceal his secret identity (A fop is a man who is overly concerned about his looks and his clothes). Zorro's adventures have thrilled Americans for generations as he has appeared in novels, film, **television** (see entry under 1940s—TV and Radio in volume 3), and cartoons, as well as in a multitude of merchandise and collectibles.

Zorro emerged from **pulp magazines** (see entry under 1930s—Print Culture in volume 2) to become a national phenomenon. Readers loved the swashbuckler as he displayed a devil-may-care attitude, great swordsmanship, and compassion for the oppressed, mistreated, and downcast members of society. McCulley penned sixty-five of the hero's adventures over nearly forty years. Zorro was successful in print, but he was even more popular on film. Douglas Fairbanks Sr. (1883–1939) first portrayed him in *The Mark of Zorro* (1920) to great acclaim. Numerous Zorro films and serials appeared into the 1970s. Perhaps the most popular depiction of Zorro was in the 1940 version of *The Mark of Zorro*. Actor Tyrone Power (1914–1958) perfectly characterized both the weak Don Diego and bold hero Zorro.

Zorro was also often featured on television. Disney produced a Zorro series in the 1950s starring Guy Williams (1924–1989) that sparked a merchandising bonanza. In 1980, George Hamilton (1939–) appeared in the campy *Zorro, The Gay Blade*. The film showed Zorro wearing a pink leather costume and was a complete disaster. Between 1989 and 1994, Duncan Regehr (1952–) appeared as the swordsman. The 1980s and 1990s witnessed several more animated Zorro programs. In 1998, Zorro again dominated the national consciousness when Anthony Hopkins (1937–) and Antonio Banderas (1960–) starred in *The Mask of Zorro,* which introduced the character to another generation of fans.

Zorro was one of the twentieth century's first popular heroic icons. He is a dashing, gentleman bandit who performs heroic feats, woos lovely ladies, and fights corruption—all with a charming elegance and flashing blade. Dozens of heroic characters, most notably **Batman** (see entry under 1930s—Print Culture in volume 2), have followed the pattern established by McCulley's masked daredevil.

Charles Coletta

For More Information

Curtis, Sandra. *Zorro Unmasked: The Official History.* New York: Hyperion, 1998.

Hutchinson, Don. *The Great Pulp Heroes.* Buffalo: Mosaic Press, 1996.

McCulley, Johnston. *The Mark of Zorro.* New York: American Reprint Co., 1924, 1976.

Toth, Alex. *Zorro: The Complete Classic Adventures.* Forestville, CA: Eclipse Books, 1988.

White, Jennifer. *The Zorro Legend Through the Years.* http://zorrolegend.com/ (accessed June 22, 2011).

1910s

Sports and Games

Baseball continued to dominate the American sports scene in the 1910s. Attendance at professional baseball games remained high throughout the decade, rising slightly from 6,206,447 in 1910 to 6,532,439 in 1919; numbers that might have been even higher without the interruptions of World War I (1914–18). The American League dominated the World Series, winning eight of ten titles in the decade. The games biggest stars were Ty Cobb (1886–1961) of the Detroit Tigers, Walter Johnson (1887–1946) of the Washington Senators, and an emerging star—George Herman "Babe" Ruth (1895–1948) of the Boston Red Sox (and later the New York Yankees). Baseball received a black eye in 1919 when several players on the Chicago White Sox were involved in throwing (intentionally losing) the World Series for money; the event became colloquially known as the Black Sox Scandal.

Aside from baseball, American professional sports were just getting started in the 1910s. Professional hockey got its start in 1911 with the founding of the Pacific Coast Hockey League, which overshadowed the fledgling National Hockey League, founded in 1917. Auto racing also got a boost in the decade with the founding of the Indianapolis 500. Ray Harroun (1879–1968) won the initial race—and the $10,000 prize—by averaging an amazing 74.6 miles an hour. Horse racing also gained respectability in the decade thanks to the introduction of the Triple

Crown, a series of horse races that included the most famous race of all, the Kentucky Derby.

College football continued to be the most popular fall spectator sport, with Notre Dame becoming a dominant team in the decade behind the play of Knute Rockne (1888–1931), who became the team's coach late in the decade. Professional football was still limited to a small league in the Midwest. Unlike professional baseball, the early pro football leagues allowed black players to participate, and several black players starred on early teams. Native American Jim Thorpe (1888–1953) was the star of the decade in professional football, and he remained so into the 1920s.

Black boxer Jack Johnson (1878–1946) continued his reign as heavyweight champion during the decade, enraging racist white fight fans who could not stand the idea of a black man being in such a position of dominance. Johnson finally lost his title to white boxer Jess Willard (1883–1968) in 1915. In 1919, a new champion, Jack Dempsey (1895–1983), took the crown. Dempsey would become the most celebrated boxer of the 1920s. Other sports also gained participants in the decade. Golf and tennis—once the exclusive domain of wealthy sportspeople—became popular among the American middle class. Golf champion Walter Hagen (1892–1969) became a minor celebrity.

Young Americans also enjoyed some fascinating new toys and games in this decade. Both Tinkertoys and Erector Sets allowed children to create toys modeled after the innovations of their day, such as cars and skyscrapers. Other children played with the newly popular Raggedy Ann and Andy dolls. Each of these toys remained in production through the early twenty-first century.

Erector Sets

Before **LEGOs** (see entry under 1950s—Sports and Games in volume 3), there were Erector Sets. The Erector Set is a popular construction toy that taught as well as amused youngsters for most of the twentieth century. The primary components of Erector Sets are nuts, bolts, and hole-filled metal girders of varying sizes. Other materials include wheels, pulleys, gears, and electric motors. Following instructions that come in each Erector Set box, children use the nuts and bolts to attach the girders, resulting in the construction of elaborate miniature buildings, airplanes, trucks, cars, bridges, ships, clocks, houses—and even robots.

The toy was first produced in 1913 by the Mysto Magic Company, which sold magic-trick components. It was the creation of A. C. Gilbert (1884–1961), the company founder. Gilbert was a man of varied interests and many talents. In 1908, he won a gold medal for pole-vaulting in the Summer **Olympics** (see entry under 1900s—Sports and Games in volume 1). The following year, he earned a medical degree from Yale University. While a passenger on a train bound from New Haven, Connecticut, to New York City, he observed workmen positioning steel beams, which inspired him to create a children's construction kit that he called the "Mysto Erector Structural Steel Builder" which eventually became commonly known as the Erector Set. Gilbert was aware of similar construction toys already available in the marketplace, such as the English Meccano. However, his sets were an improvement over the competition, because he included square girders and pieces that could bend to a ninety-degree angle. Gilbert's goal was to create a toy that was fun to play with but also allowed the user to gain an increased understanding of science and technology. He believed that "playing is essential to learning."

The instructions that accompanied Erector Sets from decade to decade paralleled twentieth-century technological advances. As architects designed great urban **skyscrapers** (see entry under 1930s—The Way We Lived in volume 2) and expansive suspension bridges, Erector Set owners were encouraged to build their own tall buildings and elevated structures. Instructions for constructing trucks, **Ferris wheels** (see entry under 1900s—The Way We Lived in volume 1), and zeppelins were added to the sets during the 1920s. A parachute jump came in the 1940s, followed by an entire **amusement park** (see entry under 1950s—The Way We Lived in volume 3) in the 1950s.

Gilbert created and marketed additional toys, including Mysto Magic sets, American Flyer trains, a glass-blowing kit, and an Atomic

A father and son play with an erector set. Creator A. C. Gilbert once said., "Playing is essential to learning." © STEVE CHENN/CORBIS.

Energy Lab, which included authentic radioactive particles and a real Geiger counter. In his lifetime, Gilbert was credited with over 150 patents and inventions. After his death, the Meccano Company—now Meccano Toys Ltd., one of Gilbert's chief early competitors—purchased the rights to Erector Sets. The Brio Corporation, known for its wooden trains, began distributing a new line of Erector Sets in the summer of 2001. In 2010, an independent film company announced it was partnering with Meccano to create an Erector **3-D** (see 3-D Movies entry under 1950s—Film and Theater in volume 3 and New 3-D entry under 2000s—Film and Theater in volume 6) feature film.

Rob Edelman

For More Information

Bean, William M. and Al M. Sternagle. *Greenberg's Guide to Gilbert Erector Sets, 1913–1932.* Waukesha, WI: Kalmbach Publishing Company, 1993.

Bean, William M. *Greenberg's Guide to Gilbert Erector Sets, Volume Two, 1933–1962.* Waukesha, WI: Kalmbach Publishing Company, 1998.

Erector Sets Homepage. http://www.erector-sets.com/ (accessed June 22, 2011).

Indianapolis 500

The Indianapolis 500 is America's most celebrated auto race. It has been held each May on or around Memorial Day, every year since 1911 (except during the world war years), at the Indianapolis Motor Speedway. The race consists of two hundred laps around the track's two-and-a-half-mile oval.

When the race started in 1911, it was called the International Sweepstakes, and it lasted most of the day. Ray Harroun (1879–1968) earned $10,000 for his first-place finish. His car, known as the "Marmon Wasp," averaged a then-astounding 74.602 miles per hour. The car reportedly was the first single-seat race car and the first automobile ever to employ a rearview mirror. Now contrast Harroun's statistics to those of drivers and cars racing in the 500 during the final quarter of the twentieth century. By then, the race generally was completed in less than three-and-a-half hours. In 1977, Tom Sneva (1948–) became the first driver to top 200 miles per hour during a race; by the 1990s, drivers regularly topped 220 miles on the corners and 240 miles on the straightaways. In 1990, winner Arie Luyendyk (1953–) averaged a course-record 185.981

Ray Harroun drives his Marmon Wasp to victory in the first Indianapolis 500 race in 1911. © BETTMANN/CORBIS.

miles per hour. Harroun's prize money was a tidy sum back in 1911, but it does not compare with the $1,568,150 Luyendyk walked away with for winning the 500 in 1997.

Almost all of America's greatest drivers have raced at Indianapolis. In its early days, the race included barnstormers like Harroun. Between 1937 and 1940, Wilbur Shaw (1902–1954) came in first place three times. In 1946, Shaw persuaded businessman-philanthropist Anton "Tex" Hulman (1901–1977) to purchase the speedway from its ownership group. Shaw was named its president. Under his and Hulman's stewardship, the Indianapolis 500 earned its status as the world's top auto race. In the 1950s, such innovations as high-octane gasoline, fuel injection, and disc brakes all were tested at Indianapolis.

Of all the drivers to compete in the Indianapolis 500, the most celebrated is A. J. Foyt (1935–), who debuted in the race in 1958. He holds the record for most career starts (thirty-five, all consecutive) and most competitive miles driven (12,273 miles). Foyt emerged victorious a record four times, a feat equaled only by Al Unser (1939–) and Rick Mears (1951–). On the downside, forty-one drivers have been killed at Indianapolis across the decades, sixteen drivers during the actual race and twenty-five during practice and qualifying runs.

In recent years, because so much money is at stake, race-car owners have become as prominent as their drivers. Perhaps the most famous is Roger Penske (1937–), a former driver who became a car-and-track owner. The decade of the 1990s saw an increase in politics within the racing establishment, and competition between the Indianapolis Racing League (IRL), which sponsors the Indianapolis 500, and its rival Championship Auto Racing Teams (CART). For this reason, many of the sport's top drivers have been forgoing the Indianapolis 500, detracting from its traditional reputation as "the greatest spectacle in racing."

Rob Edelman

For More Information

Binford, Tom. *A Checkered Past: My Twenty Years as Indy 500 Chief Steward.* Chicago: Cornerstone, 1998.

"Indy 500." *Indianapolis Motorspeedway.* http://www.indianapolismotorspeedway. com/indy500/ (accessed June 22, 2011).

Kramer, Charles. *The Indianapolis 500: A Century of Excitement.* Iola, WI: Krause, 2010.

Leerhsen, Charles. *Blood and Smoke: A True Tale of Mystery, Mayhem, and the Birth of the Indy 500.* New York: Simon & Schuster, 2011.

Reed, Terry. *Indy: The Race and Ritual of the Indianapolis 500.* 2nd ed. Washington, DC: Potomac Books, 2005.

Taylor, Rich. *Indy: 75 Years of Auto Racing's Greatest Spectacle.* New York: St. Martin's Press, 1991.

National Hockey League

Ice hockey has been played for more than five hundred years, but the National Hockey League (NHL) has only been around since 1917. Formed by hockey team owners in the aftermath of World War I (1914–18), this new professional league succeeded where previous ones, such as the

International Pro Hockey League, the National Hockey Association, and the Pacific Coast League had failed.

The NHL originally consisted of five teams: the Montreal Canadiens, the Montreal Wanderers, the Ottawa Senators, the Quebec Bulldogs, and the Toronto Arenas. The league's first game was held December 19, 1917. By 1926, the league had expanded to include ten teams and two divisions and adopted the Stanley Cup as its championship trophy. The financial shocks of the **Great Depression** (1929–41; see entry under 1930s—The

Way We Lived) claimed four franchises, leaving the NHL as a six-team league until 1967. The period of 1942 to 1967 saw increasing dominance of the sport by Canadian players. In fact, the two premier Canadian teams, the Toronto Maple Leafs and the Montreal Canadiens, won a combined total of ten Stanley Cups during the era.

One of the NHL's first American superstars emerged in the late 1960's as defenseman Bobby Orr (1948–) led the Boston Bruins to two Stanley Cup victories. Orr's success and the development of college hockey programs in the United States spurred renewed American enthusiasm for the sport during the 1970s. In 1979 the league merged with its rival, the World Hockey Association, adding five teams in one stroke of a pen.

The NHL continued to grow in the 1980s, following the gold medal performance by the U.S. men's team at the 1980 Winter **Olympics** (see entry under 1900s—Sports and Games in volume 1) in Lake Placid, New York. **Wayne Gretzky** (1961–; see entry under 1980s—Sports and Games in volume 5) and his Edmonton Oilers became the dominant team in the sport during the 1980s. The high-scoring Mario Lemieux (1965–) emerged as a star in the 1990s. The collapse of the Soviet Union spurred the emigration of a number of talented Eastern European players, such as Jaromir Jagr (1972–) and Dominik Hasek (1965–). The influx of new players and styles made the game of hockey more dynamic than ever before, and this period saw the NHL enjoy its greatest growth. A number of new franchises were added, while others, particularly those based in Canada, relocated to growing American cities like Phoenix, Arizona, and Denver, Colorado. A players' strike in 1995 briefly curtailed the NHL's growth, and in 2004 labor negotiations resulted in a league lockout that ultimately canceled an entire season of play. Despite the disruption, the popularity of the NHL has grown in recent years. This is due in part to the "Winter Classic," a popular match played outdoors— sometimes amidst the snow—each New Year's Day since 2008.

Robert E. Schnakenberg

For More Information

Goyens, Chrys, and Frank Orr. *Blades on Ice: A Century of Professional Hockey.* Markham, Ontario: TPE, 2000.

NHL.com. www.nhl.com (accessed June 22, 2011).

Pincus, Arthur, David Rosner, Len Hochberg, and Chris Malcolm. *The Official Illustrated NHL History.* Toronto: Carlton, 2010.

Strachan, Al, ed. *One Hundred Years of Hockey.* San Diego, CA: Thunder Bay Press, 1999.

Raggedy Ann and Raggedy Andy

A quarter of a century before the 1995 film *Toy Story* (see entry under 1990s—Film and Theater in volume 5) explored the hidden lives of toys, a writer named Johnny Gruelle (1880–1938) wrote about the adventures of a pair of dolls and their toy friends and the lives they lived when "real" people were not looking. First created in 1918, Raggedy Ann and Andy are still loved by children all over the world.

Dolls made of rags were not uncommon in the eighteenth and nineteenth centuries, when most toys were handmade and not manufactured. In the early 1900s, Gruelle's daughter Marcella had loved a little rag doll she named Raggedy Ann. Marcella died while still a child, and her grieving father began to write down stories about his daughter's favorite doll. Raggedy Ann, and later her brother Raggedy Andy, appeared in a series of popular books with titles like *How Raggedy Ann Got Her Candy Heart* and *Raggedy Ann and Raggedy Andy and the Camel with the Wrinkled Knees.*

Soon, toymakers began making dolls that looked like the ones in Gruelle's books. Modern children cannot only read Raggedy Ann and

Raggedy Ann and brother Raggedy Andy have comforted children for decades. © PHOTOSPIN/ALAMY.

Andy books and own the dolls, but can also watch Raggedy Ann and Andy videos and dress in Raggedy costumes on Halloween.

Tina Gianoulis

For More Information

Hall, Patricia. *Raggedy Ann and Andy: A Retrospective Celebrating 85 Years of Storybook Friends.* New York: Simon and Schuster, 2001.

Hall, Patricia. *The Real-for-Sure Story of Raggedy Ann.* Gretna, LA: Pelican Publishing, 2001.

"History of Raggedy Ann." *The Raggedy Ann and Andy Museum.* http://www .raggedyann-museum.org/ra_history.html (accessed June 22, 2011).

Hudson, Patricia L. "Still Smiling at Seventy-Five: What a Doll!" *Americana* (Vol. 18, no. 5, December 1990): pp. 52–56.

Babe Ruth (1895–1948)

"The Sultan of Swat": Babe Ruth in the New York Yankees dugout in 1926. © UNDERWOOD & UNDERWOOD/CORBIS

With due respect to baseball stars like **Ty Cobb** (1919–1972; see entry under 1900s—Sports and Games in volume 1), **Jackie Robinson** (1919–1972; see entry under 1940s—Sports and Games in volume 3), and Mickey Mantle (1931–1995), many fans view Babe Ruth as the most celebrated **baseball** (see entry under 1900s—Sports and Games in volume 1) hero of the twentieth century.

For over two decades beginning in 1914, George Herman Ruth—whose nicknames included "the Bambino" and "the Sultan of Swat"—ruled the world of baseball. His most prominent records have been broken. His record of sixty home runs in a season, set in 1927, was eclipsed thirty-four years later by Roger Maris (1934–1985) and broken yet again by McGwire and Sammy Sosa (1968–) in 1998 and **Barry Bonds** (1964–; see entry under 2000s—Sports and Games in volume 6) in 2001. Ruth's career record of 714 round-trippers was bested in the early 1970s by Hank Aaron (1934–), whose record, in turn, was bested in 2007 by Bonds.

Yet Ruth remains the most enduring of all baseball immortals for many reasons.

His larger-than-life presence, his lovable personality, and his Hall of Fame–caliber pitching skills are all factors that figure into his reputation. The most significant reason, though, is his single-handed rescue of baseball in the wake of the Black Sox gambling scandal that forever tainted the 1919 World Series, leading to a questioning of the game's integrity by a wary public. In this regard, Ruth was key to the sport's resurgence during the 1920s. In fact, Ruth became so popular and successful with the New York Yankees in the 1920s that he became the subject of a superstition known as the "Curse of the Bambino" in Boston. The **Boston Red Sox** (see entry under 200s–Sports and Games in volume 6), traded Ruth to the Yankees in 1919, and then proceeded to go eighty-five years without winning the World Series. The Yankees, meanwhile, became one of baseball's top teams. The "curse" brought on by trading Ruth was finally broken (see entry under 200s–Sports and Games in volume 6) when Boston swept the St. Louis Cardinals in the 2004 World Series.

Rob Edelman

For More Information
Creamer, Robert W. *Babe: The Legend Comes to Life.* New York: Simon and Schuster, 1974.

Jacobs, William Jay. *They Shaped the Game: Ty Cobb, Babe Ruth, Jackie Robinson.* New York: C. Scribner's Sons, 1994.

Macht, Norman L. *Babe Ruth.* New York: Chelsea House, 1990.

Miller, Ernestine. *The Babe Book: Baseball's Greatest Legend Remembered.* Kansas City: Andrews McMeel, 2000.

Montville, Leight. *The Big Bam: The Life and Times of Babe Ruth.* New York: Doubleday, 2006.

Ruth, George Herman. *Babe Ruth's Own Book of Baseball.* Lincoln: University of Nebraska Press, 1992.

Tinkertoys

Like **LEGOS** (see entry under 1950s—Sports and Games in volume 3), **Lincoln Logs** (see entry under 1920s—Sports and Games in volume 2), and **Erector Sets** (see entry under 1910s—Sports and Games in volume 1), Tinkertoys have an ageless appeal. Introduced in 1914, the simple wooden sticks with connecting wooden hubs remain a favorite among kids into the twenty-first century. In many ways, Tinkertoys are the

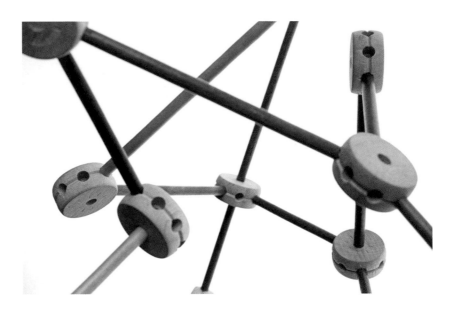

perfect toy. Simple and durable, they have the capacity to engage a child's imagination as he or she creates an unlimited variety of structures.

Tinkertoys were invented by Charles H. Pajeau, a stone mason. He thought up the toy after watching children play with pencils and wooden spools. Pajeau drilled holes around the sides of a spool and sawed thin wooden dowels into various lengths to create the first set of Tinkertoys. The sticks and spools could be combined to create a huge number of shapes, from cars to boats to the Tinkertoy classic **Ferris wheel** (see entry under 1900s—The Way We Lived in volume 1). Pajeau joined with former stock trader Robert Pettit to form a company called The Toy Tinkers of Evanston, Illinois. In 1914, they set up Tinkertoy Ferris wheels in shop windows in Chicago, Illinois, and their toy became an immediate hit. For the next several decades, demand for their product was high. In 1952, the original owners sold their company. The Tinkertoy brand passed through several owners before being purchased by toy-industry giant Hasbro in 1986.

Tinkertoys have gone through a number of changes over the years. Sets have been sold in different sizes and with motors. Beginning in 1992, wood was replaced with plastic in the majority of Tinkertoys sets. In 2000, however, Hasbro took Tinkertoys back to its roots and began marketing wooden Tinkertoys in the characteristic cardboard canister.

Nearly ninety years after their introduction, classic wooden Tinkertoys remain a favorite among American kids. In recognition of their enduring status, in 2001 Tinkertoys were named "Toy of the Year" in their category by the Toy Manufacturers of America.

Tom Pendergast

For More Information

Jailer, Mildred. "Construction Toys." *Antiques and Collecting Hobbies* (May 1988): p. 38.

Strange, Craig. *Collector's Guide to Tinker Toys.* Paducah, KY: Collector Books, 1996.

"Tinker Toys." *Yesterdayland.* http://www.retroland.com/?s=tinkertoys (accessed June 30, 2011).

1910s

The Way We Lived

Like the decade before it, the 1910s were characterized by a slow but steady modernization trend. American society became more urban. People left rural areas for suburbs. Cities expanded thanks to the ease of travel provided by automobiles, buses, and streetcars. As American factories grew larger and more capable of producing a variety of goods, more Americans stopped making their own clothes, food, and other household goods at home. Instead, they bought those goods from retail stores and from the growing variety of catalog retailers, such as Sears, Roebuck and Co.; L. L. Bean; and others.

Several dramatic social movements also helped reshape America in the decade. Racism grew even more intense in the South, as demonstrated by the growing number of Jim Crow laws (which forced blacks into separate and inferior public facilities) and the increase in lynchings (illegal mob killings). By mid-decade blacks began leaving the South in huge numbers, heading north to fill the expanding factories of manufacturers in cities such as Detroit, Michigan; Chicago, Illinois; Cleveland, Ohio; and New York City. This movement of African Americans, quickened by the involvement of the United States in World War I (1914–18) in 1917, is known as the Great Migration (1900–60).

Two other social movements led to constitutional amendments. As more and more women left their roles as homemakers and moved into the workplace, they clamored for the full rights enjoyed by men, including the right to vote. Thanks to leadership from organizers like Carrie Chapman Catt (1859–1947) and Alice Paul (1885–1977), a women's suffrage amendment passed through Congress in 1919 and became law in 1920 as the Nineteenth Amendment. Temperance crusaders led a campaign to ban the sale and distribution of alcohol, which culminated in the Eighteenth Amendment, ratified in 1919 (and repealed in 1933 after the disastrous social experiment known as Prohibition).

World War I brought major changes to the way Americans lived during the decade as well. American leaders kept the United States out of the war for the first three years, but when America joined the Allied forces in 1917, Americans threw their support behind the war effort. Two million American soldiers joined the war effort, including several thousand African Americans. Millions more Americans supported the war by purchasing war bonds. Though war brought unity to many Americans, it also created several social and political divisions. German immigrants were singled out for mistreatment, even though most committed themselves to their new country. Political radicals like Socialists and Communists faced hostility during the Red Scare of 1919.

Despite these major social changes, people still found time for new forms of amusement. There were popular crazes for new games like the card game bridge. Americans by the thousands went to see a new circus that billed itself as the "Greatest Show on Earth"—the Ringling Bros. and Barnum & Bailey Circus. Boys and girls across the nation enjoyed joining the Boy Scouts and the Girl Scouts, two popular organizations that tried to build character in their participants.

Bridge

One of the most popular card games in the world, bridge has been played in one form or another since the sixteenth century. Since modern contract bridge was developed in 1925, the game has become by far the most organized card game, with bridge clubs and leagues all over the world sponsoring highly competitive tournaments. Though often associated with well-to-do older ladies trading gossip and nibbling delicate snacks between hands, bridge actually requires significant skill and strategy. Enthusiasts include all sorts of people from college students to business executives.

Although some claim that the game of bridge has its roots in Turkey or Russia, the first real documentation of a bridge-like card game comes from sixteenth-century England. That game, called whist, whisk, triumph, or trump, introduced the "trick," where each player in turn lays a card down, following suit, and the highest ranking card wins the round.

The game went through various stages of development, but modern contract bridge was invented in 1925 by wealthy American business-man Harold S. Vanderbilt (1884–1970), supposedly to pass the time while cruising through the Panama Canal. Within two years, three major national contract bridge clubs had formed. In 1928, the first national bridge championship tournament was played. The winner of that tournament, Ely Culbertson (1893–1955), went on to popular-ize bridge nationwide. Culbertson founded *Bridge World* magazine and wrote the *Blue Book,* which laid out rules and strategies for playing the game. In the 1940s, another champion, Charles Goren (1901–1991), became the national bridge expert, writing a daily newspaper column on bridge tactics.

Though bridge is often thought of as an old-fashioned game, it still has an enormous following. As of 2011, the American Contract Bridge League had 160,000 members nationwide, and the **Internet** (see entry under 1990s—The Way We Lived in volume 5) is also bringing bridge to a wider and younger audience than ever. There are dozens of bridge Web sites where players who are home alone can find partners with whom to play. One of the largest, OKBridge.com, claims thirteen thousand mem-bers from over one hundred countries.

Tina Gianoulis

For More Information

American Contact Bridge League. http://www.acbl.org/ (accessed June 22, 2011).

D'Amato, Brian. "Bridge: The Game People Play." *Harper's Bazaar* (August 1994): pp. 66–68.

Goodwin, Jude, and Don Ellison. *Teach Me to Play: A First Bridge Book.* Roswell, GA: Pando Publications, 1988.

Grant, Audrey. *Bridge Basics 1: An Introduction.* Louisville, KY: Baron Barclay Bridge, 2006.

Koczela, Catherine. "Bridge, Handed Down; Among High Schoolers, Old Game Gaining New Following." *Washington Post* (October 16, 1997): p. M1.

Father's Day

On Father's Day, the third Sunday in June, children young and old show appreciation for their dear-old dads—and uncles, grandfathers, and godfathers. The day serves as a symbol of America's regard not only for fatherhood but also for the sanctity of the American family.

The roots of the day are imprecise. In 1910, Sonora Smart Dodd, of Spokane, Washington, wished to honor her father—a man who had raised his six children upon the death of his wife—successfully petitioned the Spokane Ministerial Association to set aside a day of reverence for all fathers. Yet Vancouver, Washington, claimed to be the first American city to officially sanction Father's Day, in 1912. Three years later, Harry Meek, the president of the Uptown Lions Club in Chicago, Illinois, was recognized as the "Originator of Father's Day" when he proposed that the third Sunday in June be set aside to honor fatherhood. He selected that date because it was closest to the birthday of the then–U.S. president, Woodrow Wilson (1856–1924). In 1924, President Calvin Coolidge (1872–1933) advocated the official acknowledgment of Father's Day across the country. Finally, in 1972, President Richard Nixon (1913–1994) signed a law making the day an official national holiday.

Today, Father's Day is exploited commercially, as children are expected not just to honor their fathers but to shower them with cards and gifts. Each year, approximately one hundred million Father's Day cards are purchased, along with endless neckties, power tools, sports shirts, golf balls, and other "male" attire and accessories. Nonetheless, the day remains a reminder of the sacrifice and devotion of fathers across the nation.

Rob Edelman

For More Information

Klebanow, Barbara, and Sara Fischer. *American Holidays: Exploring Traditions, Customs, and Backgrounds.* 2nd ed. Brattleboro, VT: Pro Lingua Associates, 2005.

Myers, Robert. *Celebrations: Complete Book of American Holidays.* New York: Doubleday, 1972.

Santino, Jack. *All Around the Year: Holidays and Celebrations in American Life.* Urbana: University of Illinois Press, 1995.

Schmidt, Leigh Eric. *Consumer Rites: The Buying and Selling of American Holidays.* Princeton, NJ: Princeton University Press, 1995.

Greyhound Buses

With the advice to "Go Greyhound—and leave the driving to us," Greyhound buses have become part of the mythology of the American road. In 1968, songwriter **Paul Simon** (1941–; see Simon and Garfunkel entry under 1960s—Music in volume 4) wrote of exploring America, and finding himself, on a Greyhound bus. Often operating out of bus stations in neglected areas of urban areas, Greyhound still represents the best way to, as Simon sang, "look for America."

Founded by Carl Eric Wickman (1887–1954) in 1914, Greyhound Buses started life as the Mesaba Transportation Company. Wickman's first bus, a seven-passenger Hupmobile, carried mineworkers between the towns of Hibbing and Alice, Minnesota. The company grew quickly. By 1935, there were seventeen hundred buses with the "racing Greyhound" logo, covering over forty-six thousand route miles. In 2000, the

"Go Greyhound—and leave the driving to us!" A Greyhound bus travels through Detroit. © IMAGES-USA/ALAMY.

company carried over nineteen million passengers. Over two thousand people every day travel its busiest route, between New York City and Atlantic City, New Jersey.

Chris Routledge

For More Information

Gabrick, Robert. *Going the Greyhound Way: The Romance of the Road.* Hudson, WI: Iconografix, 2009.

Greyhound.com. http://www.greyhound.com/ (accessed on June 22, 2011).

Jackson, Carlton. *Hounds of the Road: A History of the Greyhound Bus Company.* 2nd ed. Bowling Green, OH: Bowling Green University Popular Press, 2001.

Schisgall, Oscar. *The Greyhound Story: From Hibbing to Everywhere.* Chicago: J. G. Ferguson, 1985.

Ku Klux Klan

The Ku Klux Klan is America's oldest white supremacist organization. It first gained prominence in the South during Reconstruction (1865–77; the period following the American Civil War during which the federal government assisted and policed the former Confederate states), which the Klan resisted with beatings, murder, and terrorism. Although the organization has splintered and its fortunes have declined somewhat, the Klan still maintained a high level of awareness within the collective American consciousness in the twenty-first century.

The organization's name is derived from the Greek word *kuklos,* meaning "circle," and a corruption of "clan," or family. Its origins lie with a group of six Confederate war veterans who returned to Pulaski, Tennessee, when the Civil War (1861–65) ended in 1865. They relieved boredom by dressing up in white sheets and playing pranks on their neighbors at night. The Klan might have remained a mere gang of bullies were it not for the Congressional Reconstruction Act of 1867. This law mandated Federal military occupation of the South, declared Southern state governments illegitimate, and said that the rights of newly freed black slaves would be guaranteed by the U.S. Army.

The Klan, whose membership grew quickly, responded with violence toward anyone—black or white—who appeared to threaten the traditional Southern way of life. There are no reliable statistics for the number of people intimidated, beaten, shot, or lynched (murdered by a

A cross burning at a North Carolina Ku Klux Klan rally, October 8, 1989. © JIM MCDONALD/CORBIS.

mob, usually by hanging) by the Klan, but the violence was bad enough for Congress to pass anti-Klan legislation in 1871 and again in 1872, and to back it up with Federal troops. The Klan did not disappear, but its more public outrages stopped.

The Klan first entered popular culture in 1905, with the publication of a novel by Thomas Dixon Jr. (1864–1946), *The Clansman.* Dixon was a virulent racist. His book both criticized Reconstruction and praised the Klan's response to it. He did the same in the sequel, *The Leopard's Spots,* which appeared the following year. Both books were popular in the South, but their greatest influence involved filmmaker D. W. Griffith (1875–1948), who used material from the two novels in his 1915 epic film **The Birth of a Nation** (see entry under 1910s—Film and Theater in volume 1).

The film, regarded as one of the classics of early American cinema, is nonetheless thoroughly racist. Blacks are portrayed as either sex-crazed rapists or as moronic victims of "carpet-baggers," Northerners who moved south after the war to take advantage of post-war conditions in the South. The film's protagonists, the Stonemans, are saved from a mob of blacks only by the intervention of the Ku Klux Klan.

The Klan is also portrayed positively in 1918's *The Prussian Cur,* an anti-German propaganda film released in the last year of World War I (1914–18). Director Raoul Walsh (1887–1980) tells the story of a German spy in the United States who is caught and put in jail. A group of disloyal German Americans try to free him, but they are stopped by a patriotic group of robed Klansmen.

The Klan itself began to show renewed signs of life in 1915, courtesy of William Joseph Simmons (1880–1945), who even hired a public relations firm to drum up membership for the organization, now known as the Knights of the Ku Klux Klan. The new Klan reached out to those whites who were troubled by the social changes taking place in America. Consequently, its recruiting material stressed the Klan's opposition to the rising social position of blacks, Jews, Catholics, immigrants, suffragettes, and labor unions. The public relations firm arranged for journalists to interview Simmons, planned elaborate initiation ceremonies for new Klansmen, and even had newspaper ads and billboards spreading the Klan's message.

The Klan played an important role in the best-selling novel **Gone with the Wind** (see entry under 1930s—Film and Theater in volume 2) by Margaret Mitchell (1900–1949), published in 1937. Most of the male characters in the book become Klan members. Even protagonist Rhett Butler is sympathetic to the group's aims. However, movie producer David O. Selznick (1902–1965) eliminated all mention of the Klan in his 1939 movie version of the book.

The Klan appeared only sporadically in the popular culture of the next several decades, mostly in films. *The Burning Cross* (1948) has its war-veteran hero confront the Klan's power in his hometown. In *Storm Warning* (1951), a crusading district attorney, played by Ronald Reagan (1911–2004), sets out to convict a group of murderous Klansmen. In *The FBI Story* (1959), Special Agent Chip Hardesty, played by Jimmy Stewart (1908–1997), fights Klan violence in a Southern town.

Portrayals of the Klan surged in the 1980s and beyond. A segment of *Twilight Zone: The Movie* (1983) turns the tables on a bigot, portrayed by Vic Morrow (1929–1982), and includes a scene in which he is the victim of a Klan lynching. Set in 1964, the grimly powerful film *Mississippi Burning* (1988), directed by Alan Parker (1944–), follows the investigation of FBI agents into the Klan murder of three civil rights workers. Klan violence is also portrayed in the films *Fried Green Tomatoes* (1990); *Sommersby* (1992); *A Time to Kill* and *The Chamber* (both 1996 films based on novels by John Grisham, 1955–); and *O Brother, Where Art Thou?* (2001).

The actual Klan has not been idle, either. In some areas, Klan groups utilize local public access TV to broadcast their propaganda. Klan leaders have also appeared on talk shows ranging from *Oprah* to *The Jerry Springer Show.* The biggest boost to the Klan has come from the World Wide Web. Klan organizations have learned that they can reach far more people with a Web site than they ever could with their rallies and leaflets. And so they do—with a message of hate that remains fundamentally unchanged since 1915. At the same time, those who oppose the violence of the Klan are also hard at work. In 2007, for example, a federal jury convicted an alleged member of the Klan, James Ford Seale (1936–), for his involvement in the 1964 kidnap and murder of two African Americans. Seale was sentenced to life in prison.

Justin Gustainis

For More Information

Bartoletti, Susan Campbell. *They Called Themselves the KKK: The Birth of an American Terrorist Group.* Boston: Houghton Mifflin Harcourt, 2010.
Chalmers, David Mark. *Hooded Americanism: The History of the Ku Klux Klan.* 3rd ed. Durham, NC: Duke University Press, 1987.
Cutlip, Scott M. *The Unseen Power: Public Relations, A History.* Hillsdale, NJ: Lawrence Erlbaum Associates, 1994.
Dessomes, Nancy Bishop. "Hollywood in Hoods: The Portrayal of the Ku Klux Klan in Popular Film." *Journal of Popular Culture* (Spring 1999): pp. 13–22.
McVeigh, Rory. *The Rise of the Ku Klux Klan.* Minneapolis: University of Minnesota Press, 2009.
Riley, Michael. "New Klan, Old Hatred." *Time* (July 6, 1992): pp. 24–27.

Mother's Day

Since 1914, Mother's Day has been celebrated as a national holiday. On the second Sunday of May, children of all ages honor the parent who by tradition has raised them, as well as paying homage to the strength and integrity of the American family. However, because they express their appreciation by giving gifts and sending flowers and greeting cards, Mother's Day has also evolved into a commercial entity.

The roots of the holiday are based on love and respect for motherhood rather than on commercial exploitation. They may be traced to Anna Jarvis (1864–1948), a West Virginian who wished to perpetuate the memory of her own mother while honoring the contributions of all mothers. The intention of Jarvis—who, ironically, was neither wife nor parent herself—was to establish a day of reverence for mothers, to be celebrated across the country. The initial public memorial for her own mother took place in 1907, and the following year similar services were held for all mothers, throughout the nation.

One reason that Mother's Day was embraced as a holiday was that it helped allay fears about the then-emerging "new woman." The new woman was the suffragette who was not satisfied to be compliant in the presence of men. The new woman demanded the right to vote and might even brazenly smoke **cigarettes** (see entry under 1920s—Commerce in volume 2) or offer her own opinions in public.

Today, Mother's Day primarily is associated with commerce. Children not only pay homage to their mothers but present them with cards, flowers, boxes of candy, and other gifts. Each year, approximately 150 million Mother's Day cards are purchased; this compares to 100 million **Father's Day** (see entry under 1910s—The Way We Lived in volume 1) cards, and 900 million Valentine's Day cards. As early as 1910, the Florists' Telegraph Delivery Service (FTD) began encouraging sons and daughters living far away from their mothers to send them flowers. Candy makers, stationers, jewelers, and clothing manufacturers conduct pre–Mother's Day advertising campaigns to boost sales of their products.

Indeed, what Anna Jarvis envisioned as a "holy day" has evolved into a commercial holiday in which the buying, selling, and marketing of products certainly rivals her initial intention. Similar holidays have followed: Father's Day is easily the most popular; others include Bosses' Day, Secretary's Day, and Grandparents' Day. While Mother's Day does remain a time to honor the sacrifice and devotion of mothers across the nation, as of 2010 it also has evolved into a $24.6 billion industry, according to the National Retail Federation.

Rob Edelman

For More Information

Klebanow, Barbara, and Sara Fischer. *American Holidays: Exploring Traditions, Customs, and Backgrounds.* 2nd ed. Brattleboro, VT: Pro Lingua Associates, 2005.

Myers, Robert. *Celebrations: Complete Book of American Holidays.* New York: Doubleday, 1972.

Santino, Jack. *All Around the Year: Holidays and Celebrations in American Life.* Urbana: University of Illinois Press, 1995.

Schmidt, Leigh Eric. *Consumer Rites: The Buying and Selling of American Holidays.* Princeton, NJ: Princeton University Press, 1995.

Refrigerators

Today, refrigerators are taken for granted as one of the most common appliances in America, but it was not always so. Before refrigerators, people tried to preserve their food in cool places like streams, caves, and snow banks. As more people moved into cities, however, a better solution was needed.

By the early 1800s, people kept blocks of ice in insulated wooden cabinets called "ice cabinets." The widespread use of ice cabinets created an ice-harvesting industry in the northern states. Ice harvesters cut blocks of ice from frozen lakes and shipped them to warmer parts of the country. When the Civil War (1861–65) broke out in 1861, ice was one of the first supplies to be cut off from the southern states, leaving southerners' ice cabinets empty and their food rotting. By the early 1890s, warm winters caused ice supplies throughout the United States to diminish, providing an opportunity for other refrigeration techniques to gain attention.

Several inventors experimented with mechanical refrigeration techniques in the 1800s. A method using liquefied ammonia, created by French inventor Ferdinand Carré became the basic system used by modern refrigerators. Carré obtained a patent in France in 1859 and in the United States in 1860. It was not until 1914, however, that the first home-use refrigerator, the Dolmere, was introduced in Chicago, Illinois.

Refrigerators soon became tremendously popular; finally, homemakers had a convenient way to store perishable products. By 1916, more than two dozen refrigerator brands were sold on the market; a number that had increased to

What every family wanted in 1939: a new electric refrigerator. © SCHENECTADY MUSEUM; HALL OF ELECTRICAL HISTORY FOUNDATION/CORBIS.

two hundred by 1920. The first freezers came on the market in the late 1920s. Modern refrigerators started to be mass-produced after World War II (1939–45), making home refrigerators a common consumer product. Home refrigeration systems have not lost their appeal over the years, they have only become more efficient and more environmentally friendly. By the end of the century, refrigerators had become the most common product in American homes; 99.5 percent of American homes had at least one.

Sara Pendergast

For More Information

Jones, Joseph C., Jr. *American Ice Boxes: A Book on the History, Collecting, and Restoration of Ice Boxes.* Humble, TX: Jobeco Books, 1981.

Preville, Cherie, and Chris King. "Cooling Takes Off in the Roaring Twenties." *The Achrnews.com.* http://www.achrnews.com/Articles/Feature_Article/f9721aeb4695a010VgnVCM100000f932a8c0 (accessed July 22, 2011).

Wilsdon, Christina. *How Do Refrigerators Work?* New York: Chelsea Clubhouse, 2010.

Yenne, Bill. *100 Inventions That Shaped World History.* San Mateo, CA: Bluewood Books, 1993.

Ringling Bros. and Barnum & Bailey Circus

Going to a circus and delighting in the antics of clowns, lion tamers, acrobats, and trapeze artists is one of the rites of childhood. The most famous American circus company is the Ringling Bros. and Barnum & Bailey Circus ("Bros." is the abbreviation for Brothers).

The first circuses in the United States appeared in the late eighteenth century. The traditional ones are presented in tents, a practice that dates from 1825. The initial tent circuses were small and featured a single ring in which the entertainers performed. As the years passed, the tent size expanded, and the number of rings increased to two and three. Of all the nineteenth-century American circuses, easily the best known was the Barnum & Bailey. It was the brainchild of two men: Phineas T. Barnum (1810–1891) and James A. Bailey (1847–1906), who initially operated their own separate circuses. Barnum was a flamboyant master showman. In 1842, he purchased a five-story building in New York City and converted it into the American Museum, in which he presented freak shows,

The Ringling Bros. and Barnum & Bailey Circus combined under one big top in 1919. © BETTMANN/CORBIS.

beauty contests, and theatrical shows. Among his early stars: the Feejee Mermaid, a woman dressed in a fish costume; conjoined twins Chang and Eng (1811–1874); and Charles S. Stratton (1838–1883), a twenty-five-inch-tall (63.5 centimeters) man nicknamed General Tom Thumb. In 1871, Barnum began what he labeled "The Greatest Show on Earth," in which he combined traditional circus acts with sideshow performers and caged wild animals. Another of his many successes was his purchase and exploitation of Jumbo, a six-ton elephant.

Bailey, meanwhile, began traveling with circuses while still a boy, and worked his way up to managerial positions with various concerns. In 1872, he became a partner in James E. Cooper's Circus, which first was renamed the Great International Circus and then the Cooper, Bailey & Company Circus. In 1881, Barnum and Bailey merged their operations. For decades, their circus traversed the United States by train, bringing thrills and excitement to towns large and small. After Barnum's death in 1891, Bailey took the show to Europe. Then he expanded it to five rings plus additional stages, and it crossed the country in eighty-five railroad cars. In 1897, the circus spotlighted an act using a record seventy horses, performing together in the same ring. After Bailey died in 1906, the Ringling Brothers Circus, which began as a tent show in 1884, purchased the Barnum & Bailey for $400,000. The two operated as separate entities until 1919, when they combined into one immense enterprise.

Among the most fabled twentieth-century Ringling Bros. and Barnum & Bailey attractions were the Flying Wallendas, a family of high-wire artists founded by Karl Wallenda (1905–1978); Con Colleano (1900–1973), an acrobat known as the Toreador of the Tight Wire; aerialist Lillian Leitzel (1882 or 1892–1931); lion-tamer Clyde Beatty (1903–1965), who later had his own circus; and Emmett Kelly (1898–1979), a sad-faced clown whose best-known character was called Weary Willie.

Despite the popularity of other entertainment media, including motion pictures, **radio** (see entry under 1920s—TV and Radio in volume 2), and **television** (see entry under 1940s—TV and Radio in volume 3), the American circus—and the Ringling Bros. and Barnum & Bailey programs—endures as a special treat for people of all ages. Across the decades, it remains unchanged in the type of merriment and spectacle it offers as well as in the manner in which it transports itself by rail across the country.

Rob Edelman

For More Information

Apps, Jerold W. *Ringlingville USA: The Stupendous Story of Seven Siblings and Their Stunning Circus Success.* Madison: Wisconsin Historical Society Press, 2005.

Apps, Jerold W. *Tents, Tigers, and the Ringling Brothers.* Madison: Wisconsin Historical Society Press, 2007.

Barnum, P. T., and James W. Cook. *The Colossal P. T. Barnum Reader.* Urbana: University of Illinois Press, 2005.

Hammarstrom, David Lewis. *Behind the Big Top.* New York: Barnes & Noble, 1980.

Hammarstrom, David Lewis. *Fall of the Big Top: The Vanishing American Circus.* Jefferson, NC: McFarland, 2008.

North, Henry Ringling, and Alden Hatch. *The Circus Kings: Our Ringling Family Story.* Garden City, NY: Doubleday, 1960.

Ringling Bros. and Barnum & Bailey Online. http://www.ringling.com/ (accessed June 22, 2011).

Slout, William L. *A Royal Coupling: The Historic Marriage of Barnum and Bailey.* San Bernadino, CA: Borgo Press, 2000.

Taylor, Robert Lewis. *Center Ring: The People of the Circus.* Garden City, NY: Doubleday, 1956.

Wallace, Irving. *The Fabulous Showman: The Life and Times of P. T. Barnum.* New York: Knopf, 1959.

Scouting (Boy and Girl)

Around the world, scouting was the most popular youth movement in the twentieth century. By 2001, scouting organizations for boys and girls were in all but five of the world's countries. Founded in Britain by Robert Baden-Powell (1857–1941), the Boy Scouts reached the United States in 1909, when Ernest Thompson Seton (1860–1946) was appointed Chief Scout of America. In Britain, the Girl Scouts (then called Girl Guides) started their own movement in 1910, led by Baden-Powell's sister Agnes (1858–1945). Scouting offered young people the chance to explore the countryside and learn skills such as woodcraft, tracking, and first aid. In 2001, the Boy Scouts of America (BSA) stated that it aimed to help boys build character and physical fitness and become good citizens. Above all, both boy and girl scouts are expected to "Be Prepared."

Scouting began when General Baden-Powell returned from the British campaign at Mafikeng in the South African Boer War (1899–1902). His handbook, *Scouting for Boys,* was published in 1908 and immediately became a **best-seller** (see entry under 1940s—Commerce in volume 3). Chapters entitled "Scoutcraft," "Woodcraft," "Chivalry," and "Our Duties as Citizens" gave advice on subjects such as tying knots, blazing a trail, running a successful camp, and caring for others. Perhaps reflecting Baden-Powell's military background, the handbook even explains what to do if you find a dead body. Through the Boy Scouts and the Girl Guides, Baden-Powell instructed British boys and girls to become loyal subjects of the British Empire.

In the United States, scouting began for different reasons. After the declared "closure" of the frontier in 1893, many Americans worried that the country would lose its pioneering spirit. In 1902, Seton set up the "Woodcraft Indians," a troop of boys who learned how to follow a trail; to recognize different animals, birds, and plants; and to work together as a team in the wilderness. Seton visited Baden-Powell in London in 1906 to exchange ideas. Two years later, scouting came to the attention of American William D. Boyce (1858–1929). Finding himself lost in London, Boyce asked a small boy the way back to his hotel. Boyce was surprised when the boy led him all the way there. He was even more surprised when the boy refused to take money for his trouble, telling Boyce that this was his good turn as a Boy Scout. Impressed, Boyce sought out Baden-Powell to find out about scouting. On his return to the United States, Boyce contacted Seton and together they founded the BSA. The organization was granted its Congressional charter in 1916.

Baden-Powell's aim for the Boy Scouts was to turn boys into "handy, capable men." Organized in army-style "patrols," boy scouts learned teamwork, loyalty, and respect for authority. Early scouting laid down very clear rules about what boys and girls could and should do with their lives. Unlike the boys, who would learn to be leaders and adventurers, Girl Guides would learn to become good companions to their husbands, brothers, and sons. Juliette Gordon "Daisy" Low (1860–1927) began the first American Girl Guide troop in Savannah, Georgia, in 1912. They became known as Girl Scouts in 1915. Already moving away from Baden-Powell's ideas for Girl Guides, Low envisioned an organization that would help girls enjoy an active life outside of the home. Although the first Girl Scout handbook, *Scouting for Girls* (1920) emphasizes domestic skills such as cooking, sewing, and household hygiene, the Girl Scouts also gave girls the chance to live more active and independent lives than before.

Low's Girl Scouts were encouraged to help in their communities, fundraising through annual bake sales and cookie drives. In 1912, ankle-length blue uniforms reflected the accepted view that respectable girls did not play sports, but Low had the girls playing basketball and tennis. Girl Scouts went on hiking and camping trips as well. By 1926, the Girl Scouts had 137,000 members and a national training center in upstate New York. The Girl Scouts organization was always less similar in structure to the military than the Boy Scouts. Its religious views sit more easily with modern attitudes and beliefs, and the organization has made a great effort to be tolerant and inclusive. In 2011, it boasted 3.2 million members worldwide, ranging from the kindergarten "Daisies" to seventeen-year-old "Seniors." Remarkably, cookie sale drives remain an important source of income for the Girl Scouts.

For almost fifty years, parents welcomed scouting as a wholesome influence on youth. But as society became more liberal in the 1960s, the movement lost momentum. Many of the attitudes in *Scouting for Boys* and *Scouting for Girls* seemed very outdated. In the 1990s, the Boy Scouts' opposition to homosexuals and religious nonbelievers drove away many natural supporters. Highly publicized cases of sexual abuse of scouts also turned many away. Many people dislike the military style and conservative approach of scouting in general. Even some critics of scouting, however, accept that its core values of loyalty, honesty, and respect for others are also the essential qualities of any good citizen.

Chris Routledge

For More Information

Boy Scouts of America. http://www.scouting.org/ (accessed on June 22, 2011).

Brown, Fern G. *Daisy and the Girl Scouts: The Story of Juliette Gordon Low.* Niles, IL: Whitman, 1992.

Christiansen, Betty. *Girl Scouts: A Celebration of 100 Trailblazing Years.* New York: Stewart, Tabori & Chang, 2011.

Girl Scouts of the U.S.A. http://www.girlscouts.org/ (accessed on June 22, 2011).

Peterson, Robert W. *Boy Scouts: An American Adventure.* New York: American Heritage, 1985.

Wills, Chuck. *Boy Scouts of America: A Centennial History.* New York: DK Publishing, 2009.

Titanic

· ·

The largest and most luxurious ocean liner of the time, the R.M.S. *Titanic* was a wonder of its age. (The R.M.S. stands for Royal Mail Steamer.) The ship was a symbol of the industrial age and an emblem of the power of the British Empire. However, the fame of the *Titanic* before it sailed was nothing compared with that following its maiden voyage. Retold in numerous books, documentaries, and films, the story of the *Titanic* has become a modern folk tragedy. A warning against pride and overconfidence, it is also a fable of lost dreams, dignified bravery, and greedy self-interest.

The story of the *Titanic* begins in 1907. J. Bruce Ismay (1862–1937), head of the White Star shipping line, commissioned the shipbuilders Harland and Wolff of Belfast, Ireland, to create three new ships for crossing the North Atlantic. The resulting *Olympic,* the *Titanic,* and the *Britannic* would carry passengers and mail between Britain and the United States. Built alongside the larger second vessel, the *Olympic* was the first to be finished. But the *Titanic* was the masterpiece. White Star's ships offered greater stability, luxury, and sheer size than rival Cunard's fleet. The *Titanic,* then the largest moving object ever made, was launched into the river Langan on May 31, 1911.

The ill-fated maiden voyage of the R.M.S. *Titanic* began from Southampton on April 10, 1912. The ship stopped at Cherbourg, France, and Queenstown (now Cobh), Ireland. Then the *Titanic* left for New York carrying over 2,200 passengers and hundreds of mail bags on April 12. The *Titanic* struck an iceberg on April 14 and sank off Newfoundland, causing the loss of 1,513 lives. Touted as a practically unsinkable vessel, the ship carried lifeboats for only half its passengers. The inquiries that followed pointed blame in many directions, including at Captain Edward John Smith (1850–1912) for hurrying through dangerous waters and at White Star for ignoring the need for lifeboats. The sinking led to stricter safety regulations for the shipping industry, including instructions for dealing with disasters, and the establishment of the International Ice Patrol.

While the *Titanic* disaster had a huge effect on rules for shipping, its influence on popular culture was nothing short of profound. Some religious leaders claimed the wreck was a warning from God against the excesses of the Gilded Age (the period of rapid industrialization in the early 1900s). Some women survivors were criticized for not staying behind with their husbands. Groups campaigning for women's rights actually complained about the unfair treatment of men left behind on the sinking ship. At a time when the social classes were strictly divided, the *Titanic* revealed the different experiences of people from different backgrounds. Passengers in the cheaper "steerage" cabins were much less likely to have survived than first-class passengers. It was suspected that lower-class passengers were never intended to be rescued.

Just one month after the disaster, *Saved from the Titanic* was filmed on the *Olympic,* starring survivor Dorothy Gibson (1884–1946). Lawrence Beesley (1877–1967) published the first survivor's account of the tragedy, *The Loss of the S.S. Titanic,* six weeks after the event. Numerous books, magazine articles, and popular songs appeared in the aftermath of the disaster, but by 1913, the intensity of *Titanic* mania had eased. Among the most interesting of the many early movies are *Atlantic* (1929) and *Titanic* (1943), a German propaganda film. The *Titanic* experienced renewed notoriety in the 1950s. One of the most popular of the films about the disaster from that decade is *A Night to Remember* (1958). In 1960, there was even a popular Broadway musical telling the story of survivor Margaret Tobin Brown (1867–1932), entitled *The Unsinkable Molly Brown. Titanic: A New Musical* revived the story for the stage in 1997.

A second revival in the 1970s included the best-selling novel by Clive Cussler (1931–), *Raise the Titanic* (1976). Many real-life attempts have been made over the years to find and raise the *Titanic*. One of the more unlikely plans was to freeze the water inside the ship. It would then rise to the surface like, of all things, an iceberg. But it was not until September 1985 that American Robert Ballard (1942–) and Frenchman Jean-Louis Michel finally located the wreck. After much debate about whether the ship should be left untouched as a grave site, artifacts were finally recovered from the wreck. An exhibition of objects from the *Titanic* went on tour around the world.

In the twenty-first century, a *Titanic* industry produces everything from models of the ship to reproductions of china and silverware. There is a Titanic Historical Society dedicated to all things *Titanic,* and there are many small *Titanic* museums in Britain, Ireland, and America. Perhaps the most lavish tribute to the ship, its passengers, and its crew is the 1997 film by James Cameron (1954–), *Titanic,* co-starring young heartthrob Leonardo DiCaprio (1974–) and Kate Winslet (1975–). Using near-life-sized models and enhancing them with computer-generated images, Cameron's film was the most expensive ever made. Despite historical inaccuracies, *Titanic* the movie is as much a cultural phenomenon of its own age as the ship was in 1912.

Chris Routledge

For More Information

Butler, Daniel Allen. *"Unsinkable": The Full Story of the RMS Titanic.* Mechanicsburg, PA: Stackpole, 1998.

Encyclopedia Titanica. http://www.encyclopedia-titanica.org/ (accessed on June 22, 2011).

Hill, Christine M. *Robert Ballard: Oceanographer Who Discovered the Titanic.* Berkeley Heights, NJ: Enslow, 1999.

Lynch, Don. *Titanic: An Illustrated History.* New York: Hyperion, 1992.

Marshall, Logan. *The Sinking of the Titanic.* Halifax, NS: Nimbus, 1998.

RMS Titanic Home. http://www.rmstitanic.net/ (accessed on June 22, 2011).

Spignesi, Stephen J. *The Complete Titanic: From the Ship's Earliest Blueprints to the Epic Film.* Secausus, NJ: Carol Publishing Group, 1998.

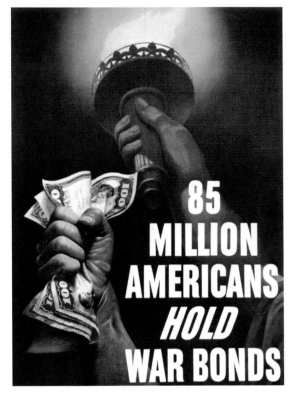

A World War II war bonds poster. © PICTORIAL PRESS LTD./ ALAMY.

War Bonds

Wars are expensive, and nations at war need to raise a great deal of money. Higher taxes raise some money, but usually not enough. The solution in the United States during the first half of the twentieth century was war bonds.

In buying a war bond, a citizen is loaning money to the government, at a given rate of interest, to be repaid years later, when the war is over. In World War I (1914–18), these notes were called Liberty Bonds. They were touted at bond rallies, endorsed by movie stars, and the subject of speeches by civilian volunteers called the Four Minute Men. Similar strategies were used during World War II (1939–45) to sell bonds. Some of the most successful bond rallies, attended by thousands of people and often broadcast live over the **radio** (see entry under 1920s—TV and Radio in volume 2), featured popular entertainer Kate Smith (1907–1986) singing "God Bless America." It is notable that during conflicts in Korea, Vietnam, Afghanistan, Iraq, and elsewhere, the U.S. government did not sell war bonds. Perhaps this is related to the fact that the last time the United States formally declared war was in 1941, after the Japanese bombing of Pearl Harbor.

Justin Gustainis

For More Information

Blum, John Morton. *V Was for Victory: Politics and American Culture during World War II.* New York: Harcourt Brace Jovanovich, 1976.

Kimble, James J. *Mobilizing the Home Front: War Bonds and Domestic Propoganda.* College Station: Texas A&M University Press, 2006.

O'Neill, William L. *A Democracy at War: America's Fight at Home and Abroad in World War II.* New York: Free Press, 1993.

Where to Learn More

The following list of resources focuses on material appropriate for middle school or high school students. Please note that the Web site addresses were verified prior to publication, but are subject to change.

Books

America A to Z: People, Places, Customs and Culture. Pleasantville, NY: Reader's Digest Association, 1997.

Beetz, Kirk H., ed. *Beacham's Encyclopedia of Popular Fiction.* Osprey, FL: Beacham, 1996.

Berke, Sally. *When TV Began: The First TV Shows.* New York: CPI, 1978.

Blum, Daniel; enlarged by John Willis. *A Pictorial History of the American Theatre, 1860–1985.* 6th ed. New York: Crown, 1986.

Brinkley, Douglas. *The Great Deluge: Hurricane Katrina, New Orleans, and the Mississippi Gulf Coast.* New York: Morrow, 2006.

Brooks, Tim, and Earle Marsh. *The Complete Directory to Prime Time Network and Cable TV Shows, 1946–present.* 9th ed. New York: Ballantine, 2007.

Cashmore, Ellis. *Sports Culture: An A to Z Guide.* New York: Routledge, 2000.

Condon, Judith. *The Nineties (Look at Life In).* Austin, TX: Raintree Steck-Vaughn, 2000.

Craddock, Jim. *VideoHound's Golden Movie Retriever.* Rev. ed. Detroit: Gale, 2011.

Daniel, Clifton, ed. *Chronicle of the Twentieth Century.* Liberty, MO: JL International Pub., 1994.

Dunning, John. *On the Air: The Encyclopedia of Old-Time Radio.* New York: Oxford University Press, 1998.

Dunning, John. *Tune in Yesterday: The Ultimate Encyclopedia of Old-Time Radio 1925–1976.* New York: Oxford University Press, 1998.

Ehrenreich, Barbara. *Nickel and Dimed: On (Not) Getting By in America.* New York: Metropolitan Books, 2001.

Epstein, Dan. *20th Century Pop Culture.* Philadelphia: Chelsea House, 2000.

Finkelstein, Norman H. *Sounds of the Air: The Golden Age of Radio.* New York: Charles Scribner's, 1993.

Flowers, Sarah. *Sports in America.* San Diego: Lucent, 1996.

Friedman, Thomas L. *Hot, Flat, and Crowded: Why We Need a Green Revolution—and How It Can Renew America.* New York: Picador, 2009.

Gilbert, Adrian. *The Eighties (Look at Life In).* Austin, TX: Raintree Steck-Vaughn, 2000.

Godin, Seth. *The Encyclopedia of Fictional People: The Most Important Characters of the 20th Century.* New York: Boulevard Books, 1996.

Gore, Al. *An Inconvenient Truth.* Emmaus, PA: Rodale Press, 2006.

Grant, R. G. *The Seventies (Look at Life In).* Austin, TX: Raintree Steck-Vaughn, 2000.

Grant, R. G. *The Sixties (Look at Life In).* Austin, TX: Raintree Steck-Vaughn, 2000.

Green, Joey. *Joey Green's Encyclopedia of Offbeat Uses for Brand-Name Products.* New York: Hyperion, 1998.

Green, Stanley. *Encyclopedia of the Musical Theatre.* New York: Da Capo Press, 1976.

Hischak, Thomas S. *Film It with Music: An Encyclopedic Guide to the American Movie Musical.* Westport, CT: Greenwood Press, 2001.

Katz, Ephraim. *The Film Encyclopedia.* 6th ed. New York: Collins, 2008.

Kirkpatrick, David. *The Facebook Effect: The Inside Story of the Company That Is Connecting the World.* New York: Simon & Schuster, 2011.

Lackmann, Ron. *The Encyclopedia of American Radio: An A–Z Guide to Radio from Jack Benny to Howard Stern.* New York: Facts on File, 2000.

Lebrecht, Norman. *The Companion to 20th-Century Music.* New York: Simon & Schuster, 1992.

Levitt, Steven D., and Stephen Dubner. *Freakonomics: A Rogue Economist Explores the Hidden Side of Everything.* Rev. ed. New York: Harper, 2009.

Lissauer, Robert. *Lissauer's Encyclopedia of Popular Music in America: 1888 to the Present.* New York: Facts on File, 1996.

Lowe, Denise. *Women and American Television: An Encyclopedia.* ABC-CLIO: Santa Barbara, CA, 1999.

Maltin, Leonard, ed. *Leonard Maltin's Movie Encyclopedia.* New York: Dutton, 1994.

Martin, Frank K. *A Decade of Delusions: From Speculative Contagion to the Great Recession.* Hoboken, NJ: Wiley, 2011.

McNeil, Alex. *Total Television: The Comprehensive Guide to Programming from 1948 to the Present.* 4th ed. New York: Penguin, 1996.

National Commission on Terrorist Attacks. *The 9/11 Commission Report: Final Report of the National Commission on Terrorist Attacks Upon the United States.* New York: Norton, 2004.

Newcomb, Horace, ed. *Encyclopedia of Television.* 2nd ed. Chicago: Fitzroy Dearborn, 2004.

Packer, George. *The Assassins' Gate: America in Iraq.* New York: Farrar, Straus, and Giroux, 2005.

Rosen, Roger, and Patra McSharry Sevastiades, eds. *Coca-Cola Culture: Icons of Pop.* New York: Rosen, 1993.

Schlosser, Eric. *Fast Food Nation.* New York: Houghton Mifflin, 2001.

Schwartz, Herman M. *Subprime Nation: American Power, Global Capital, and the Housing Bubble.* Ithaca, NY: Cornell University Press, 2009.

Schwartz, Richard A. *Cold War Culture: Media and the Arts, 1945–1990.* New York: Facts on File, 1997.

Sennett, Richard. *The Culture of the New Capitalism.* New Haven, CT: Yale University Press, 2007.

Sies, Luther F. *Encyclopedia of American Radio, 1920–1960.* 2nd ed. Jefferson, NC: McFarland, 2008.

Slide, Anthony. *Early American Cinema.* Rev. ed. Metuchen, NJ: Scarecrow Press, 1994.

Tibbetts, John C., and James M. Welsh. *The Encyclopedia of Novels into Film.* 2nd ed. New York: Facts on File, 2005.

Tibbetts, John C., and James M. Welsh. *The Encyclopedia of Stage Plays into Film.* New York: Facts on File, 2001.

Vise, David A. *The Google Story.* Updated ed. New York: Delacorte Press, 2008.

Weisman, Alan. *The World Without Us.* New York: St. Martin's Press, 2007.

Wilson, Charles Reagan, James G. Thomas Jr., and Ann J. Abadie, eds. *The New Encyclopedia of Southern Culture.* Chapel Hill: University of North Carolina Press, 2006.

Woodward, Bob. *Bush at War.* New York: Simon & Schuster, 2002.

Web Sites

Bumpus, Jessica. "The Noughties' Fashion Highlights." *Vogue* (December 22, 2010). http://www.vogue.co.uk/spy/celebrity-photos/2010/12/22/the-noughties (accessed September 23, 2011.)

Markowitz, Robin. *Cultural Studies Central.* http://www.culturalstudies.net/ (accessed August 7, 2011).

"The Noughties: Year by Year." *The Sunday Times,* October 20, 2009. http://women.timesonline.co.uk/tol/life_and_style/women/the_way_we_live/article6881549.ece (accessed September 23, 2011).

"100 Songs That Defined the Noughties." The *Telegraph,* September 18, 2009. http://www.telegraph.co.uk/culture/music/rockandpopfeatures/6198897/100-songs-that-defined-the-Noughties.html (accessed September 23, 2011).

"Pictures of the Decade." *Reuters.* http://www.reuters.com/news/pictures/slideshow?articleId=USRTXRYG2#a=1 (accessed September 23, 2011.)

"A Portrait of the Decade." *BBC News,* December 14, 2009. http://news.bbc.co.uk/2/hi/8409040.stm (accessed September 23, 2011).

Washington State University, American Studies. *Popular Culture: Resources for Critical Analysis.* http://www.wsu.edu/%7Eamerstu/pop/tvrguide.html (accessed August 7, 2011).

Yesterdayland. http://www.yesterdayland.com/ (accessed August 7, 2011).

Zupko, Sarah. *Popcultures.com: Sarah Zupko's Cultural Studies Center.* http://www.popcultures.com/ (accessed August 7, 2011).

Index

Italic type indicates volume number; **boldface** indicates main entries; (ill.) indicates illustrations.

C

E

Goulding, Ray, *3:* 773

"Gourmet" coffee, *5:* 1440

Gourmet grocery stores, *6:* 1518–20

GPS (global positioning device), *3:* 861

Grabeel, Lucas, *6:* 1605 (ill.)

Grable, Betty, *3:* 552

Grace, Maggie, *6:* 1607 (ill.)

Grace, Princess of Monaco. *See* Kelly, Grace

Grace Under Fire, 4: 1173–74

Graceland, 4: 943

Graceland (Nashville, Tennessee), *3:* 758

Gracie Jiu-jitsu, *6:* 1580–81

The Graduate, *1:* 26–27; *4:* 868, **901–3,** 902 (ill.), 943

Graff, Robert de, *2:* 484

Graffiti, *5:* 1254

Graham, Billy, *1:* 137; *3:* 556

Graham, Jefferson, *3:* 815

Graham, Martha, *2:* 393

Grahame, Gloria, *3:* 585

Grammar, Kelsey, *5:* 1286 (ill.), 1287, 1413, 1414 (ill.)

Gramophones, *1:* 72

Grand Ole Opry, *2:* 253, **315–16;** *3:* 605

Grand Slam (Serena Williams), *6:* 1585–86

Grand Theft Auto video games, *4:* 1113

Grandy, Fred, *4:* 1139, 1139 (ill.)

Grange, Harold "Red," *2:* 343, 354

Granger, David, *2:* 481

Granjean, Arthur, *3:* 786

Granny Doodle, *2:* 401

Grant, Cary, *2:* 425–26, 426 (ill.); *3:* 702

Grant, Maxwell, *2:* 494

The Grapes of Wrath, *2:* 391, 396, 465, **484–85**

Graphical User Interface (GUI), *4:* 1166–67, 1183; *5:* 1347

Grassle, Karen, *4:* 1137

Grateful Dead, *4:* 934–35, 1019, 1023; *5:* 1241

Graves, Peter, *5:* 1221 (ill.), 1222

Gray, Billy, *3:* 832, 832 (ill.)

Gray, Harold, *2:* 330

Gray, John, *5:* 1337

Gray, William S., *2:* 476

Gray flannel suit, *3:* 722

"Great American Smokeout," *2:* 267

"Great Bambino," *1:* 101

Great Britain, skinhead movement, *5:* 1328

Great Depression, *2:* 256, 389, 394, 395–96, 531–32, **540–41,** 541 (ill.); *3:* 673

  big bands, *2:* 458–60

  Empire State Building, *2:* 430, 431 (ill.), 538 (ill.), 538–39, 545; *6:* 1561

  fashion, *2:* 403

  food, *2:* 403, 449, 453

  The Grapes of Wrath, 2: 391, 484–85

  hot rods, *3:* 686, 686 (ill.)

  jukeboxes, *2:* 462 (ill.), 462–63

  movie palaces, *1:* 45

  movies, *2:* 407–8

  music, *2:* 457–58

  New Deal, *2:* 389–90, 396, 408, 531–32, 541

  poverty, *3:* 673

  radio, *2:* 513, 525

  repeal of Prohibition, *2:* 449

  Rodgers, Jimmie, *2:* 316–17

  Route 66, *2:* 384

  sports, *2:* 501–2

  toys, *2:* 400–401

  The Waltons, 4: 1161–62, 1162 (ill.)

The Great Gatsby, 2: 259; *4:* 1049

Great Migration, *1:* 160, 229

The Great One, *5:* 1272

Great Performances, 4: 999

The Great Train Robbery, *1:* 3, 5, **39–41,** 40 (ill.); *2:* 445

"Great White Hope," *1:* 107

Great White Way (Broadway), *1:* 34–36, 35 (ill.); *3:* 574

The Great Ziegfeld, 1: 54

"The Greatest Gift," *3:* 584

"The Greatest Show on Earth," *1:* 241

Greece, *6:* 1467

"Greed decade," *5:* 1333

"Greed is good," *5:* 1200

Greek mythology, in *Percy Jackson* series, *6:* 1560–61

Green, Brian Austin, *5:* 1409, 1410 (ill.)

Green, Robert, *1:* 69

Green Acres, 3: 833; *4:* 976, 979, 1136

Green Bay Packers, *4:* 969

Green Day, *3:* 761; *6:* 1549

K

M

423

Mary Hartman, Mary Hartman, 2: 526
Mary Kay Cosmetics, *4:* **890–91**
Mary Poppins, *4:* 913 (ill.), **913–14**
The Mary Tyler Moore Show, *3:* 833; *4:* 1140 (ill.), **1140–42**
M*A*S*H, *4:* 1042, **1143–45,** 1144 (ill.)
"Mash me a fin," *3:* 552
The Mask of Zorro, *1:* 214
Mason, Bobbie Ann, *3:* 621
Mason, Perry. *See* Perry Mason
Mass market, *1:* 88; *2:* 249; *3:* 693
Mass murders, *4:* 1189
Mass production, of houses, *3:* 690–91, 862
Mass suicides, Jonestown, Guyana, *4:* 1170
Masscy, Raymond, *4:* 988
Massively multiplayer online role-playing games (MMORPGs), *6:* 1574
Master Charge (MasterCard), *3:* 711
"Master of Suspense," *4:* 918
Masters, William H., *4:* 1034
Masters of Deceit (Hoover), *3:* 684
Match Game, *3:* 816
Mathers, Deborah, *6:* 1533–34
Mathers, Jerry, *3:* 825, 826 (ill.)
Mathers, Kimberley Scott, *6:* 1534
Mathers, Marshall. *See* Eminem
Mathers, Marshall, III, *6:* 1464
Mathis, June, *2:* 300
Matlock, Glen, *4:* 1085
Mattel, *2:* 401; *3:* 708–10, 709 (ill.)
Matthau, Walter, *4:* 915, 916
Matthews, Dave, *5:* 1241
Mauch Chunk Switchback Railway, *1:* 147
Maugham, Somerset, *3:* 666
Max Payne, *4:* 1114
Maxwell House Coffee, *1:* 2
May, Robert L., *2:* 270; *3:* 632
"May the Force be with you," *4:* 1070
Mayberry R.F.D., *4:* 977
Mayer, Louis B., *2:* 295
Mayfield, Curtis, *4:* 1074
Mays, Willie, *3:* 785
Mazes and Monsters, *4:* 1104
McAuliffe, Christa, *4:* 1030
McAvoy, Mary, *2:* 293 (ill.)

McBeal, Ally, *2:* 260; *5:* 1400–1402, 1401 (ill.)
McCain, John, *4:* 1196
McCall, C. W., *4:* 1124
McCall, David, *4:* 1156
McCarthy, Charlie, *2:* **416–17,** 417 (ill.)
McCarthy, Joseph, *3:* 703, 848–50, 849 (ill.)
McCarthy-Army hearings, *3:* **848–50,** 849 (ill.)
"McCarthyism," *3:* 704, 850
McCartney, Paul, *4:* 906, 927
McCay, Winsor, *1:* 157, 185–87
McConnell, David, *1:* 124
McCormack, Eric, *6:* 1620, 1620 (ill.)
McCormick, Maureen, *4:* 1119 (ill.), 1120
McCorvey, Norma, *4:* 1187–88
McCoy, Sherman, *5:* 1260–61
McCoy, Van, *4:* 1074, 1078
McCrane, Paul, *5:* 1412 (ill.)
McCulley, Johnston, *1:* 213
McDaniel, Hattie, *2:* 425
McDaniels, Daryl "DMC," *5:* 1256, 1257 (ill.)
McDonald, Christopher, *3:* 827
McDonald, Dick and Mac, *3:* 596
McDonald's, *2:* 302–3; *3:* **595–97,** 596 (ill.), 747, 749
McDonough, John, *3:* 808
McDonough, Mary Elizabeth, *4:* 1162 (ill.)
McDowall, Roddy, *4:* 916
McDowell, Malcolm, *4:* 1054, 1131
McEntire, Reba, *3:* 606
McFarlane, Leslie, *2:* 327
McFarlane, Seth, *6:* 1600
McGarrett, Steve, *4:* 994
McGovern, George, *4:* 943
McGowan, Rose, *5:* 1363
McGraw, Tim, *3:* 607
McGwire, Mark, *1:* 103; *5:* 1341
McInerney, Jay, *5:* 1316, 1333
McIntyre, Trapper John, *4:* 1143
McKay, Jim, *4:* 972–73
McKernan, Ron, *4:* 935
McKinley, William, *1:* 3–4
McLachlan, Sarah, *5:* 1377
McLamore, James, *3:* 746
McLaren, Malcolm, *4:* 1085
McLaughlin, John, *1:* 74
McMahon, Ed, *3:* 839–40; *4:* 984 (ill.), 985

O

Paranormal, *5:* 1230–32

The Paranormal Activity, 2: 410

Parapsychology, *5:* 1230

The Parent Trap, 4: 1174

Parental units, *5:* 1336

Parents Music Resource Center, *5:* 1243

Paretsky, Sara, *2:* 474

Paris, France, *2:* 286

"Park," *2:* 250

Park, Maud Wood, *2:* 254

Parka, quilted down, *2:* 271

Parker, Alan, *1:* 236

Parker, Bonnie, *2:* 534

Parker, Charlie, *1:* 73; *3:* 554

Parker, Dorothy, *2:* 281, 331

Parker, Fess, *3:* 809, 809 (ill.)

Parker, Peter, *4:* 958

Parker, Ray, Jr., *5:* 1231

Parker, Sarah Jessica, *6:* 1613

Parker, Trey, *5:* 1423, 1425

Parker Brothers, *1:* 119

Parks, Gordon, *4:* 1067–68

Parks, Wally, *3:* 687

Parliament/Funkadelic, *4:* 1074, 1077

Parodies

    The Daily Show, 6: 1591–93

    of horror movies, *4:* 909

    MAD magazine, 3: 772–73

    The Simpsons, 5: 1303

Parrish, Maxfield, *1:* 67

Parsley, Sage, Rosemary and Thyme, 4: 943

Parsons, Gram, *5:* 1370

Parsons, Louella, *2:* 326

Parton, Dolly, *5:* 1201

The Partridge Family, *4:* 1149 (ill.), **1149–50**

"Party" direct sales system, *3:* 564 (ill.), 565

The Passion of the Christ, *6:* **1507–9,** 1508 (ill.)

Passion pit, *3:* 708

Passos, John Dos, *2:* 481

Password, 3: 816

Pat the Bunny, 3: 628

Patch, Sam, *5:* 1392

Patel, Dev, *6:* 1512

Patman, Wright, *3:* 711

Patrick, Dan, *4:* 1129

Patriot Act, *6:* 1641

Patriotism, *3:* 623; *5:* 1219

Patten, Fred, *2:* 324

Patten, Gilbert, *1:* 2

Patterson, Lorna, *5:* 1221 (ill.)

Patton, Charley, *2:* 458

Patton, Gene, *4:* 1132

Patton, George S., *3:* 556–57

Paul, Alice, *1:* 230; *4:* 1178

Paul, Les, *3:* 755

The Paul Harvey News, 3: 555

Pauley, Jane, *3:* 837

Paxson, Lowell "Bud," *5:* 1204

Pay-per-view, *5:* 1280; *6:* 1581

"Payola" scandal, *3:* 753

PayPal, *6:* 1473–74

Payton, Walter, *2:* 309

PBS (Public Broadcasting System), *3:* 668–69

    Barney and Friends, 5: 1404–5, 1405 (ill.)

    Thomas the Tank Engine, 5: 1425–26, 1426 (ill.)

PC (political correctness), *5:* 1198, **1322–23**

PCs (personal computers). *See* Personal computers (PCs)

PDAs (personal digital assistants), *4:* 1184

Peale, Norman Vincent, *3:* 701

Peanut Gallery *(Howdy Doody Show), 3:* 659

Peanuts, *3:* **778–80,** 779 (ill.)

Pearce, Alice, *4:* 980

Pearl, Minnie, *4:* 1136

Pearl Harbor, *2:* 362

Pearl Jam, *5:* 1372

Peary, Robert, *1:* 93

Peck, Harry Thurston, *3:* 570

Peer-to-peer file sharing, *6:* 1543

Pegleg Pete, *2:* 297

Pekar, Harvey, *2:* 472

Pelley, Scott, *3:* 663

Pemberton, John "Doc," *1:* 58

Pen, ballpoint, *2:* **397–98**

Pendleton, Karen, *3:* 827

Penguin Books, *2:* 489

The Penguins of Madagascar, 4: 1003

Penicillin, *2:* **378–79**

Television (*Continued*)
high-definition (HDTV), *6:* 1633–35, 1634 (ill.)
holiday special, *3:* 771
Home Shopping Network (HSN), *5:* 1204–5
Lassie, *3:* 586–87
late-night, *4:* 870
live drama *(Studio One), 3:* 666–67
Monday Night Football, 4: 1108 (ill.), 1108–10
MTV (Music Television), *4:* 1122; *5:* 1200,
    1237, 1252 (ill.), 1252–54
"Must See TV," *5:* 1399
networks, *3:* 704–5; *5:* 1399–1400
news programming, *3:* 661–63, 662 (ill.)
pay-per-view, *5:* 1280
Peyton Place, 3: 701, 737–39
program schedule, *3:* 783–84
public debut, *2:* 514
public vs. commercial, *4:* 999
from radio, *2:* 361
reality *(see* Reality TV)
soap operas, *2:* 525–26 *(see also* specific soap
    opera, e.g. Guiding Light)
TV dinners, *2:* 351–452
TV Guide, 3: 783–84
World Wrestling Federation (WWF),
    5: 1279–81, 1280 (ill.)
Television directors
Fernandez, Peter, *4:* 1007
Harrison, John, *4:* 953
Landon, Michael, *4:* 1137–38
Lubin, Arthur, *4:* 996
Mann, Michael, *5:* 1224–25
Studio One, *3:* 667
Television journalism, *4:* 1005
Television producers
Abrams, J. J., *6:* 1606
Barris, Chuck, *4:* 1132–33
Borden, Bill, *6:* 1604
Cherry, Marc, *6:* 1596
Crane, David, *5:* 1415
Davies, Michael P., *5:* 1427–28
Freeman, Leonard, *4:* 994
Hamner, Earl, Jr., *4:* 1161
Hewitt, Don, *4:* 1005–6
Kauffman, Marta, *5:* 1415

Kelley, David E., *5:* 1401
Landon, Michael, *4:* 1137–38
Lear, Norman, *4:* 1116
Lindelof, Damon, *6:* 1606
Marshall, Garry, *4:* 1133
Michaels, Lorne, *4:* 1153–54; *6:* 1610
Rafelson, Bob, *4:* 936
Roddenberry, Gene, *4:* 1008
Schneider, Bert, *4:* 936
Schwartz, Sherwood, *4:* 993
Spelling, Aaron, *4:* 1131, 1139; *5:* 1409
Webb, Jack, *3:* 812
Weiner, Matthew, *6:* 1608
Television programming
daytime talk shows, *4:* 986–87
early morning, *3:* 837
late night, *5:* 1295; *6:* 1609–11
"magazine format," *4:* 1005
MTV, *5:* 1253
news, *4:* 1005–6
Saturday morning cartoons, *4:* 1001–4
sitcoms, *3:* 831–33, 832 (ill.)
sports, *5:* 1271
Television shows. *See* Television; specific type of
    television show, e.g., Comedies, TV; "TV and radio"
    listing in "Entries by Topic Category" on p. lviii
Television sports shows
ESPN, *4:* 973
Monday Night Football, 4: 973
Wide World of Sports, 4: 972–73
Television trials, *5:* 1340, 1451–54, 1452 (ill.)
Television violence, *5:* 1408
Telstar, 3: 860
Temperance, *1:* 230
Temple, Shirley, *2:* **440–41,** 441 (ill.)
Temptations, *4:* 939
The Ten Commandments, 2: 252; *3:* 702
Tennis
1990s, *5:* 1392
Williams sisters, *6:* 1585–86
Tennis shoes, *1:* **173–74,** 174 (ill.)
The Terminator, 5: 1219
Terrorism
9/11, *6:* 1461–62, 1641 (ill.), 1641–43
and nuclear weapons, *3:* 679

U

W

X

Y